CONTENTS

BIOGRAPHICAL DETAILS OF CONTRIBUTORS

Gillian Pugh is chief executive of Coram Family, England's oldest childcare charity. She was previously director of the Early Childhood Unit at the National Children's Bureau. She has worked nationally and internationally in the fields of early childhood education and parenting education and support and is author of a number of books including *Training to Work in the Early Years* (with Lesley Abbott; Open University Press, 1998), *Confident Parents, Confident Children* and *Preventive Work with Families*. She is also co-editor of the journal *Children and Society*. She was a member of the Rumbold Committee on the education of children aged 3–5 years, of the RSA Start Right enquiry and of the Audit Commission study of early education. She was a founder member and chair of the Early Childhood Education Forum, is a founder member and chair of the Parenting Education and Support Forum and a trustee of the National Family and Parenting Institute. She is chair of governors of the Thomas Coram Early Excellence Centre.

Peter Moss is Professor of Early Childhood Provision at the Institute of Education, University of London and, between 1986 and 1996, was Coordinator of the European Commission Childcare Network. His research interests include services for children and the staffing of these services; parental employment trends; parental leave; and the relationship between care and employment. Recent publications include *Beyond Quality in Early Childhood Education and Care: Postmodern Perspectives* and *Parental Leave: Progress or Pitfall?* (with F. Deven; NIDI/CBGS, 2000).

Gerison Lansdown is currently a freelance writer and researcher in the field of children's rights. She was the founder director of the Children's Rights Office (now known as the Children's Rights Alliance for England), and has published and lectured widely in the field of children's rights. She also works as a consultant for the UNICEF Innocenti Research Centre in Florence.

Penny Lancaster is the project co-ordinator of Coram Family's 'Listening to Young Children' project. Her background is in education, social development and humanitarian relief. Before coming to the UK she worked in Serbia, Kosova and Albania where she managed a peace-building initiative between Serbs and Kosovar Albanians and developed educational projects for Kosovar Albanian children during their experience of forced migration. She is a graduate of the Refugee Studies programme (Oxford) and has an MA in education.

Tricia David is a professor of education (early childhood) at Canterbury Christ Church University College, a past president of OMEP (UK) (OMEP is the World Organisation for Early Childhood Education) and a past editor of its international journal. Tricia's earlier experience includes teaching and headships at nursery and primary schools and research, lecturing and community education work in universities – but she values the continuing opportunities to enjoy learning from family life (especially from her three grandchildren all of whom are under 5 years of age). Among Tricia's 12 books and over 70 articles, her best-known publications include *Under Five – Under-educated?* (Open University Press, 1990); *Effective Teaching in the Early Years* (with Audrey Curtis and Iram Siraj-Blatchford; Trentham Books, 1992); and two books with CCCUC colleagues about early childhood education (birth to 8 years) – *Young Children Learning* and *Teaching Young Children* (Paul Chapman Publishing/Sage, 1999). Tricia is currently very involved in cross-cultural research about early literacy (in France and Spain, funded by the Esmée Fairbairn Charitable Trust) and local developments with Kent's Early Years Development and Childcare Partnership and Sure Start programmes.

Cathy Nutbrown is Lecturer in Early Childhood Education and Director of the MA in Early Childhood Education at the School of Education, the

University of Sheffield. Her teaching and research has focused on early literacy, assessment of children's learning, curriculum and children's rights in early education. Her many publications include *Threads of Thinking* (Paul Chapman Publishing, 1999) and *Recognising Early Literacy Development* (Paul Chapman Publishing, 1996).

Dorothy Selleck is an early years advisory teacher in the London Borough of Hammersmith and Fulham, Early Years Development and Childcare Partnership. Her work is with practitioners from all settings so as to develop quality experiences for children, from babies to children in primary school reception classes. Her observations and conversations with children, parents, practitioners, researchers and policy-makers are the force for her chapter and for playing a part in the contemporary management of change in early years provision for play, care and education.

Iram Siraj-Blatchford is Professor of Early Childhood Education and Head of Child Development and Learning at the University of London Institute of Education. She has been an early years teacher and advisory teacher. She is co-director of the major five-year DfEE 'Effective Provision for Preschool Education' project and the 'Effective Pedagogy in the Early Years' project. Iram is committed to research and practice which combats disadvantage for children and families.

Sheila Wolfendale is an educational psychologist and is the course director of a doctorate programme in educational psychology for practising educational psychologists at the University of East London. She has written and published extensively on topics such as early years, special needs, educational psychology and parental involvement.

Margy Whalley has managed multidisciplinary early years services in Brazil, Papua New Guinea and England. She was the founding head of the Pen Green Centre for Under Fives and their Families and has worked there for 18 years. She has undertaken a secondment to The Open University where she wrote course materials for parents wanting to increase their knowledge and understanding of child development. She was invited to be part of the Labour Party enquiry team into under-5s' education and care and was the Association of County Councils' representative on the national Audit Commission concerned with children under 5 years. She has also been a member of the QCA Advisory Group on the framework for the Foundation stage. Currently she is Director of the Research, Development and Training Base at the Pen Green Centre and is involved in research in this country and Europe. The primary function of the research programme over the last five years has been involving parents in their children's learning. The new research project at Pen Green focuses on children's resilience and well-being and how parents can support children's emotional lives. The research base also delivers a training and consultancy service throughout the UK.

Lucy Draper is the Co-ordinator of Coram Parents Centre, which offers a wide range of parenting support and education to families from the Kings Cross area of the London Borough of Camden. She originally trained as a teacher, and has since worked in a variety of early years settings, as an early years training officer and as a counsellor and groupworker with parents.

Bernadette Duffy is currently Head of the Thomas Coram Early Childhood Centre in Camden which, with the Coram Parents Centre, has been designated as an Early Excellence Centre by the DfEE. The centre offers fully integrated care and education for young children in partnership with their parents and local community. Bernadette originally trained as a teacher and since then has worked in a wide range of early years settings over the last 20 years. She has also been head of an NVQ assessment centre. Bernadette is currently a member of the QCA's working party on the Foundation stage. She has contributed to a number of publications and is the author of *Supporting Creativity and Imagination in the Early Years* (Open University Press 1998).

James Walker-Hall graduated with a psychology degree in 1998. He is currently involved in various early years research projects at the Department of Educational Studies, University of Oxford. He is a research officer working mainly on the 'Effective Provision of Preschool Education' project and the 'Families, Children and Childcare' project and also works with research students, tutoring them on research design and statistical analysis.

Kathy Sylva is Professor of Educational Psychology at the University of Oxford Department of Educational Studies. After earning a PhD at Harvard University she moved to Oxford where she taught psychology while serving on the Oxford Preschool Research Group. Her book *Childwatching at Playgroup and Nursery School* (with C. Roy and M. Painter; Grant McIntyre, 1980) broke new ground by questioning an unbridled 'free play' ideology. With Teresa Smith and Elizabeth Moore, she evaluated the High/Scope preschool programme with its emphasis on 'plan, do, review' in each session. She moved to London to begin research on assessment and curriculum in primary schools. In *Early Intervention in Children with Reading Difficulties*, she and Jane Hurry showed that

Reading Recovery is a successful intervention and cost-effective as well. During this period she was co-director of the Royal Society of Arts' Enquiry into Early Years Education (Start Right report). She has returned to Oxford and is one of the leaders of the DfEE research on effective provision of preschool education. A dominant theme throughout her work is the impact of education not only on 'subject knowledge' but on children's problem-solving, social skills and commitment to the community. A related theme in her work is the impact of early intervention in combating social disadvantage and exclusion. She was Specialist Adviser to the House of Commons Select Committee on Education and Employment during their enquiry into early childhood education.

Lesley Abbott is Professor of Early Childhood Education in the Institute of Education, Manchester Metropolitan University, where she heads the Early Years Multiprofessional Centre. She was a member of the committee of enquiry into the quality of education experiences offered to 3- and 4-year-olds (the Rumbold Committee) and the Royal Society of Arts 'Early Learning' project. She is firmly committed to multiprofessional training and the development of a 'climbing frame' of training opportunities for all those involved in the 'educare' of young children. She directed the research project 'Educare for the Under Threes' and produced a video training and resource pack – *Shaping the Future – Working with the Under Threes*. She is currently working on support materials for the implementation of early learning goals and co-editing, with Cathy Nutbrown, a book on Reggio Emilia.

As founder and Director of the Open University's Vocational Qualifications Centre, **Denise Hevey** heads up a small, specialist team of vocational education and training experts within the UK's largest higher education institution. A psychologist by background, she spent some years researching support services for families with young children before joining The Open University in 1983. She has contributed to a variety of open-learning courses, including 'Child Abuse and Neglect', 'Working with Children' and 'Young People and Key Skills: Making a Difference'. She has also been actively involved in a voluntary capacity with the childcare sector and was President of the National Childminding Association for six years. In 1989 she was seconded to the Local Government Management Board to manage the 'Working with Under Sevens' project, which was responsible for developing the first NVQ in Childcare and Education. Since then she has been regularly involved as a consultant to the DfEE, the QCA and the Quality Assurance Agency for Higher Education on research projects related to vocational qualifications.

Coram Family

Coram Family is thought to be the UK's first childcare charity. It has a reputation for pioneering work in difficult areas, maintaining the spirit of its founder, Captain Thomas Coram who established the Foundling Hospital for abandoned children in London in 1739. Coram runs about 30 projects, working with over 1,000 children and young people in the care system and 600 families and young children in the local community. The work includes:

Intervention – enabling children who have experienced trauma and dislocation in their lives, and who have been separated from their parents, to develop a sense of self-esteem, to find stability and lead fulfilling lives.

Prevention – supporting vulnerable children and families in order to promote positive outcomes and prevent later difficulties.

Promotion – drawing on their experience to influence policy and practice, and to raise public awareness of the needs of children and young people.

INTRODUCTION

Gillian Pugh

Since the first edition of this book was published in 1992 there have been very considerable changes in the circumstances of children's lives but, more particularly, in the levels of service provision for young children and the commitment of government to take children and families seriously. The central focus of the book, however, remains the same – how we can work better together to meet the needs of young children and their families. The authors, some of them contributing to the book for the first time, have all brought a completely new perspective to their chapters in the light of the changes of the last decade. But with advances in our understanding of early brain development and an ever-growing awareness of the importance of the early years of life, all the authors focus on young children – children who may be powerless and vulnerable, but children who are intensely curious and energetic, children who are instinctive and enthusiastic learners.

Running through the book is a concern about the environment and the experiences we offer to children: a concern for equality of opportunity for all children, for respecting and valuing children, for observing and listening to children, for understanding how to support and enable children's learning and for planning how to meet their needs as individuals now and in the future. But the book is also about relationships between adults and children, and about relationships between the adults – parents and educators – who work with and care for children. And it is about working across boundaries, boundaries between parents and professionals, and between 'carers' and 'educators', and finding time to care for each other as well as for our children.

If we look at the circumstances in which children are growing up and at key demographic changes in family life at the beginning of the new century, four key issues stand out.

The first is that the UK is an ageing society. The numbers of children in the population and the percentage of children are both decreasing. In 1971, children and young people under 20 years of age comprised 31% of the population. By 1996 it had fallen to 25%. For children under 5 years, a population of 3.2 million in 1975 had dropped to 3 million in 1999, accounting for just over 6% of the population.

The second is the change in family patterns. Although four fifths of children live with both their natural parents, just under one in five families are now headed by a lone mother. The majority of lone mothers are divorced or separated, but an increasing number of women have never married. One third of children are born outside marriage, compared to one in ten 20 years ago, although four fifths are registered by both parents. The annual divorce rate is now six times higher than 30 years ago, with one child in 25 experiencing the divorce of their parents before their fourth birthday, and one in four by the time they are 16 years of age. One in six fathers live apart from their children, and 8% of children live in stepfamilies. Although there is concern at the impact on children of increasing instability in family life, there is no straightforward relationship between family disruption and the consequences for children – other than a clear message about the impact of the ensuing financial hardship. The key factor that comes through from research is that what matters above all is the nature and quality of parenting, and the extent to which children are able to keep in touch with both parents.

Changing employment patterns are the third most notable change in the last decade, with two out of three mothers with dependent children now working or looking for work compared with less than half 20 years ago. In the last decade, mothers with children under 5 years working outside the home rose from 32% to 51%, with some evidence this figure would be higher if there were more adequate childcare. A much smaller percentage of lone parents work, again linked to the shortage of childcare facilities. A number of commentators have pointed to the growing division between 'work rich' families with two full-time earners and 'work poor' families with no earner. There is also concern that British men, particularly those with dependent children, work longer hours overall than their European counterparts.

The fourth, and most distressing, trend is that between 1979 and 1994 the number of children living on or below the poverty line rose from one in ten to one in three. Over 4.3 million children live in households with below half the average income. The reduction and eventual eradication of childhood poverty is a key target of the current Labour government and lies behind most of the new initiatives that have been launched since the government came into power in 1997.

If we look at the main headlines of current government policy for children, these can be summarised as follows:

- *Joined up thinking* – the need to link together at central policy level and at local planning and delivery level services that are provided for children.

- *Reducing child poverty* – a commitment to halve poverty by 2010 and eradicate it within 20 years.

- *Supporting families* – a range of initiatives summarised in the green paper, *Supporting Families* (Home Office, 1999), including the Sure Start initiative.

- *Reducing social exclusion*, through a range of measures being driven by the Cabinet-level Social Exclusion Unit and the recently formed Children and Young People's Unit.

- *Improving health*, as outlined in the *NHS Plan* (NHS, 2000).

- *Raising educational standards*, through a range of measures, including expansion of nursery education and the literacy and numeracy strategies.

- *Improving access to work*, underpinned by the childcare strategy and central to the drive to reduce child poverty.

- *Basing services on the needs of consumers* rather than the wishes of service providers.

- *Taking seriously the state's role as corporate parent*, particularly through the Quality Protects initiative, which recognises that children 'looked after' in the care system have consistently been let down by the state.

This broad-ranging policy agenda has spawned a huge number of initiatives, units and zones. Amongst those most relevant to young children and their families are the Children and Young People's Unit, bringing a strategic planning role to services nationally, and the locally based Children's Fund; the Sure Start initiative (£1.4 billion over six years to establish 500 community-based schemes for parents and children under 4 years of age in areas of high need); the National Childcare Strategy (providing for a huge expansion in childcare facilities, particularly after-school and holiday play schemes); the establishment in every local authority of Early Years Development and Childcare Partnerships; and a network of 30 'early excellence centres'. These, and other initiatives, are covered in the chapters that follow.

The very considerable additional investment in services for young children and their families is welcomed by all the contributors to this book.

However, as several point out, we are still some way from a child-centred society in which children, and those who work with them, are understood, valued and taken seriously.

The book is in two main parts – policy and practice (both of them informed by research) – but with additional chapters on research and on training.

The first three chapters are principally concerned with policy. In the opening chapter, Gillian Pugh reviews the main developments within a national policy context over the past four years. Whilst she finds much to celebrate, with considerable improvements in the range and level of provision for young children and services for children and families higher on the national agenda than at any time in living memory, there is still a lack of overall vision and coherence, and too much dependence on short-term funding. This theme is taken up by Peter Moss in Chapter 2, who draws on his extensive cross-national experience to compare early childhood services and related policies in Britain to those in the rest of Europe, and particularly Sweden, the only other country in the world apart from Britain to bring all services within the education department. This chapter finds the UK response to be a pragmatic one to a huge and varied existing market, lacking in the vision required to develop a truly child-centred society.

Gerison Lansdown and Penny Lancaster explore a child welfare model that builds on a respect for children's rights. They draw on an exploratory project that is creating different methods to enable young children to articulate their feelings, experiences, concerns and anxieties.

The second and longer section of the book focuses on practice in the early years and includes five chapters on the quality of the experiences we offer young children. Tricia David explores what we mean by curriculum in the context of the first national curriculum guidelines for 3–5-year-olds and the 'early learning goals'. We are challenged to rethink how young children learn, and to remember the importance of play and of child-directed learning – and of the skills required by early educators – in a world dominated by national assessments. Cathy Nutbrown develops the theme of assessment in her chapter on how early childhood educators can understand the capabilities of the children they teach, looking particularly at the role of child observation as one of the best 'tools of the trade'. Observation is also central to Dorothy Selleck's chapter on providing a high-quality environment for children under 3 years of age. As more and more parents use care outside the home for their very young children, this chapter looks at how early years settings can complement the home, with a particular emphasis on observation, on early attachments and on continuity of experiences.

Although the central tenet of each chapter is that of equality of opportunity and a quality service that meets individual needs, two chapters look at specific issues. In her chapter on diversity and learning, Iram Siraj-Blatchford challenges the hidden assumptions which oppress particular groups and individuals: children who may be disadvantaged on grounds of ethnic background, language, gender or socioeconomic class. Sheila Wolfendale picks up these themes in relation to children with special needs, examining key concepts, principles and values in the context of special needs legislation and policy development.

Two chapters focus on relationships between the adults who work with children. Margy Whalley describes the process of developing and supporting a multiprofessional staff team, working with parents, volunteers and staff from other agencies. Lucy Draper and Bernadette Duffy draw on their experience in an early excellence centre to explore the many ways in which parents and professionals work together in early years settings, for the benefit of children, parents and staff.

In a completely new chapter, James Walker-Hall and Kathy Sylva draw on US evidence to describe which programmes are most effective for parents whose children are exhibiting serious behavioural problems from a very young age, looking particularly at the work of Carolyn Webster-Stratton, whose approach is now being developed in the UK.

And finally Lesley Abbott and Denise Hevey confront what has been described as the early years training muddle, in a chapter which traces recent developments in National Vocational Qualifications, in teacher training and in the establishment of early childhood studies degrees. The climbing frame of qualifications is under construction, but there are still many rungs missing.

The contributors to this book are all nationally and internationally known for their contributions to the early childhood debate over the last 20 years. All recognise the very different climate within which a new government is trying to catch up with levels of service provision elsewhere in Europe, and to challenge the huge divisions within society which give some children so much more of a head start than others. Children and families are now a priority within national policy, and attempts are being made at all levels to 'join up' the thinking and bring us out of our professional boxes. But there is still a long way to go and still the danger we may lose sight of services which are truly child-centred. If the considerable progress that has been made in the last four years is not to be lost, we must ensure those responsible for the development of policy and practice across all sectors take account of and build on these changes.

PART 1
POLICY

1

A POLICY FOR EARLY CHILDHOOD SERVICES?

Gillian Pugh

Within the context of the major demographic and policy changes of the last four years, summarised briefly in the Introduction, this chapter considers the progress that has been made towards the development of a coherent national policy on services for young children under the age of 8 years and their families. Since the election of a Labour government in 1997, services for children and families have been higher on the public agenda than at any time in living memory. Much has been achieved, but where do the gaps remain?

INTRODUCTION

Since the establishment of the first nursery school by Robert Owen, in Scotland in 1816, the development of early education in the UK has been remarkably slow by comparison to much of mainland Europe. In 1870, publicly funded education became compulsory at the age of 5 years, but from the earliest days children as young as 2 years were admitted to primary schools. During the course of the twentieth century successive governments supported the principle of free nursery education but seldom found the resources to fund it. Even with the gradual establishment of nursery schools and, during the 1914–1918 war, some public day-care centres, the predominant form of early education in the UK has always been state primary schools. The lack of appropriate provision within the education system led to two parallel developments: on the one hand the emergence during the 1960s, through the voluntary sector, of the playgroup movement; and, on the other, the growth during the 1990s, through the private sector, of day-care centres to meet the needs of working parents who needed full day care for their children.

This legacy is important in understanding the state of early childhood services at the beginning of the twenty-first century. A review in 1988 found a patchwork of fragmented and uncoordinated services, showing wide variations between one part of the country and another, within the context of a 'low national commitment to developing and resourcing pre-school services, and the absence of a national policy on what services should be provided, for whom and by whom' (Pugh, 1988). This review concluded that the challenge for government was to provide an overall framework within which services could be developed flexibly at local level. The previous edition of this book (Pugh, 1996) described services in the UK as follows:

- Discretionary, with considerable variations between local authorities as to the level of services provided.

- Having very low levels of public funding by comparison to the rest of Europe.

- Having a heavy reliance on the private and voluntary sectors.

- Having diversity of provision, but very little choice for parents.

- Lacking in co-ordination between services, with services run by education, social services, health, leisure departments, employers, private and voluntary organisations.

- Comprising different services having very different aims and purposes.

- Having different services used by different client groups: children of working parents in private provision, children 'in need' in local authority nurseries, and children for whose parents part-time provision in nursery classes and playgroups is convenient.

The levels of concern expressed here were reflected in a number of prestigious national reports published during the 1990s, including the Rumbold Report *Starting with Quality* (DES, 1990), largely ignored by the government at the time but very widely used as the basis for best practice in early years settings; the National Commission on Education's *Learning to Succeed* (1993), which made the expansion of nursery education its highest recommendation; the Royal Society of Arts' *Start Right: The Importance of Early Learning* (Ball, 1994), an authoritative report which re-emphasised the importance of the early years and recommended that the school starting age should be raised to 6 years; and the Audit Commission Report *Counting to Five* (1996), which pressed for greater coherence between the different types of provision.

During the 1980s and early 1990s there was a lack of political conviction that young children mattered and a view that children were the private responsibility of their parents. But there were also unclear and conflicting messages about what was required – should an early years policy be most concerned with preparing children for school or with day care for working parents; should it provide stimulation for a developing brain or equal opportunities for women; was it about cost savings for employers, able to retain staff when they became parents, or about reducing the benefit bill for single parents; or was prevention the main driving force – whether of developmental delay in children or juvenile crime?

The establishment of the Early Childhood Education Forum in 1993, bringing together all the national agencies in the field, was one response to the lack of clarity over what a policy for early childhood services should look like. As the forum gathered strength, with a membership of 45 national organisations by 1998, and as report after report called for an expansion in services, the government took action. In 1995 additional funding for the education of 4-year-olds was announced but, controversially, the funding was to be made available to parents through vouchers which could be redeemed in private, voluntary or local authority nurseries. A pilot scheme was rolled out across four local authorities, amidst mounting criticism (Owen and McQuail, 1997), but full implementation was stopped by the election of a Labour government in 1997. We will now turn to an analysis of policy at the beginning of the new millennium.

AN INTEGRATED NATIONAL POLICY?

Since coming into power, the government's over-riding policy commitment has been to reduce the huge numbers of children living on or below the poverty line. The range of initiatives that has been established as part of this drive includes many focused on families with young children:

(1) Transference of responsibility for children under the age of 8 years from the Department of Health to the Department for Education and Skills, with the DfES taking the lead on issues concerning young children.

(2) The establishment of the Foundation stage of early education, for children aged from 3 years to the end of the reception year of school.

(3) Increased expenditure on nursery education, with a place for all 4-year-olds and for all 3-year-olds by 2004 (though these places may be in any of the wide range of types of provision noted below).

(4) The National Childcare Strategy, which is bringing an additional £470 million to expand and improve childcare services for children from birth to 3 years of age and out-of-school provision for children under 14 years.

(5) The working families tax credit, which provides £70 towards the cost of childcare for one child, and £105 for two or more children for low-income families.

(6) More family-friendly policies in the workplace – improved parental leave and more flexible working arrangements.

(7) The introduction of Early Years Development and Childcare Partnerships in local authorities (see below).

(8) The establishment of the Early Excellence Centres pilot programme (see below).

(9) The establishment of the Sure Start initiative, which is bringing £1.4 billion to 500 high-need communities to develop services for children under 4 years and their parents over a five-year period.

(10) The establishment of an Early Years National Training Organisation and the production of a national qualifications and training framework for the early years (QCA, 1999b).

(11) An integrated inspection service from autumn 2001.

(12) A recognition that early years services must meet the needs of parents as well as children.

This level of investment would have been inconceivable ten years ago, and those working in the field have been astonished at the speed with which the new developments have been implemented. However, in relation to an aspiration for an integrated policy, whilst much has been achieved, there has been no national debate as to what a coherent early childhood policy should look like, there is still no overall vision, and the various elements are still far from 'joined up'. Within the DfES, for example, there are still divisions between Early Years (with a focus on universal nursery education for 3- and 4-year-olds), Childcare (developing a fee-paying service in response to parental employment), and Sure Start (developing community-based services for children under 4 years of age as part of the anti-poverty strategy). This feels more like a bolt-on approach to policy-making than the coherent policy for children from birth to 6 years that many commentators have been calling for (see Ball, 1994; Moss and Penn, 1996; Pugh, 1996; Moss, 1999). As Moss has noted (1999), in the flurry of activity to increase levels of provision, 'the opportunity to *transform* a neglected and incoherent confusion of services' has been missed (see also Chapter 2).

Whilst there has been a considerable increase in the level of funding going into early years services, there is a continuing lack of coherence between the many new initiatives, with several different departments in control of different sources of funding. A recent report noted 45 distinct streams of funding for childcare, many of them so complex and diverse that key players are often unaware of all the potential sources and so unable to make the most of them (Day Care Trust, 2000).

Whilst there has been a general welcome for the integration of responsibility for all young children's services within the DfES, there is some concern that children's heath and welfare could be neglected at the expense of their education. By comparison with much education legislation, the Children Act was a child-centred Act that was carefully considered and broadly supported. In the drive to raise standards there are those who fear the needs of the most vulnerable children could be at risk.

Levels of provision

The lack of co-ordination in service provision is mirrored by a lack of co-ordination in the collection of data about the use of services, and it is only through the services of the NCB Early Childhood Unit that it is possible to get some sense of the current usage by comparison to that in previous years. The increase in funding for the sector is evident in Table 1.1, which provides comparative data for services in England over a 24-year period.

Table 1.1   Under-5s in England: use of services, 1975/1999

	1975	1985	1994	1999
Places per 100 children 0–4				
LA day nurseries	0.8	1.0	0.7	0.50
Private nurseries	0.8	0.8	3.8	7.25
Childminders	2.6	4.7	11.0	11.00
Places per 100 children 3–4				
Playgroups	23.3	33.8	31.3	30.00
Pupils as % of 3- and 4-year-olds				
Nursery schools and classes	10.0	22.5	26.4	30.00
Under-5s in infant classes	18.9	20.7	25.0	29.00
Indepedent schools	2.1	2.5	3.7	5.60

Source: Early Childhood Unit, National Children's Bureau; based on government statistics.

The trends evident in 1994 have continued. The amount of publicly funded day care continues to decrease, whilst the percentage of children in private nurseries has increased substantially, and those with childminders by a small margin. As far as part-time education is concerned, the percentage of children in playgroups continues to decrease as more statutory provision comes on stream, and increasing numbers of 3- and 4-year-olds find places in nursery schools and classes and in infant classes.

What these figures are unable to show is a small but growing number of combined centres, 'early excellence centres' and family centres which attempt to provide a more integrated service for local families.

Until very recently, the figures have has been very approximate due to the fact that different data have been collected by different departments. The DfES, for example, collected pupil figures, whereas the Department of Health collected numbers of places. The new Early Years Census and the Day Care Survey, both initiated in 1999, should help to provide more reliable statistics, and an annual census combining both these was launched in 2000.

Access to services

A decade ago the Rumbold report was concerned that 'access to services is still largely determined by where a child lives, when his or her birthday is, whether the parents have access to information about services, and whether they can afford the fees where there is no public provision' (DES, 1990, pp. 27–8). Whilst the government is attempting to address long-standing inequities in access to early years services, there are still some considerable gaps in the levels of provision.

Although many 4-year-olds are in nursery or infant schools for a school day, most nursery education is sessional (i.e. a two and half hour session in the morning or afternoon). In Europe, on the other hand, the norm is full-time nursery provision for three years up until the start of school at 6 (see Chapter 2). For those 4-year-olds who are in infant schools, there is growing concern about the inappropriateness of this provision for such young children.

With the main statutory funding for children limited to the provision of education during the school day, those parents who are working or studying (now the majority of parents with young children) must cobble together a range of care arrangements to 'wrap around' the school day and to take care of the holidays. And for children under 3 years of age there is almost no state-funded provision at all. Despite the expansion of additional places through the National Childcare Strategy, and the additional funds for parents through the working families tax credit, access to affordable childcare is still a major problem for large numbers of parents. There is still a shortage of affordable, quality childcare, particularly for children under 3 years of age.

AN INTEGRATED POLICY AT LOCAL LEVEL

When the Conservative government was considering the introduction of the voucher scheme in 1995 as a way of broadening the market in the provision of services and loosening the hold of the local authorities, the Early Childhood Education Forum (ECEF) proposed an alternative approach. With a membership representing all the major players in the early years field, they proposed the establishment of forums in each area, bringing together statutory, voluntary and private sector providers around the table to hammer out policy and expenditure at a local level.

With the arrival of a new government, the setting up of Early Years Development and Childcare Partnerships (EYDCP) in every local authority – a very similar arrangement to that recommended by ECEF – became mandatory. Partnerships consist of representatives from the maintained, private and voluntary sectors, local education, social service and health representatives, employers, training institutions, and parents. Working in partnership with the local education authority, each partnership is required to draw up an annual local plan, linked into the government's targets for early education places for 3- and 4-year-olds and the expansion of childcare. This has required every EYDCP to undertake a childcare audit to assess shortfall of supply in relation to demand – a considerable challenge in its first year. A review of the first two years of the operation of the partnerships pointed to the challenges posed by the tight timetables and detailed demands of the EYDCP plan, and noted the importance of recognising the process of partnership as the key dynamic, rather than simply achieving targets (Jamieson and Owen, 2000). But every local authority did set up a partnership and complete both an audit and a plan. The challenge now is the extent to which the partnerships can involve local people in creating real change within their community.

Although there are as yet only a few Sure Start schemes established nationwide, it will be interesting to see the impact such schemes have on planning and delivering services at local level. Despite the goals and targets set by the scheme nationally, the local programmes will vary in their response to local need. A significant element of every scheme will be the partnership approach both to defining local need and to delivering local services, with parents and community organisations playing a significant role in the board that will manage each scheme (Sure Start, 1999a).

Structures for running early years services

In the previous editions of this book I have considered the range of administrative arrangements local authorities have made in managing services at local level. In the last five years there have been significant changes in local authority organisation. Some have encouraged new structures, whilst others have put a stronger emphasis on joint planning. Local government reform, the establishment of some unitary authorities, the Health Act 1999 which enables local authorities and health authorities to devise integrated structures, responsibility for early years services at national level passing to the DfES and the requirement for local EYDCPs have all impacted on the provision of services at local level. Nevertheless it is worth noting that those local authorities which had well developed early years policies and structures in place were best able to make progress on their plans (Jamieson and Owen, 2000).

A review of effective structures for early years services concluded that:

> Structures are important, but so too are relationships between key individuals who must be able to transcend the barriers of professional jealousies and vested interests and work openly together in the best interests of children and their parents The key is to develop strategies for planning, resourcing and reviewing high quality services that are 'owned' by all elected members and senior officers. These strategies need to be supported by the capacity to make executive decisions, which requires some control over budgets. An overall vision, shared by all the 'stakeholders' and which takes account of local circumstances and traditions, together with the means of implementing it, is as important as the type of political or management structure (Pugh and McQuail, 1995, p. 16).

Drawing on this study, on the evaluation of the Children Act reviews (Elfer and McQuail, 1996) and on work with local authorities over many years, it can be concluded that effective co-ordination or integration depends on:

- A clear policy agreed by all the main providers, setting out the principles upon which services should be based, the aims and objectives for the service, an EYDCP plan, and a clear process for implementation and review.

- A committee structure and administrative structure which can support the EYCD partnership and, through it, an integrated approach to planning.

- A children's committee with delegated powers for policy development and resource deployment.

- Clear support from senior elected members and chief officers. This is particularly important in areas of discretionary expenditure.

- Clarity about roles and about management responsibility, and clear lines of communication both within departments (between senior management, middle management and front-line workers) and between departments.

- Clarity about relationships with health authorities and trusts and primary care groups and trusts.

- Real partnership with the voluntary and private sectors.

- A role for local forums, and links between local forums and Sure Start partnerships and the EYCDPs.

- A senior-level post within the local authority responsible for early years.

FLEXIBLE SERVICES TO MEET THE NEEDS OF CHILDREN AND THEIR PARENTS

The demand for early childhood services still far outstrips the supply and, even where services have expanded, they still do not always meet the needs of parents in terms of availability, accessibility and affordability. Surveys of parents' needs show considerable variety, reflecting different local circumstances and expectations. The need for flexibility in the provision of services has been well documented, but the development of such services has been extraordinarily slow. Although the first combined nursery centre opened in 1971, the complexity of bringing together funding across different departments and of employing staff under different terms and conditions has proved too much for many who have attempted it over the years. Yet for parents who are working, two and a half hours of nursery education or three mornings a week at a playgroup is hardly likely to be suitable, and the importance of linking existing services to each other, or of running a range of services from one base, is slowly beginning to be understood. There is also a growing realisation that early childhood services can provide important support for parents in their role as parents and in supporting their children's learning, as well as helping them to access training and employment.

The government's 'early excellence centre' programme has given the development of more flexible and responsive services a much-needed boost. Although most of the 30 current centres have been established for many years, the high-profile nature of the programme has drawn attention to the principles that underpin such services, and an ongoing evaluation study will bring evidence of what can be achieved through such approaches. Early excellence centres are expected to provide:

- Excellence in integrated education and care services.

- Access to extended day and holiday childcare for children from birth.

- Support for families, including parenting education.

- Links to other key services, such as community health services.

- Accessible and affordable adult training opportunities.

- Outreach through local EYCD partnerships to improve the quality of other early years services through training and practical example.

Early evidence from the first centres shows that not only are the centres having a substantial and positive impact on children and families but also that they are supporting practitioners through additional training and are making significant cost savings (DfEE, 1999a).

Recent announcements from the DfES have suggested that Sure Start schemes should be more closely linked into early excellence centres. Most centres do in fact already provide most of the services for children under 4 years of age and their families that are envisaged in Sure Start – for example home visiting schemes, family support, drop-in centres and crèche provision – but the strong emphasis on community health care is not always so evident in school-based centres.

A diagram showing the services provided by the Thomas Coram Early Excellence Centre is given in Figure 1.1. This centre is part of the Coram Community Campus, based in the Kings Cross area of London and working with 600 local families in the most deprived ward in Camden. Our aim has been to provide a 'one-stop shop', offering high-quality, open-access services, provided by the five voluntary organisations working in partnership with the local authority (education and social services) and the community health trust. (For an evaluation, see Wigfall and Moss, (2001). Chapter 10 in this book considers work with parents in the centre.)

It is interesting to reflect on why the 'vision' for early childhood units of the future as being based in every primary school (Pugh and McQuail, 1995) has failed to take root. Only two of the current 'early excellence centres' are based in primary schools – perhaps because primary headteachers are too preoccupied with the government's many other demands on them?

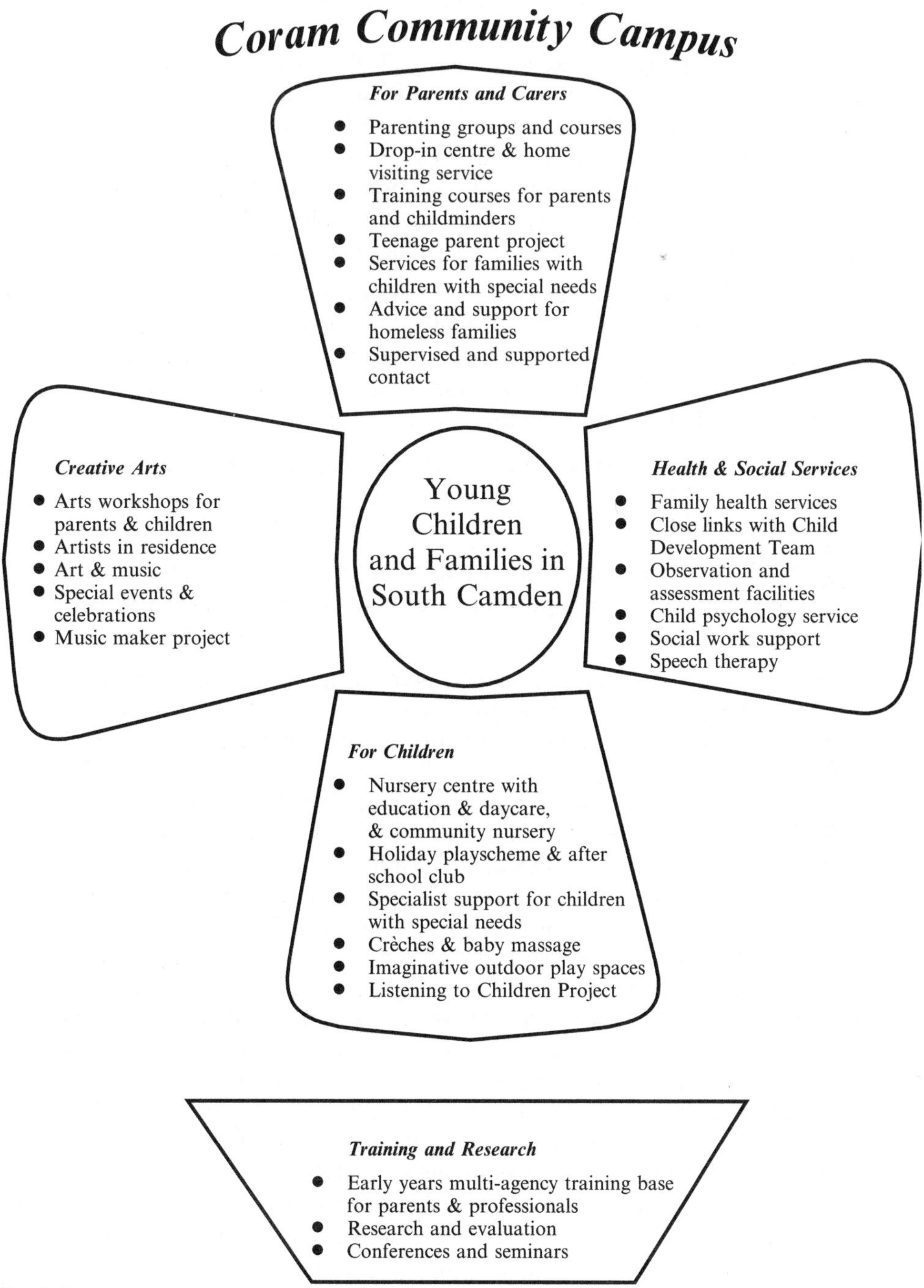

Coram Community Campus

For Parents and Carers

- Parenting groups and courses
- Drop-in centre & home visiting service
- Training courses for parents and childminders
- Teenage parent project
- Services for families with children with special needs
- Advice and support for homeless families
- Supervised and supported contact

Creative Arts

- Arts workshops for parents & children
- Artists in residence
- Art & music
- Special events & celebrations
- Music maker project

Young Children and Families in South Camden

Health & Social Services

- Family health services
- Close links with Child Development Team
- Observation and assessment facilities
- Child psychology service
- Social work support
- Speech therapy

For Children

- Nursery centre with education & daycare, & community nursery
- Holiday playscheme & after school club
- Specialist support for children with special needs
- Crèches & baby massage
- Imaginative outdoor play spaces
- Listening to Children Project

Training and Research

- Early years multi-agency training base for parents & professionals
- Research and evaluation
- Conferences and seminars

Fig 1.1.

A HIGH-QUALITY SERVICE

The issue of quality has been discussed in almost every book on early childhood services published during the past decade (see, for example, Abbott and Roger, 1994a,b; Moss and Pence, 1994; Pascal *et al.*, 1994; Williams, 1994; Woodhead, 1996) and has to be seen as a complex process rather than a set of tidy outcomes. Dahlberg *et al.* (1999, pp. 5–6) point to the growing awareness of context, complexity, plurality and subjectivity noted by these and other writers, whom they say have:

- identified the importance of the *process* of defining quality – who is involved and how it is done – and questioned how that process has operated in the past, arguing that it has been dominated by a small group of experts, to the exclusion of a wide range of other stake holders with an interest in early childhood institutions;

- understood quality to be a *subjective, value-based, relative* and *dynamic* concept, with the possibility of *multiple perspectives* or understandings of what quality is;

- argued that work with quality needs to be *contextualised*, spatially and temporally, and to recognise cultural and other significant forms of *diversity*.

Within the context of these remarks, perhaps the three most important elements of a quality early years service are an appropriate curriculum, well trained staff and good relationships between staff and parents, all of which are covered in later chapters.

With regard to curriculum, there have been growing concerns that the introduction of the National Curriculum and, more recently, the national literacy and numeracy strategies, are leading to pressure to formalise education at the earliest opportunity. The Rumbold report (DES, 1990) argued that the *context* of learning and the *process* of learning – the way in which young children acquire the disposition to learn – are as important as *what* children learn, and the report argued against the early introduction of formal learning. Much of the debate about young children's learning in the past decade has centred on attempts by those who work with young children to convey this understanding to those responsible for policy and national guidance – in the DfEE, the Teacher Training Agency, OFSTED, and the Qualifications and Curriculum Authority (QCA).

The Foundation stage curriculum guidance (QCA, 2000a), prepared by a working party of early years experts including many of those who have contributed to this book, provides a clear and unambiguous statement of the principles which should underpin both learning and teaching. The guidance argues that:

- Effective early education requires a relevant curriculum, one that builds on what children can already do and which includes opportunities for children to engage in activities planned by adults as well as those they plan or initiate themselves. Children are innately curious and eager to learn. They learn best through play, through talk and through direct experience; and they learn when they feel confident and secure. Early learning experiences should encourage in children a positive attitude and disposition towards learning, and the confidence to work on their own and with others to solve problems and make choices.

- Effective early education requires practitioners who understand how young children learn and develop; who can observe children and respond appropriately, planning for children's learning, both as individuals and in groups; who can create a stimulating and well-organised learning environment; and who can work in partnership with parents.

There are two particular areas of concern. The first relates to the considerable and growing number of 4-year-olds who are going early into primary school, often into classes where ratios may be as high as 1:30, where many teachers will not be trained to work with such young children, and where the curriculum is unlikely to be appropriate (see Pugh, 1996). There is clear evidence there are no educational advantages of entering school early, and a growing body of research shows the adverse effects of introducing children too early to an inappropriately formal curriculum. It is to be hoped the introduction of the new 'foundation stage' for children from 3 to 6 years of age, up to the end of the reception year, will lead to improvements in this area, but it will need the understanding and support of headteachers, governors and OFSTED.

The other relates to children under 3 years of age. The QCA guidance provides for children aged 3–5 years and does not consider birth to 6 years as the first phase of education. Yet children are of course learning from birth or even earlier and we know from research into early brain development how important the first three years of life are, in terms of the speed at which the brain is developing and its susceptibility to environmental influences. As services for children under 3 years of age slowly develop, it is important there is a clearer understanding of what constitutes 'good practice', whether in nurseries or at home with parents or childminders. (See, for example, Chapter 6 and Sure Start, 2000.)

SETTING STANDARDS AND MONITORING QUALITY

One of the concerns of an uncoordinated system of early years provision has been the considerable variation in quality between different types of provision. Another has been the different regulation and inspection regimes, where OFSTED has been operating two separate systems, one for schools and one for other early years settings, and local authorities have been inspecting all registered settings under the requirements of the Children Act. A single inspection system under the direction of OFSTED, to include registration and inspection, comes into operation during 2001 and the national standards have recently been published. In the tension between the need to expand services but yet maintain standards, there is some concern these are too low.

Whilst external inspection will always be part of a quality assurance system, the UK has one of the most over-regulated and inspected services in Europe. If services are really to improve, and if staff are to take responsibility for that improvement, then self-assessment through professional development and training has to be an important strand of all service provision. Over the past decade there has been an increasing number of developments that have supported this approach to improving quality, including *Quality in Diversity in Early Learning* (Early Childhood Education Forum, 1998), the 'Effective Early Learning' project (Pascal *et al.*, 1997) and the 'Day Care Self Evaluation' scheme (Munton and Mooney, 1998). It is to be hoped that the new inspection regime will build on the current developments in self-appraisal and self-evaluation and link them into centre action plans, supported by early years advisers.

STAFF TRAINING AND QUALIFICATIONS

The quality of provision in early years settings is clearly linked to the quality of the staff who work in them. All the major reports over the last ten years have pointed to:

- A chronic shortage of trained staff in all sectors.

- A lack of qualifications amongst those working with children under 5 years of age in the private and voluntary sectors.

- A huge range of different qualifications – one study identified 329 recognised qualifications (HERA 2, 1999).

- The inappropriateness of the content of teaching training for nursery and infant teachers, with a curriculum that neglects child development.

- The high proportion of teachers in reception classes in schools who are not trained to work with such young children (only 37% with some relevant training in a recent QCA survey).

- A lack of funding for training, whether through the NVQ route or through teacher training.

- A lack of interface between the developing Early Years National Training Organisation (responsible for accrediting NVQ-related qualifications taken by playgroup leaders, nursery nurses, child-minders, etc.) and the Teacher Training Agency's role in training teachers.

Effective early education requires a well qualified workforce, all of whom should be appropriately trained. All early years settings should employ or have access to early years teachers, as is now recognised in government guidance, and yet the recent expansion in provision has not been paralleled by an expansion in training. Teaching young children is a skilled and demanding job. As the RSA report (Ball, 1994) argued, early years teachers require a breadth of knowledge, understanding and experience that is not required of those training to teach older children.

There are two other major areas of concern. The first is the importance of access to inservice training and continuous staff development, which should be a right of all early years practitioners. Schools have five days a year for staff training; many private and voluntary sector groups have little or no inservice training.

The second is the huge differentials in pay and conditions between the various staff working with young children, and generally low levels of pay across the sector. There are also high rates of turnover, with an estimated 30% of staff in nurseries leaving their jobs every year (Day Care Trust, 1997). This is a professional job that does not, at present, command a professional salary.

Whilst there have been many encouraging developments, such as the expansion of integrated early years degrees and the recognition of these as the basis for teacher training, there has been no major investment in training, and no national commitment to resolving the continuing divisions in training and conditions of service between teachers and non-teaching staff. Elements of the climbing frame are being put in place (see Abbott and Pugh, 1998), but the government has not as yet developed a strategic approach to staff training and qualifications nor to recruitment, retention and improved working conditions. These issues are further discussed in Chapter 12.

IN CONCLUSION

The last decade has seen considerable improvements in the range and level of provision for young children in the UK and the many achievements have been noted in this chapter. But there is still a long way to go. Whilst services may be more joined up, there is no coherent overall policy that brings together the needs of children (as seen within the education system) with the needs of parents to reconcile employment with family life (as seen within the day-care system), and no broader and longer-term vision of an integrated approach to services for children under 6 years of age. Many children still use several different services before they start school, sometimes indeed in the course of a week, and there is still a severe shortage of affordable day care for children under 3 years of age. The introduction of a Foundation stage for children aged 3–5 years is to be welcomed, but there is a continuing lack of continuity between services for children under 3 years of age and those over 3. It also remains to be seen whether the existence of the Foundation stage will successfully push good child-centred practice up into the primary schools, or whether the downwards push of the National Curriculum will prevail.

Whilst there is additional funding, and some services have expanded, much of this is for short-term initiatives that will finish in three or five years' time. The complexity of the different funding streams presents huge challenges for those running services in local areas. And there is still a severe shortage of trained early years workers and no overall strategy to improve training, pay and conditions in the sector.

2

BRITAIN IN EUROPE: FRINGE OR HEART?

Peter Moss

Britain's relationship to the rest of Europe (or, for the purposes of this chapter, that part of it within the European Union) sits at the centre of British politics. As an off-shore island, with an imperial and maritime history, Britain often looks across the Atlantic and to the rest of the English-speaking world for comparison and inspiration. Yet as an island close to the shores of the European landmass we can never escape the gravitational pull of Europe. Our relationship, however, is deeply ambivalent. We like to make comparisons to show how much better 'Europe' does this or that, yet we get readily defensive.

In this chapter, I want to compare early childhood services and related policies in Britain[1] with those in our European partners, identifying some similarities and some differences. But before making this comparison, I want to flag up some features of the social, economic, demographic and political context which have had a bearing on shaping recent developments in early childhood services in Britain. I then want to make a more specific comparison. In the late 1990s, both Britain and Sweden moved responsibility for early childhood services and school-age childcare services (called 'free-time' services in Sweden) into education, becoming the only countries in the world where these services and schools fall within the same administrative framework. I shall look at this reform process in both countries, including the extent and nature of restructuring and rethinking. Finally, I shall conclude by asking why should we bother with making cross-national comparisons: what, if anything, is to be gained from the exercise?

---

[1] I recognise there are some significant differences between England and other parts of Britain, in particular Scotland (e.g. Scotland has no National Curriculum and takes few 4-year-olds into reception classes).

PUTTING THINGS INTO CONTEXT

Like the rest of Europe, Britain has been experiencing historically low fertility rates for many years – well below the rate needed for population replacement. Partly as a consequence of changing fertility, Europe is ageing:

> The mean age of the European population is higher than that of any other region in the world, and gets older year by year. In exact figures, the population of the European Union ages by 2.5 months each year or by two years each decade. This trend is likely to continue well into the twenty-first century. The proportion of the population below age 20 is likely to decline further while the proportion of those above 60 will increase from 21 percent to 34 percent. Simultaneously, the mean age of the European population, which presently is around 39 years is likely to reach 45 years by 2030 (Lutz, 1999, p. 8).

Not only is the European population ageing in the sense of fewer young people and more old people: most key stages of the life course are taking place at ever older ages – finishing full-time education, starting employment, marriage, having children and so on. The main exception is the age of leaving employment, which has been getting earlier, leading to a concentration of employment on 25 to 55-year-olds.

There are many uncertainties. Fertility rates can change: low fertility today may be due to decisions by women to defer having children until later in their lives, and there may be a catching up. Increasing numbers of elderly people may put pressure on resources at the expense of children or governments may be encouraged to invest more in children, on the grounds of making the most of a diminishing resource or to encourage women and men to have more children. Perhaps least certain of all are the consequences of these trends for the experience of childhood itself and how parents view and relate with children.

However, on several parameters Britain stands out, creating a context that, if not unique, is at least rather distinctive. Britain has one of the highest levels of lone-parent families in the EU, second only to Sweden (UNICEF, 2000). It also has the highest level of poverty amongst children. In the case of Britain, the two are related: 46% of children in lone-parent families live in poverty. But the connection is not inevitable: only 7% of Swedish children in lone-parent families live in poverty. Other factors contribute to high levels of poverty in Britain. Overall, Britain:

> has a more generous level of social expenditure [than the USA] but a high proportion of children in lone-parent families and of households with children without an employed adult. At another extreme, Sweden, also with a high proportion of children in lone parent

families, has low rates of worklessness, low wage inequality and a high volume of social transfers – leading to a low child poverty rate (UNICEF, 2000, p. 16).

What also needs to be taken account of in Britain is the rapidity of change: lone parenthood, workless households and poverty amongst children increased very substantially over a short period in the 1980s and 1990s. But other rapid changes were occurring at the same time. Employment rates amongst women in Britain were relatively high in 1980, but they were distinguished by a large difference between women with young children and other women. Women's, and especially mothers', employment in Britain was also marked by high levels of part-time work. But from the late 1980s, employment rates amongst women with young children rose rapidly, beginning to close the employment gap with other women; the same trend was apparent in the rapid increase in women resuming employment after maternity leave. Moreover, a large part of this increased employment amongst women with young children was due to growth in full-time employment (Brannen *et al.*, 1997).

How does this square with a picture of increasing poverty, linked to growing numbers of workless households? Growth in maternal employment was not evenly spread but focused on more advantaged groups of women, in particular those with high levels of education and living with an employed partner. Employment growth was therefore part of a process of polarisation in Britain, producing more workless and poor families as well as more parental employment and affluence (for a fuller discussion of these trends, see Brannen and Moss, 1998).

What caused this enormous social upheaval and dislocation in the 1980s and 1990s? For part of the answer perhaps we have to look to the political and economic climate of the time. While free-market philosophies have become more influential throughout Europe, neoliberalism – with the value it attaches to market fundamentalism, economic individualism and deregulation, inequality and a minimal 'safety net' welfare state – has made more impact on the UK than most other countries in continental Europe (Giddens, 1998). Perhaps we should seek explanations for the massive growth of such phenomena as child poverty over the last 20 years in the interaction of neoliberalism with a class-ridden social structure and an outdated manufacturing base playing second fiddle to a powerful financial sector. Developments that might have been due to happen in any case, such as the growth of employment amongst women with young children, took a particularly polarised course for similar reasons.

Britain and the rest of Europe

Having set the scene, I want to locate early childhood services and policies in Britain in relation to the rest of Europe. These exercises carry a built-in risk: it is all too easy to offer generalisations with strong distinctions when the reality is much more nuanced, both between Britain and the rest of Europe and between those diverse countries that make up 'the rest of Europe'. For example, there are some respects in which Britain, Ireland and The Netherlands seem to have more in common with each other (for example, in starting many children at school at the age of 4 and in a commitment to employer funding for childcare) than with other countries in Europe.

So while there are some distinctive differences between Britain and many other countries in Europe, I want to start by seeking some common ground. As a broad generalisation, we can see the emergence of a common agenda for European early childhood policy:

- A legal right to parental leave.

- Public support for the childcare needs of employed parents.

- Public support for at least two years education for *all* children before they start compulsory schooling (an aim either already achieved or set as an objective of public policy).

(For those wanting more detailed comparisons between countries, see Table 2.1; also EC Childcare Network, 1995; Karlsson, 1995; Oberheumer and Ulich, 1997; OECD 2001.) Britain has now signed up to this policy agenda. However, in all cases Britain signed up late, with a clear commitment to each item only since 1997.

A combination of coming late and some of the contextual features outlined above has meant our implementation of this policy agenda has been rather distinctive. Provision of parental leave in the rest of Europe is very varied and often rather weak as judged in terms of criteria such as payment and flexibility. But neoliberalism, with its emphasis on economic deregulation, has influenced a parental leave scheme in Britain of unique weakness: unpaid and limited in duration to only four weeks in any one year and intended to have minimal implications for employers (for a fuller discussion of parental leave in Europe, see Moss and Deven, 2000). Significantly, responsibility for parental leave, whose main purposes concern child and family welfare and gender equality, has fallen to the Department of Trade and Industry, whose main concern is business competitiveness. At the time of writing, parental (and maternity) leave are the subject of government review, which may lead to a stronger measure, even including some payment.

Table 2.1   Summary of provision in EU member states for children under compulsory school age

Belgium	*Leave:* 9 months (9) (additional 'career break' period is also available); *CSA:* 6 years; *services:* split system; *publicly funded provision:* 0–3 years HIGH, 3–6 years HIGH; *tax relief:* 0–3
Denmark	*Leave:* 14 months (14); *CSA:* 7 years (early start 6); *services:* integrated system (welfare); *publicly funded provision:* 0–3 years HIGH, 3–6 years HIGH
Germany	*Leave:* 36 months (24*); *CSA:* 6 years; *services:* limited integration (welfare); *publicly funded provision:* 0–3 years LOW, 3–6 years HIGH (LE)
Greece	*Leave:* 9 months (3); *CSA:* 5½ years; *services:* split system; *publicly funded provision:* 0–3 years LOW, 3–6 years MEDIUM; *tax relief:* 0–6
Spain	*Leave:* 36 months (4); *CSA:* 6 years; *services:* partially integrated (education); *publicly funded provision:* 0–3 years LOW, 3–6 years HIGH; *tax relief:* 0–3, for low-income families
France	*Leave:* 36 months (36*); *CSA:* 6 years; *services:* split system; *publicly funded provision:* 0–3 years MEDIUM, 3–6 years HIGH; *tax relief:* 0–6
Ireland	*Leave:* 10 months (3); *CSA:* 6 years (early start 4); *services:* split system; *publicly funded provision:* 0–3 years LOW, 3–6 years MEDIUM (mainly primary school)
Italy	*Leave:* 13 months (13); *CSA:* 6 years; *services:* split system; *publicly funded provision:* 0–3 years LOW, 3–6 years HIGH (LE)
Luxembourg	*Leave:* 14 months (8); *CSA:* 4 years; *services:* split system; *publicly funded provision:* 0–3 years no information, 3–6 years HIGH; *tax relief:* 0–6
The Netherlands	*Leave:* 15 months (3); *CSA:* 5 years (early start 4); *services:* split system; *publicly funded provision:* 0–3 years LOW, 3–6 years MEDIUM (mainly primary school); *tax relief:* 0–6
Austria	*Leave:* 24 months (4); *CSA:* 6 years; *services:* limited integration (welfare); *publicly funded provision:* 0–3 years LOW, 3–6 years HIGH
Portugal	*Leave:* 10 months (5); *CSA:* 6 years; *services:* split system; *publicly funded provision:* 0–3 years LOW, 3–6 years MEDIUM (LE, 4 and 5-year-olds)
Finland	*Leave:* 36 months (36); *CSA:* 7 years; *services:* integrated system (welfare); *publicly funded provision:* 0–3 years MEDIUM (LE), 3–6 years MEDIUM (LE)
Sweden	*Leave:* 18 months (15); *CSA:* 7 (early start 6); *services:* integrated system (education); *publicly funded provision:* 0–3 years HIGH (LE from 12 months), 3–6 years MEDIUM (LE)
UK	*Leave:* 9 months (4); *CSA:* 5 (early start 4); *services:* partially integrated (education); *publicly funded provision:* 0–3 years LOW, 3–6 years MEDIUM (mainly primary school); *tax relief:* 0–6

Notes:

Leave: maximum period of post-natal maternity and parental leave in months *per family*; figure in brackets indicates period of leave for which some payment is made (often at a low flat rate). * Indicates paid to certain families only.

CSA: compulsory school age. 'Early start' indicates age at which children may start primary schooling on a voluntary basis.

Publicly funded provision: shows amount of provision directly funded publicly, expressed as full-time equivalent places. Figures are for early/mid-1990s and will have increased since then in most countries. For 0–3 years (i.e. up to 36 months), LOW = coverage for less than 10% of children; MEDIUM = 10–24%; HIGH = 25% or more. For 3–6 years (i.e. from 36 to 71 months), LOW = under 50%; medium = 50–74%; high = 75% or more. Figures based on full-time equivalent places and include children under 6 in primary school.

LE = legal entitlement.

Tax relief: indicates some form of tax relief/credit available for age-group.

When we turn to public support for early childhood services, we can see the significance of government coming late to the scene. Decades of official neglect created a vacuum that was filled by a mix of private provision and providers. For example, when maternal employment surged in the late 1980s, especially among more advantaged groups, a neoliberal government responded by asserting that childcare (and other forms of support for working parents) was a private matter for parents (in practice, mothers) to resolve for themselves. The result was a boom in private, 'for-profit' nurseries and domestic forms of care, such as nannies.

It would be misleading to suggest there were no publicly supported early childhood services but, again, they took very particular forms and left a very particular legacy. On the welfare side, there was a growth of publicly supported provision for 'children in need' and family support, in particular family centres serving a mainly poor and workless constituency. On the education side, there was a steady growth in two types of provision, both in primary schools: nursery classes and reception class for 4-year-olds.

In most of the rest of Europe, the emerging policy is access to at least three years of publicly funded provision prior to compulsory schooling at the age of 6, usually in a fairly uniform system of institutions – nursery schools or kindergartens or, in the Nordic countries, often centres taking children across the early childhood age-range. Provision is usually available for at least a full school day. By contrast, the emerging British system is a two-year offer of *part-time* preschool education, available in a diversity of institutions (and at childminders) until children start compulsory schooling at the age of 5 (or are admitted at 4 years to reception class).

The effects of public policy coming late can also be seen when it comes to 'childcare' provision for working parents. Most other European countries have some publicly supported provision for working parents, such as nurseries or organised family day-care schemes. The principle that parental employment should be a criterion for family support has been accepted in most countries for some time, although levels of provision have varied considerably, often veering on the low side; public provision for children under 3 years of age in particular has been low in many cases – relatives continuing to be the main form of childcare in most countries. Provision may be mainly made directly by local authorities or involve public support for private non-profit organisations, while a number of countries have also provided some form of subsidy to parents, but always in addition to direct subsidy of provisions.

Government interest in Britain, when it came, was confronted by a large and diverse private market, dominated by childminders and a 'for-profit' nursery sector far outstripping anything to be found in the rest of Europe (arguably because in other parts of Europe, a combination of demand and supply factors has made nurseries run as businesses less viable). This situation on the ground, plus (neo)liberal beliefs about parental responsibility and markets, has led in Britain to a particular reliance on demand subsidies (tax credits) and public/private partnerships. Direct support for early years provision outside the school sector remains largely confined to welfare roles, such as children in need, family support and (recently announced) nurseries in deprived areas.

Public support for childcare and preschool education can therefore be seen in terms of a pragmatic and ideological concern with stimulating, shaping and giving increased access to a market, mostly private but also including a public sector of primary schools eager to woo new pupils through offers of 'preschool' provision. Comparison with other European countries shows, however, that certain types of provision are under-represented in the market: Britain has many private nurseries, family centres, playgroups and nursery classes, but it has few nursery schools, organised family day-care schemes or publicly supported nurseries. With its strong market orientation, polarised employment and high levels of poverty, the British system is more socially divisive than most other countries: there is a system for the poor, workless and disadvantaged, and another for the affluent, 'work rich' and advantaged. The relationship of preschool and school systems, and how far the latter does or should influence the former, is an issue in many European countries; but because primary schooling reaches down the age-range so far, to encompass many 4-year-olds, the early childhood system in Britain is inherently weaker and more liable to domination by school agendas than in most other countries.

So far I have focused on 'mainstream' policy: parental leave, childcare for working parents, preschool education. But there is a fourth component in the new surge of government interest in early childhood: the Sure Start programme, which targets children under 4 years of age and their families in disadvantaged areas. The theme is prevention of social exclusion through early intervention, and the focus is on multi-agency and multidisciplinary working.

Within a European context, Sure Start is unique. No other country has introduced such a concerted programme of early childhood intervention targeted at reducing poverty: indeed, the British government has looked to the USA rather than Europe in developing this policy. One reason is because, as already noted, levels of poverty in Britain are the highest in Europe. Nordic countries such as Sweden have used other social policies, with a strong egalitarian orientation, to prevent poverty getting out of hand in the first place; Britain, by contrast, looks to early intervention as a cure for the epidemic of poverty. In all this, young children are assigned a redemptive role. Sure Start can be seen as the latest in a history of interventions stretching back at least a century (cf. Rose, 1990), based on a belief that the right technology applied at the right time will resolve the problem presented by a large underclass (Moss, 2000).

INTEGRATING EARLY CHILDHOOD SERVICES

An important dividing line in Europe is whether early childhood services are integrated or split. In many countries, responsibility for these services is divided between welfare and education authorities. This administrative division carries over into other areas, including funding, costs to parents, legislation, opening hours, purposes and, perhaps most important, staffing. The 'classic' example of a split system is France, where the welfare system provides a range of services for children under 3 years of age, including nurseries and organised family day care, while the education system provides another range of services for children from 2 years until 6, in nursery schools. Welfare system nurseries are headed by nursing-trained directors and staffed by a mixture of other staff, some having a 2½-year post-18 training, others a one-year post-16 training. Open all day and all year, the main purpose of these nurseries has been to provide 'childcare' for working parents, who contribute to the cost. Nursery schools, in contrast, are staffed by teachers with a five-year post-18 degree training, are open during school terms and school hours and have always had a primarily educational orientation (though most are also linked to out-of-school services for working parents). Being part of the education system, attendance is free.

In 1998, Britain took the significant step of moving responsibility for all early childhood services into the education system. It joined four other member states that already had administrative integration for early childhood services. One of these member states, Spain, took the step at the beginning of the 1990s. The other three, Denmark, Finland and Sweden, have a long-established tradition of integrated services (as have the other Nordic countries of Norway and Iceland). However, in 1997 Sweden took a significant step, moving responsibility for early childhood services from the welfare system (where all Nordic countries had located early childhood previously) to the education system. Britain and Sweden therefore found themselves sharing a unique European (indeed world) position as the only countries that have brought into one administration early childhood services, schools and school-age childcare services. Indeed only two other countries (Spain and New Zealand) have placed all early childhood services within education.

What have been the consequences of these moves in Britain and Sweden? The situations are, of course, very different. Swedish early childhood services have been integrated for many years, not just administratively but in all respects, including legislation, types of provision, funding and staffing. They have also been built up over the years through sustained public policy support: when reform came in the late 1990s, Sweden had a strong and extensive system of preschool provision.

This can be exemplified in two ways. Legislation in 1993 placed a duty on local authorities to provide a place in a publicly funded service for children between the ages of 12 months and 12 years if their parents are employed or studying or if the children have a special need: in 1998, 95% of local authorities stated they could meet this duty within a 3–4 month waiting period (Gunnarsson *et al.,* 1999, p. 39). Second, like other Nordic countries, most early childhood workers (60% in 1998, and a growing proportion (*ibid.*)) are pedagogues (or 'preschool teachers') with a basic training of three years at the post-18 (higher education) level, and have pay and other working conditions not far below those of school teachers. Sweden therefore has already addressed one of the central problems facing Britain: a workforce mainly consisting of poorly trained and poorly paid early childhood workers (Cameron *et al.,* 2001).

Sweden was transferring a well funded, already-integrated and well established system from welfare to education. Britain, by contrast, was transferring one half of a split system ('childcare') from welfare to join the other half ('early education') already in education. The Swedes might therefore have been excused for doing little more once responsibility was transferred. In fact, the transfer has been just one event in an ongoing reform process.

For many years, Sweden has had high employment rates amongst mothers and fathers, reflecting a combination of low unemployment and a strong emphasis on the importance of employment as a means of social inclusion. This has produced a policy of well paid but relatively short parental leave, followed by a right of access to a publicly funded service once children reach the age of 12 months (hence very few children in Sweden under 12 months are in services, but three quarters of children between 12 months and 6 years of age go to a publicly funded service). However, the right to a place has been linked to parents' labour-force participation, and the growth of unemployment in the 1990s emphasised how children whose parents were not employed could lose, or not get, places.

One result of the move to education is the extension (from July 2001) of the right to an early childhood place to *all* children, detaching access to early childhood provision from labour market participation:

Children between the ages of 1–5 years old, whose parents are unemployed or on parental leave shall have the same right as children

of employed parents or full-time students to be included under the
municipality's responsibilities to provide places in the pre-school
system...Children are to be guaranteed a stay of at least 3 hours per
day (Swedish Ministry of Education, 2000a, p. 2).

The move to education has also highlighted another anomaly. Under
welfare, parents were expected to make a contribution to the costs of all
services used. With the move to education, 4- and 5-year-olds will now get
about three hours a day of free attendance while, for the remainder of
children's attendance, the government is proposing a maximum fee parents
should pay (*ibid.*).

So integration into education has involved the infusion of educational
principles concerning access. More fundamentally, integration has led to a
rethink of training, not just of early childhood workers but of *all* workers
in the education system working with children up to 18 years of age. From
2001 a new integrated system of teacher training will be introduced, to
replace eight of the present eleven teaching qualifications. All teachers,
including early childhood teachers, will do a degree course of at least 3½
years (except upper secondary vocational teachers who will only do three
years). Moreover, 1½ years of the course will involve common studies by
all students – whether proposing to work with 18-month-olds or 18-year-
olds. This general field of education 'should comprise, on the one hand,
areas of knowledge that are central to the teaching profession, such as
teaching, special needs education, child and youth development, and on the
other hand, interdisciplinary subject studies' (Swedish Ministry of
Education, 2000b, pp. 1–2). The remainder of the course will involve
more specialised studies (for example, in early childhood work).

This reform is driven by several influences, including the promotion of
team working involving different types of pedagogues and teachers. But
most important, *restructuring* administrative responsibility and teacher
training is linked to a radical process of *rethinking*: of childhood,
knowledge, learning and teaching. The rethinking process involves schools
as much as preschools and recognises, for example, that aspects of
preschool pedagogy should inform new ways of working in the school – up
to and including education for 16–19-year-olds. Integration of early
childhood services (and free-time services) into education is understood not
to involve a 'take-over' by one pedagogical tradition and perspective, a sort
of triumph of one professional culture, but should instead be based on a
general rethinking and the search for new and shared understandings.

A discussion paper, commissioned by the government from two leading
pedagogical researchers in Sweden, Gunilla Dahlberg and Hellevi Lenz
Taguchi, has been one important influence in this process of rethinking.
Titled *Pre-school and School – Two Different Traditions and the Vision of a*

Meeting Place, the paper begins by identifying different pedagogical traditions in preschool and school, each produced by a different social construction of the child: 'the analysis shows that the view of the child which we call the child as nature is, for the most part, embodied in the pre-school, while the child as producer of culture and knowledge is, for the most part, embodied in the school.' These different constructions have had 'direct consequences on the content and working methods of pedagogical activity, and in that way affected the view of the child's learning and knowledge-building'. The paper goes on to suggest an alternative construction of the child – the child as a constructor of culture and knowledge – which could 'create a meeting place where both the pre-school teachers and the primary school teachers are given the possibility to develop their pedagogical practices':

> We do not wish to present a new pedagogical method or model, but a vision of a possible meeting place. This vision can be seen as a provisional, holistic picture of the educational institutions we need in a quickly changing society. The vision deals with a way of relating and a working process in relation to the child's creation of knowledge and everyday reality which is based upon continual discussions and common values which one wants to permeate the child's upbringing and education. This way of relating starts from the view of the child as a competent and capable child, a rich child, who participates in the creation of themselves and their knowledge – the child as a constructor of culture and knowledge. In this pedagogical approach, this way of relating is characterised by a researching, reflective and analytical approach at different levels.

This sort of analysis is related to an understanding that Sweden is moving from an industrial society into a post-industrial, information and knowledge society – a learning society. There is also recognition of a profound change – a paradigmatic shift – in how people understand and create meaning in their lives, which has consequences for understandings of children and childhood.

New ways of understanding childhood, knowledge and learning require new ways of understanding (and training) the teacher, whatever age-group he or she works with:

> The view of the child as co-constructor implies a view of the teacher as co-constructor of culture and knowledge. This view means a twofold professional responsibility, which partly is about going into a dialogue and communicative action with the child, the group of children and colleagues, partly about a reflecting and researching attitude in which the starting point is the work and learning process of

both the children and the teacher ... The work of the teacher is mainly
to be able to listen, see and let oneself be inspired by and learn from
what the children say and do (Dahlberg, 1997, p. 23).

It would be misleading to suggest the new ways of working and thinking
outlined above are universally adopted. There is considerable diversity
between local authorities in Sweden, and there are resistances among many
practitioners to working in teams. Not everyone would accept a social
constructionist analysis or these new ideas about learning. However, what
is impressive about today's Sweden is an openness to new ideas, to new
relationships, to new ways of working – and a general sense of optimism
amongst practitioners.

As already noted, Britain started integration far further back than
Sweden, with a much poorer legacy in terms of investment in services and
the great disadvantage of huge social problems, including higher levels of
poverty. However, much work has been undertaken since 1997, as Gillian
Pugh sets out in Chapter 1. Indeed, more has been done in the last three
years in Britain than in the previous 30 years. However, what is lacking in
the British reforms so far is any sense of vision – how a truly integrated
early childhood service might look and how it might relate to other parts of
the educational system – or the related searching for any critical questions.
Instead, reform has been an extremely pragmatic, very British affair, strong
on making things work better, adapting the existing system rather than
taking a longer-term view. Nothing illustrates this better than the approach
to staffing.

All countries that have established an integrated early childhood service
have based this on a core worker specialising in work across the early
childhood age-range and in all settings. In the case of the Nordic countries,
this has been a pedagogue, a well trained educator but not a teacher.
Sweden has now moved to bring preschool and free-time pedagogues
within the reformed system of teacher training so that the future core
worker will be a teacher, with an early childhood (or free-time) specialism.
New Zealand and Spain, both of which have integrated services in
education, have also opted for an early childhood teacher as their core
worker. What all these workers – pedagogues or teachers – have in
common is a high-level basic training: at least three years at a post-18
higher-education level.

So far, however, British integration has assumed a continuance of a split
system of staffing: an elite of teachers (trained for work in primary schools)
in school-based services, and a majority workforce of 'childcare' workers
with a low level of training. While existing training is being rationalised, so
far there has been no sign of taking the major step of rethinking the work
of the early childhood worker. Part of the problem may be cost: the British

system relies on a workforce that is poorly trained and poorly paid, and reform along the lines of Sweden would mean not only rethinking the work but also revaluing it – increasing costs significantly.

A central issue is the relationship between education and childcare and between preschool and school. Swedish early childhood services gained momentum in the 1970s as a response to increased maternal employment; their aim was to provide 'childcare' for children with parents in the labour market. However, they also carried educational traditions and objectives, and the pedagogical work has come to be increasingly emphasised. Now with inclusion in education, some of the existing differences between childcare and education are being removed, as already described. In a sense, the need for childcare is taken for granted; services have to address this need. But having taken this on board, the focus is now on other social purposes, including learning.

In contrast, and despite some progress, the British system remains divided, conceptually and in practice, between 'childcare' and 'early education'. Instead of immediately bringing 'care' and 'school-based' services for young children into one strong and integrated 'early childhood' division, responsibility remained divided between two parts of the DfEE for three years – the 'early years division' and the 'childcare unit'. Certainly government policy emphasises the close relationship between care and education. But underlying thinking often appears still compartmentalised. This is reflected in the continuing use of the language of 'childcare', the emphasis attached to a 'National Childcare Strategy' and the exception of early years education and teachers in the maintained school sector from the reforms of early years regulation and training. These and other signs appear to add up to a decision not to take the transformatory step of committing to an integrated and coherent early childhood service, covering *all* services up to compulsory schooling.

The relationship between preschool and school is also fundamentally different. In Sweden, early childhood goes up to the age of 6 years. There is a strong, well established early childhood sector, quite separate from compulsory schooling, with a workforce that is well trained and has its own identity. The early childhood sector has its own curriculum, which falls into the category described as 'framework, consultative curricula' rather than 'central, competency orientated curricula'. A framework, consultative curriculum

> provides the main values, orientations and goals for pedagogical programs, but does not enter into the details of how these goals should be achieved. Its actual interpretation and implementation is left to the local level, which has full responsibility for the pedagogical programs that are put into practice in the early childhood center. The

framework curriculum generally stresses multiple aspects of the
child's development, but the well-being of the child and her holistic
development are major concerns...[This type of curriculum] restores
the responsibility to early childhood professionals and parents of
formulating their own pedagogical programs (Bennett, 2001, pp. 229,
233)

Rather than a merger of (near) equals, with both sides rethinking and
adapting, in Britain integration not only leaves clear fissures within early
childhood (the fissures now being within one department rather than
running between two departments) but also appears to be nearer to a take-
over in which compulsory school agendas increasingly determine early
childhood agendas.

One final difference is worth noting. Britain has always prided itself on
having a diverse early childhood system offering parents choice. Britain
certainly has considerable diversity in types of provision (playgroups,
nursery classes, day nurseries, etc.) But, since 1997, this diverse system is
being subjected to very strong processes of standardisation, through a
combination of strong central government, the development of a national
system of standards and regulation, and the introduction of a curriculum
framework and guidance on how to deliver it. In Sweden, by contrast, a
rather uniform system of provision, mostly in local authority nurseries,
now has far more possibility for diversity, with a broad framework
curriculum, no national standards or regulation, and strong decentralisa-
tion to local authorities and individual institutions:

> The provision of early childhood services has become program-
> matically far more diversified than in the past. Curricular strategies
> are becoming more diverse, as are the options that are afforded
> parents. This diversification underscores the respect for individuality
> and for parents' differing needs. Yet, supported by a common
> curriculum and organisational framework, there is a coherence to the
> services without over-formalisation and over-bureaucratisation
> (OECD, 1999, p. 32).

CONCLUSION

Having spent many years undertaking cross-national comparisons, I am
forced to ask myself increasingly what their purpose is. Some see them as a
resource for advocacy. Arguing a case these days often falls back on the 'it
will save billions of pounds' line or 'we lag behind Europe' line. How far
this sways governments is a moot point. Another reason is the search for
'programmes' or 'models' that can be exported. This raises many problems,

not least how to take account of context, including values. At the very least, it suggests the need to adapt the export to local conditions; but, in many cases, this may simply prove impossible.

In my view, at least in the field of early childhood, one of the main values of cross-national comparisons is as a tool to aid critical thinking. Understanding of other countries – and not just how they do things but also why – can help create local solutions by enabling us to view what exists critically, to reveal the many assumptions underlying what we do, and to ask critical questions. Being at the heart of Europe means having a mature and sustained engagement with other countries, using this opportunity to exchange experience, discuss issues of shared interest and reflect on policy and practice.

Further reading

The 30-plus reports of the European Commission Childcare Network cover a wide range of relevant issues, and include reviews of services for children aged 0–10 years. See in particular *A Review of Services for Young Children in the European Union, 1990–95* and *Quality Targets in Services for Young Children*, both published in 1995. More recently, the OECD (Organisation for Economic Co-operation and Development) has conducted a cross-national review of early childhood education and care policies and services, which covers 12 countries, most in Europe. A full report was published in 2001. Background reports (prepared by the countries prior to review) and country notes (prepared by the review teams) are available for a number of countries, including Sweden, at the OECD website http://www.oecd.org/els/education/eec/docs.htm

For staffing issues, see Oberhuemer, P. and Ulich, M. (1997) *Working with Young Children in Europe: Provision and Staff Training* (London: Paul Chapman Publishing) and Moss, P. (2000) Training of early childhood education and care staff: *International Journal of Education Research*, Vol. 33, pp. 31–53. For a discussion of parental leave and its relationship to early childhood services, see Moss, P. and Deven, F. (eds.) (2000) *Parental Leave: Progress or Pitfall?* (The Hague and Brussels: NIDI/CBGS) (available from London University Institute of Education Bookshop). Finally, Dahlberg, G., Moss, P. and Pence, A. (1999) *Beyond Quality in Early Childhood Education and Care* (London: Falmer Press) provides an account of an important European experience, the early childhood work in Reggio Emilia, in northern Italy.

PROMOTING CHILDREN'S WELFARE BY RESPECTING THEIR RIGHTS

Gerison Lansdown and Y. Penny Lancaster

Children are defined as minors in law. They do not have autonomy or the right to make choices or decisions on their own behalf. Instead, responsibility for decisions that affect them has traditionally been vested with those adults who care for them. It has always been presumed not only that adults are better placed than children (particularly when they are young) to exercise responsibility for decision-making but also that, in so doing, they will act in children's best interests. And this presumption has been established as a legal obligation on the courts, which are required to give paramountcy to the welfare of children in making decisions concerning their day-to-day lives (s. 1 Children Act 1989). This welfare model of adult/child relationships constructs the child as a passive recipient of adult protection and good will, lacking the competence to exercise responsibility for his or her own life.

In recent years, we have begun to question the adequacy of this approach and to re-examine the assumptions on which it is based:

- that adults can be relied on to act in children's best interests;

- that children lack the competence to act as agents in their own lives;

- that adults have the monopoly of expertise in determining outcomes in children's lives.

THE LIMITATIONS OF A WELFARE APPROACH

Adults can abuse their power over children

Adults in positions of power over children can exploit and abuse that power to the detriment of children's well-being. The 1970s witnessed a growing awareness of the extent to which children are vulnerable to physical abuse within their own families. The extent and scale of violence perpetrated by parents on their own children emerged through the work of Henry Kempe in the USA and was brought home forcefully in this country with the case of Maria Colwell, an 8-year-old girl who was returned from care to live with her parents who subsequently beat her to death (Howells, 1974). No opportunity then existed for her views and concerns to be taken seriously by those responsible for the decision. During the 1980s, the phenomenon of sexual abuse within families, as a day-to-day reality for many thousands of children, hit the public consciousness with the Cleveland inquiry into sexual abuse of children (Report of Inquiry, 1988). There was, and probably still is, considerable resistance to the recognition that parents and other adult relatives could and do rape and assault their children. Particularly shocking has been the realisation that even babies and toddlers are not exempt from such abuse. It challenges the very notion of family life we wish to believe exists for all children – the view children are safest within their families. It also challenges the legitimacy of the powerful cultural desire for protecting the privacy of family life because it undermines the comfortable assumption that parents can always be relied on to promote the welfare of their children.

It took until the 1990s to uncover the next scandal in the catalogue of failure on the part of responsible adults to protect and promote the welfare of children. In a series of public enquiries it became apparent not only that children in public care in a number of local authorities had been subjected to systematic physical and sexual abuse by staff in children's homes, but that these practices had been surrounded by a culture of collusion, neglect, indifference and silence on the part of the officers and elected members within those authorities. It is now acknowledged this experience of abuse was not simply the consequence of a few paedophiles entering the public care system (Utting, 1997). Rather, it is an endemic problem, affecting children in authorities across the country and symptomatic of a fundamental failure to provide effective protective care towards vulnerable children. One of the most forceful lessons to emerge from the series of public enquiries into abuse of children in public care has been the extent to which the children involved were denied any opportunity to challenge what was happening to them (Levy and Kahan, 1991; Kirkwood, 1993; Waterhouse, 2000). They were systematically disbelieved in favour of adult accounts. They were denied access to any advocacy to help them articulate their concerns. Indeed, if and when they did complain they risked further abuse. In other words, the adults involved could, with impunity, behave in ways entirely contrary to the children's welfare.

We can, then, no longer disregard the fact that children can be and are both physically and sexually abused by the very adults who are responsible for their care, both within families and in state institutions. Accordingly, it becomes necessary to move beyond the assumption that simple reliance on adults to promote the well-being of children, because of their biological or professional relationship with the child, is an adequate approach to caring for children.

Adults do not always act in children's best interests

Actions detrimental to the well-being of children do not merely occur when adults deliberately abuse or neglect children. During the course of the last century, adults with responsibility for children across the professional spectrum have been responsible for decisions, policies and actions that have been inappropriate, if not actively harmful, to children, whilst claiming to be acting to promote their welfare. One does not have to look far for the evidence – the separation of young children from parents in the war evacuations, the exclusion of mothers from hospital when their small children were sick, in pain and frightened, the failure to recognise that babies experience pain and consequent denial of analgesics, the pressure on unmarried mothers to have their babies adopted with no possibility of future contact, the placement of children in care in large, unloving institutions which stigmatised them and denied them opportunities for emotional and psychological well-being – in all these examples, there is now public recognition that children were more harmed than helped by these practices.

And the existence of public policy, which serves to act against the best interests of children, is not simply a matter of history. We continue to place disabled children in special schools on the grounds of the 'efficient use of resources' rather than the promotion of the child's best interests (s. 316 Education Act 1996). There is serious cause for concern that the current emphasis on attainment targets for preschool children will jeopardise their opportunities for play. And there is growing evidence that the massive expansion in out-of-school clubs to promote work opportunities for mothers is being developed more as a resource for parents than as a service designed to meet the best interests of children (Smith and Barker, 2000).

Parents' rights are protected over those of children

Public policy often supports the rights and interests of parents ahead of those of children, even when the consequences of so doing are detrimental to the welfare of children. There is, for example, a clear conflict of interest between children and parents in the field of assisted reproduction in which both law and practice favour the interests of prospective parents. Present legislation fails to protect the right of children born through assisted reproduction techniques to access to knowledge of their biological identity. The law actively prohibits children from access to identifying information about their biological parents, and there is no obligation or encouragement from the relevant professionals for parents to be open with their children about the origins of their birth (s. 33 Human Fertilisation and Embryology Act 1990). The desire for a pretended normality, the fear of children not loving the non-biological parent, the fear of a reduced supply of donors if anonymity were not preserved, the difficulties in confronting children with the truth all play a part in perpetuating the current collusion against a commitment to respecting the fundamental right of the child to knowledge of his or her identity (see, for example, Blyth, 1990; Freeman, 1997). It is evident that children's welfare is not the over-riding factor determining legislation and practice in this field, but rather the directly competing interests of parents to maintain secrecy and to have a child.

In 2000, the government issued a consultation paper setting out proposals to change the law on physical punishment of children in order to comply with the findings of the European Court of Human Rights that the law in the UK failed to protect a child from inhuman and degrading treatment under Article 3 of the European Convention on Human Rights (A *v.* UK, ECHR 1998). The consultation sets out three questions for consideration. Should the defence of 'reasonable chastisement' be removed from certain forms of physical punishment, such as hitting children around the head in ways that might cause brain injury or damage to the eyes and ears? Should the defence cease to be available against a charge of actual bodily harm? And should the defence be restricted to those with parental responsibility (Department of Health, 2000a)? Aside from the fact it is little short of extraordinary that we should need to consult on whether such levels of violence could even be contemplated as lawful, the consultation document fails to ask the central and most significant question – should parents be allowed to hit their children at all? The absence of this question is not accidental. There was considerable pressure on the government, from Children are Unbeatable (an alliance of some 250 organisations), to include in the consultation paper the option to change the law to remove the defence of 'reasonable chastisement' for parents and to give children the same protection from all forms of assault as adults. The government refused to do so. It is clearly recognised under international law that the continued practice of hitting children represents a breach of their human rights (Article 19 UN Convention on the Rights of the Child). The Committee on the Rights of the Child (the international body established to monitor government progress in implementing the UN Convention on the Rights of the Child) has already criticised the UK government for its failure to introduce legislation to protect children from physical punishment by parents, and recommended a review of the law to introduce appropriate protection (CRC, 1995). When the government appears before the committee again in 2002, it will be censored if it has failed to act on this recommendation. The reality is that the government is not willing even to consult on a proposal to end all physical punishment of children because to do so would be seen to interfere with the rights of parents.

There is considerable evidence that physical punishment of children is not an effective form of discipline, that it can and does cause harm, and that as a form of punishment it can and does escalate (Leach, 1999). And almost every professional body working with children is unanimous we should change the law to protect children better and to give parents a positive message that hitting children is both wrong and unnecessary (see Barnardo's, 1998b). A consultation exercise conducted by Willow and Hyder (1998) with 70 children aged 5–7 years provides graphic evidence of the humiliation, pain and rejection children experience when their parents hit them. When asked what they understood by a 'smack', they all described it as a hit. Comments such as 'it feels like someone banged you with a hammer', 'it's like breaking your bones', 'it's like you're bleeding' and 'it hurts, it's hard and it makes you sore' were amongst those used to describe how it felt. Their eloquent accounts contrast starkly with the widely promulgated view from parents that such punishment is delivered with love, does not cause real hurt and is only applied *in extremis* (Willow and Hyder, 1998).

It can also be seen from the experience of the eight countries that have banned it, that it does not lead to a rise in prosecutions of parents, it does change parental behaviour in favour of more positive forms of discipline and it does not lead to worse behaved or ill-disciplined children (see Durrant, 1999). Again, then, it is not the welfare of children that informs the law and its proposed reform, but the need to assuage adult public opinion.

Children's interests are often disregarded in public policy

Children's interests are frequently disregarded in the public policy sphere in favour of more powerful interest groups. It is not necessarily the case that children's welfare is deliberately disregarded, but rather that children, and the impact of public policy on their lives, are not visible in decision-making forums and, accordingly, never reach the top of the political agenda. Just consider, for example, the impact of public policy on children during the 1980s and 1990s. In 1979, one in ten children were living in poverty. By 1991, the proportion had increased to one in three (DSS, 1993). That alone is sufficient indictment of our neglect of children. But even more significant is that it was the children who bore the disproportionate burden of the increase in poverty during that period. No other group in society experienced a growth in poverty on a comparable scale. And the consequences of that poverty on children's life chances are profound – it impacts on educational attainment, physical and mental health, emotional well-being and employment opportunities. At a collective level, our society failed to promote and protect the welfare of children over two decades.

There is little analysis of public expenditure to assess whether the proportion spent on children and their well-being reflects either their levels of need or their representation within the community. What little we do know indicates the lack of data is likely to cover very significant inadequacies in spending on children, indicating their weak position in the lobbies that influence public agendas and expenditure. For example, we know that health authorities spend 5% of their mental health budgets on children and adolescent mental health services, even though that age-group represents 25% of the population (Audit Commission, 1999). Of course, it is likely that services for older people will necessitate a disproportionate claim on these budgets, but no systematic assessment has been made as to whether the current balance in any way reflects comparative levels of assessed needs. And as long as children lack powerful advocates in the field of health, such discrepancies will not be effectively challenged. In a completely different arena, but providing even more dramatic evidence of low priority given to children, a report by the National Playing Fields Association in 1993 estimated that the then Department of National Heritage spent 3p of its budget on children for every £100 spent on adults (NPFA, 1993).

Similarly, in the field of housing, countless estates have been built in which the needs of children have been completely disregarded – no play spaces or facilities and dangerous balconies and lifts with controls out of the reach of small children (Freeman *et al.*, 1999). And we have grown increasingly intolerant of children in the public arena. Far from developing towns and cities which are designed with children in mind, which are child-friendly as befits a society that has the welfare of children at its heart, we now tend to view children as undesirable in streets and shops, particularly when they are in groups. The introduction of powers to impose child curfews on children under 10 years of age and the refusal of many shops to allow unaccompanied children in are all testimony to a perception of children as threatening, hostile and outside the legitimate bounds of society. Too little attention has been paid to developments such as safe routes to school and home zones, which allow opportunities for younger children to play and move within their local communities although now, belatedly, the government is beginning to invest in such schemes. Public spaces are seen to be 'owned' by adults, with young people's presence in those spaces representing an unwanted intrusion. Yet these are the adults on whom children rely to promote their best interests. These are the adults who are responsible for protecting children's welfare.

MOVING BEYOND A WELFARE PERSPECTIVE

Once it is acknowledged not only that adults are capable of abuse of children but also that children's welfare can be undermined by conflicting interests, neglect, indifference and even hostility on the part of adults, then it becomes clear it is not sufficient to rely exclusively on adults to define children's needs and be responsible for meeting them. Indeed, the welfare model has failed children. Rather, there is a need to recognise children as subjects of rights – a concept that developed gradually during the course of the last century, culminating in the adoption by the UN General Assembly in 1990 of the UN Convention on the Rights of the Child. The Convention, which now has almost universal acceptance having been ratified by 191 countries throughout the world, is a comprehensive human rights treaty that encompasses social, economic and cultural as well as civil and political rights. Acknowledgement of children as rights-bearers rather than merely recipients of adult protective care introduces a new dimension in adult relationships towards children. It does not negate the fact that children have needs but argues that, accordingly, children have rights to have those needs met.

Implications of respecting children's human rights

One of the underlying principles of the Convention is that the best interests of the child must be a primary consideration in all actions concerning the child (see Article 3). But this principle does not merely take us back to a welfare approach. A commitment to respecting the human rights of children requires an acceptance that promoting children's welfare or best interests requires more than the good will or professional judgement of adults. It injects two fundamental challenges to traditional practices in respect of children.

First, the means by which the best interests of children are assessed must be the extent to which all their human rights are respected in any particular policy, action or legislation. In other words, the rights embodied in the Convention must provide a framework through which to analyse the extent to which proposals promote the best interests of children (see Hodgkin and Newell, 1998). And this approach extends both to matters affecting the rights of an individual child and children as a body. For example, in providing child protection services, do interventions that seek to protect the child from abuse also respect the child's right to privacy, respect for the child's views and evolving capacities, to continuity in family life, to contact with immediate and extended family? In a proposed local housing development, have the rights of children to adequate play facilities and to safe road crossings been fully considered? Likewise, one can apply a comparable analysis to decisions taken within families. Many parents currently drive their children to school and justify doing so in terms of the potential dangers of both traffic and abduction or assault to which children might otherwise be exposed. A rights-based approach would necessitate a broader analysis of the rights of children. What impact does driving children to school have on their right to the best possible health, to freedom of association, to play, to growing respect for their emerging competence?

In all these examples, it can be argued that, unless a comprehensive rights-based approach is taken, there is a risk that a decision or intervention is made that responds to one aspect of the child's life and, in so doing, fails to acknowledge other rights or needs. Indeed, it may inadvertently impact adversely on the child.

Secondly, if children are subjects of rights, then they themselves must have the opportunity to exercise those rights and be afforded means of seeking redress when rights are violated. In other words, they must have opportunities to be heard. Article 12 of the Convention embodies the principle that children have the right to express their views on matters of concern to them and to have those views taken seriously in accordance with their age and maturity. It is a procedural right, which has increasingly been recognised as necessary if children are to move beyond their traditional status as recipients of adult care and protection and become social actors entitled to influence decisions that affect their lives (see, for example, Lansdown, 1996; Willow, 1997). And it applies to all children capable of expressing their views, however young. Children are entitled to be actively involved in those decisions that affect them as individuals – in the family, in schools, in public care, in the courts and as a body in the development, delivery, monitoring and evaluation of public policy at both local and national levels. Listening to children and taking them seriously is important because children have a body of experience and views relevant to the development of public policy, will improve the quality of decision-making and will render it more accountable. And beyond this, it is an essential element in their protection. Children who from an early age experience respect for their views and are encouraged to take responsibility for those decisions they are competent to make will acquire the confidence to challenge abuses of their rights.

The welfare model of childcare has perpetuated the view that children lack the capacity to contribute to their own well-being or that they have a valid and valuable contribution to make. Yet failure to involve children in decisions that affect their own lives is the common thread that underpins many of the mistakes and poor judgements exercised by adults when acting on children's behalf. There is now a growing body of evidence that children, both in respect of individual decisions that affect their lives or as a body in the broader public policy arena, have a considerable contribution to make to decision-makers (see Alderson, 1993; John, 1996; Marshall; 1997). For example, the Stepney Community Nursing Development Unit research and development programme undertook a consultation with 4- and 5-year-olds living in East London on their local environment. The children highlighted more effectively than adults could have done the extent to which their lives were dominated by fear of traffic, drugs, cockroaches and violence. Whilst anxious for more trees and greenery, they rejected the idea of grass-covered play space as this would prevent them seeing abandoned needles and dog excrement. Children, even when very young, can act, for example as peer counsellors, mediators or mentors for other children. At Highfield Primary School in Plymouth, members of the school council are involved, for example, in recruitment of staff, development of all school policies and the anti-bullying strategy. Local and health authorities have successfully involved very young children in the development of new hospitals, anti-poverty strategies, advice services and planning for real initiatives. In other words, far from being 'in waiting' until they acquire adult competencies, young children when empowered to do so can act as a source of expertise, skill and information for adults and can contribute towards meeting their own needs.

Towards a rights-based model of promoting young children's welfare

The 'Listening to Young Children' project
Coram Family is undertaking a 'Listening to Young children' research and development project, in partnership with the Ragdoll Foundation, to promote resilience amongst young children so they can ultimately take responsibility for their own lives and reach their potential. The project views the young child as an active player in his or her

environment and has been shaped to reveal and promote the diversity inherent in young children. The primary aim of the project is to identify different creative methods that enable young children to articulate their feelings, experiences, concerns and anxieties. It is rooted in an acknowledgement that young children have something worthwhile to say about their lives, that they are capable of sharing their viewpoint and, when provided with information, that they are competent to make informed decisions. It seeks to move from a model of promoting young children's welfare to an approach that is rights-based.

Although a rights-based approach addresses traditional power relations it is not advocating young children should hold all or the majority of power. It is an approach that views young children as active and competent participants within their environment. Young children are not advanced the status of *the* expert, however – having the expertise to be the sole decision-makers in their lives. Addressing power relations is about advocating for the young child's views to be tabled along with the views of all the other active players. Inclusion to decision-making processes is not premised on the exclusion of another (parents, carers and significant others). It is rather about pulling up another chair alongside those already present.

In recent years, there have been numerous developments in listening to older children. There is, however, a dearth of knowledge about how to listen to young children – to provide opportunities where children are able to articulate what is important to them. The project seeks to contribute towards the body of knowledge that promotes opportunities so that the 'voices' of young children can be respected.

An ethical package: Central to the project is the respect Article 12 of the UN Convention on the Rights of the Child affords young children. The project identifies the following three stages to develop and implement a rights-based ethical package from which to undertake its investigation:

- Respecting children's right to appropriate information that will involve, for example, ensuring all children participating in the project are fully informed about its rationale and methods, their contribution, consent and their right to withdraw at any time.
- Respecting what children say – children will be provided with opportunity and time to explore what is important to them.
- Respecting children's right to participate – children will have the opportunity to be involved in contributing to the research methodology.

The ethical package has been informed by the work of Alderson (1995),

Morrow and Richards (1996) and Thomas and O'Kane (1998).

Methodology: The methodology of the project is multi-layered, working simultaneously with young children, older children, parents and professionals.

- *Younger children:* To highlight the diversity of young children, the project, which is located in five settings, has been designed to focus on asking them directly *what is important to you?* By focusing on understanding and documenting what is important to the individual child, the project is seeking to reveal the extent to which common sense homogenous descriptions about young children are 'non-sense'. They are neither homogeneous chronologically or emotion-ally, but nor is there consensus amongst them in terms of what they think is important or how they prefer to articulate their views. The project draws on the range of communication signals that are utilised by children under the age of 8 years – not only verbal language skills but also drawing, body language and photographs – to investigate the variety of creative ways that enable children under the age of 8 years to communicate what is important to them.

- *Children as consultants:* Children older than those selected in the case studies are included in the project to participate as consultants. The format of the consultancy is primarily focus-group discussions. Once children have registered their interest, a plan is made to meet regularly. Initially, children are asked about what might be important to young children, what questions would be appropriate, the obstacles that might exist and the methods that might be useful. Further meetings provide opportunities to continue to gather advice as the project proceeds and to involve these children in gathering the views of the younger children themselves. Their efforts are documented creatively, such as the production of a colourful newspaper.

- *Parent focus-group discussions:* The project is interested in facilitat-ing parents' involvement through focus-group discussions, which can be organised during the year, each month focusing on a particular issue. Parent focus-group discussions involve parents as participants in evaluating the research methodology and seek to enhance their understanding of young children's competency.

- *Professional forums:* The professionals at each setting represent social workers and teachers from nursery and primary schools. This wider professional network provides a platform for professionals to ask questions and exchange their ideas about issues around listening to young children. One group of teachers, for instance, is focusing on the 'user-friendly' nature of the different research methods, in light of curriculum demands.

Summary
The UN Convention on the Rights of the Child has played a significant role in calling for children's views to be taken seriously. Article 12 details the importance of children being given opportunities to express their opinion about issues that are important to them. The view that young children are competent to express their opinions and participate in decision-making processes evokes a range of feelings amongst parents and professionals alike – anxious that it challenges traditional ways of organising family life and that the authority they have to act in the best interests of their children may be undermined. The 'Listening to Young Children' project is seeking to develop a rights-based approach to promote the welfare of young children, but within a framework that secures that the rights of others are likewise upheld.

CONCLUSION

There is a continuing resistance to the concept of rights in this country, particularly when applied to children. It is a resistance shared by many parents, politicians, policy-makers and the media. It derives, at least in part, from a fear that children represent a threat to stability and order if not kept under control. Further, it reflects the strong cultural tradition that children are 'owned' by their parents and that the state should play as minimal a role as possible in their care. Attempts by the state to act to protect children are viewed with suspicion and hostility. But promoting the rights of children is not about giving a licence to children to take complete control of their lives irrespective of their levels of competence. It is not about allowing children to ride roughshod over the rights of others, any more than adult rights permit such abuses. It is, rather, about moving away from the discredited assumption that adults alone can determine what happens in children's lives without regard for children's own views, experiences and aspirations. It means accepting that children, even very small children, are entitled to be listened to and taken seriously. It means acknowledging that as children grow older they can take greater responsibility for exercising their own rights. It involves recognising that the state has explicit obligations towards children, for which it should be held accountable. A commitment to respecting children's rights does not mean abandoning their welfare. It means promoting their welfare by adherence to the human rights standards defined by international law.

Points for discussion

- In what ways has a reliance on an adult perspective of children's best interests failed children in your professional field?

- Could you consider undertaking an audit of your work to assess what children's rights are at stake and how well existing policy and practice serve to promote and protect those rights?

- What strategies could you develop to promote more active participation by children in decisions that affect their lives?

Further reading

Alderson, P. (2000) *Young Children's Rights: Exploring Beliefs, Principles and Practice*. London: SCF/Jessica Kingsley.

Flekkoy, M. G. and Kaufman, N. H. (1997) *The Participation Rights of the Child: Rights and Responsibilities in the Family*. London: Jessica Kingsley.

Miller, J. (2000) *All Right at Home?* London: Children's Rights for England Alliance/SCF/Children's Society/Barnardo's/ NSPCC/NCH.

Willow, C. (1997) *Hear! Hear!*. London: Local Government Information Unit.

PART 2
PRACTICE

4

CURRICULUM IN THE EARLY YEARS

Tricia David

WHAT DO WE MEAN BY 'CURRICULUM'?

Many years ago, when I was head of a nursery school, few early years practitioners set out curriculum outlines, documented plans, children's assessment records or evaluations, although they did have aims and they did plan, assess children and evaluate their own 'performance'. Sometimes a little of this would be written down but mainly it was 'in our heads'. One day, while discussing the idea of curriculum with a group of colleagues, I realised they were horrified because they confused 'curriculum' with 'syllabus' and seemed to expect they might end up being told to 'teach the life cycle of the cabbage white butterfly in Term 3' or something of that nature. In a way, the advent of the National Curriculum for children from the age 5 to 16 years in England, following the Education Reform Act 1988, may have confirmed the fear that, ultimately, the content of what young children should learn would be prescribed like a GCSE syllabus. My colleagues' horror arose out of the sense many early years teachers had that each child comes to a preschool setting with unique experiences from family, home and community; that early childhood should be a time of spontaneity and of exploration according to individual interests; and that didactic, teacher-planned instruction has no part in an early years teacher's repertoire – is in fact a waste of time – because young children learn best through 'hands-on' self-chosen play experiences. That understanding of young children's learning and development still underpins the work of early years practitioners in England (David *et al.*, 2000) and, as a result, ideas about curricula and their impact on pedagogy and children's learning demand careful consideration and articulation.

The *New Oxford Illustrated Dictionary* defines 'curriculum' as 'a course of study', while it defines 'syllabus' as 'concise statements of... [a] course of study'. There appears to be little difference between these two definitions, although 20 years ago 'curriculum' would have implied a broader meaning, focusing on general aims and processes (including the 'hidden' or 'covert' aspects of a learning setting) and 'syllabus' the narrower, more detailed and prescribed content (i.e. what was to be taught/learnt).

The new curriculum guidance for England from the Qualifications and Curriculum Authority (QCA) defines the term 'curriculum' as 'everything children do, see, hear, or feel in their setting, both planned and unplanned' (QCA, 2000a, p. 1). Thus the QCA's definition takes a broad view which includes the 'hidden curriculum' and is not unlike that proposed 20 years ago by the Schools Council (1981, p. 1): 'the effective curriculum is what each child takes away.' Rooting the curriculum in the child's earlier experience and knowledge, Tina Bruce (1987, p. 65) maintained that a curriculum for the early years should be constructed from 'the child and the processes and structures within the child; the knowledge the child already has; and knowledge the child will acquire competently but with imagination'. Such a definition then leads to the question of 'what knowledge?' Those who have feared a senseless move to the prescription of particular content, to be taught by overly formal methods, have reiterated the centrality of early years teachers' knowledge about children's development and learning. So, following the downward pressure caused by the implementation of the National Curriculum for children in primary schools, curriculum theorists such as Blenkin and Kelly (1994) have called for a reappraisal of what is considered appropriate for inclusion in an early years curriculum. Such calls impel us to recognise that as educators it is not enough to be knowledgeable about disciplines – or areas of experience and learning – we also need to be informed about children's development and learning; individual children's earlier experiences and the impact upon these of the contexts where the children are growing and learning.

The fundamental building blocks of a curriculum can be seen as the knowledge (facts), skills, concepts/understandings and attitudes to be acquired. From the moment of birth or maybe even before this, children are trying to 'make sense' of the worlds in which they find themselves. In their own way they are attempting to acquire those skills, concepts and facts given high status by their social group. At the same time they will acquire the attitudes of the group, even if they may consciously discard or challenge them later. Young children seek a place in their society, they are born to be social and they can recognise those achievements and characteristics that attract acceptance and status. Each cultural group holds particular expectations of both children and adults at different stages in their lives and so, in effect, a curriculum is being imposed on young children, even in societies, families and settings where none of the expectations are written down or made explicit.

Over ten years ago, Sally Lubeck (1986) – in her study of two preschool groups in a North American city – showed how the way in which the staff (three per group) chose to interact with the children, interacted with each other (or did not) and structured the sessions resulted in the children acquiring very different skills and achievements after attending the two different settings. Similarly, David Hartley's (1993) study of three nurseries in Scotland showed 'invisible pedagogy' being used in different ways as a regulatory mechanism. In both pieces of research it is reported the curricula the children experience unintentionally preserves social stratification, by either preparing children for a particular kind of future or by denying them access to knowledge, or cultural capital, which other children gain at home. These examples serve to emphasise that in debating the idea of the early years curriculum it is not enough to think of the curriculum as 'content to be learnt' but as 'processes of learning and teaching' too. Everything a child experiences is a learning opportunity and each child will try to make sense of that experience in the light of earlier learning. The very delineation of babyhood, early childhood and the ways in which the age-group is thought of forms part of a child's learning experiences and is thus part of his or her curriculum.

IDEAS ABOUT EARLY CHILDHOOD AND THEIR IMPACT ON CURRICULA

What is a child? According to both the UN Convention on the Rights of the Child and the UK's Children Act 1989, a child is a person aged between birth and 18 years. What happens to, or is thought to be 'right' for, young children in any society or subcultural group is related to the childhoods constructed by that society (Tobin *et al.*, 1989; Nunes, 1994; Sharpe *et al.*, 1999). Once we become aware of the ways in which childhood itself is constructed in different societies or at different times we begin to ask ourselves why children are treated in certain ways, why particular curricula are considered appropriate for children at different stages in their lives and what all this tells us about that society. Although babies and young children themselves are active, not passive, participants in the shaping of their childhoods, recent research indicates they will live 'up or down' to societal and family expectations, that they will try to please the adults around them in order to be valued, loved and accepted (e.g. Bruner and Haste, 1987; Trevarthen, 1992).

The main implication of this, then, is that the curriculum we decide on for young children, both its content and its teaching approaches, may have crucial long-term consequences for our society.

In addition to an increased acknowledgement for the ways in which children co-construct their understandings about the world through socially based learning interactions alongside more knowledgeable others (Vygotsky, 1978), research about brain development has also been enlisted to help governments recognise the need for investment in early years provision (for example, Bill and Hillary Clinton attended a White House seminar on the brain in 1998 and a government-initiated working party about early brain development was formed in the UK at around the same time).

Perhaps the most important messages for curriculum planners to come out of all the discussion on brain research are as follows:

- The 'old' debate about nature or nurture is dead – what we should be discussing is the dynamic interaction between nature and nurture – the complementary nature of genetic and epigenetic factors in human brain development (Lambert, 1996).

- Human brains are highly 'plastic'; life-long learning really should be our goal but as human brains are probably at their most plastic during the earliest years we cannot afford to waste children's time by treating them as if they have no brain or as if their brains need 'filling up' with knowledge simply transmitted (transplanted?) from our adult brains during this early phase.

- Learning through supported exploration and play is probably the most effective mode for young children.

- Babies and young children are fully human beings in their own right, as they are now, so our curriculum should take account of this and not be geared only to their future as adults (see, for example, Diamond and Hopson, 1998; Bruer, 1999; Gopnik *et al.*, 1999).

Referring to the nature–nurture debate, Allison James (1998, p. 47) points out: 'Once it had been realised that expectations about the abilities and competencies of "the child" had been shown to vary cross-culturally and over time, it was suggested that biological development must be seen as contextualising, rather than unequivocally determining, children's experience.'

So the stress is now upon enabling young children's learning through relevant and meaningful experiences with adult support (teaching) which takes account of the child's earlier experiences and existing understandings.

Further, Gardner (1983) has added another dimension to the questioning of assumptions about childhood, by questioning assumptions about what kinds of achievements we nurture through our education systems. Gardner proposes (*ibid.*) the idea of multiple intelligences, most of which we in the West appear unable to foster because we cannot 'see' and do not value many of those 'intelligences'. In other words, Gardner is calling for a change in thinking about children – not just about *how* they learn but about what is seen as appropriate for them to learn. Thus, while bearing in mind ideas about child development theory and constructions of childhood, we need to consider different curriculum models and their aims.

CURRICULUM 'MODELS' AND THEIR MEANINGS

Different types of curricula have different purposes. They are underpinned by different values and principles and are informed by different assumptions and beliefs about children. At the time when the National Curriculum was being implemented and the Education Reform Act 1988 formulated, so that for the first time the UK was to have a national curriculum, there was much debate about curriculum construction. Robin Alexander (1988) identified seven types of primary school curriculum:

(1) *Classical humanist* (initiating the child into the 'best' of cultural heritage).

(2) *Behavioural/mechanistic* (hierarchies of observable and testable learning outcomes).

(3) *Elementary* (preparation for work).

(4) *Social imperatives* (may take two forms: *adaptive* – enabling the child to meet society's economic, technological and labour needs; *reformist or egalitarian* – enabling children to fulfil their potential and contribute to the progress of society).

(5) *Progressive* (open and negotiable, enabling children to achieve individual potential).

(6) *Developmental* (underpinned by knowledge about children's psychological and physiological development and learning).

Applying the typology to different models of early years provision can highlight the importance of exploring the philosophy underpinning a model. It can also demonstrate the mix of curriculum models which may be operating in a society or setting.

For example, the feted nurseries of Reggio Emilia are deemed to have no curriculum with planned lessons based on behaviourist outcomes, according to Loris Malaguzzi, one of the founders of this system of nurseries (Edwards *et al.*, 1998). However, they have very rigorously shared aims – such as promoting the idea of young children as rich and powerful (in their thinking, learning, expressing, and so on) and the rejection of Fascism and the promotion of independent decision-making. In addition to this the staff team is not hierarchical; they celebrate certain kinds of achievements in their community (for example, by inviting recognised artists to work with the children in the ateliers); they celebrate knowledge about children's development and learning (by employing advisers called *pedagogistas*); the staff document the children's processes of learning and exhibit their products (in fact using them to raise funds to support the nurseries); and they use aspects of their civic surroundings as stimuli for the children's learning. So we can see that even though there may be no formal laid-down curriculum, there are elements of the classical humanist, developmental, social imperatives and progressive curriculum models in their approaches. Perhaps the issue is again one relating to the difference between 'curriculum' and 'syllabus'.

In a similar way, we can interrogate the curriculum models proposed by government bodies in different countries and draw out the priorities set for young children as a result.

Using information from David (1993) and Oberhuemer and Ulich (1996), Angela Anning (1998) created a table which set out the main features of curricula in different European countries – Belgium, France, Italy, Spain and England and Wales. Her aim was to show how early years curricula may or may not bear a close resemblance to a secondary sector subject-orientated curriculum. Although many of the documents produced as guidelines by different European countries appear to use similar areas of learning, the emphases, language used and the overall interpretations can be very disparate. In 1996 a document called *Desirable Outcomes for Children's Learning on Entering Compulsory Schooling* (SCAA, 1996a) was issued relating to settings wishing to access government funding for 4-year-olds. This was not intended to be taken as a curriculum statement, but as guidance. Staff teams of each setting were expected to reflect on the document's contents, especially the learning outcomes for the six areas, and define their own curriculum which would then be interpreted into a kind of syllabus of experiences and learning opportunities.

What was particularly interesting about this document was the fact that a different version appeared in England from that issued in Wales. While the English document was written in unemotional and rather boring 'administrator-speak', the Welsh version was lyrical, opening with an extract from a Welsh poem by Gerallt Lloyd Owen, entitled *Afon* (*The River*), an epic in which the poet longs for the magic of early childhood as a time when the world is there to be explored, experienced and discovered – and when children are allowed the time to do this – and adventure is all around (Curriculum and Assessment Authority for Wales, 1996). A further stark difference between these documents was the English version's almost total avoidance of the use of the word 'play' whereas the Welsh version included explicit comment devoted to advocating 'the importance of play' (Curriculum and Assessment Authority for Wales, 1996, p. 2) (see David, 1998, for further discussion of these documents).

Thus the English curriculum framework document (SCAA, 1996) appeared to be negating the importance of play and the holistic, interconnected nature of learning in these earliest years. It also stressed the emphasis on 'early literacy, numeracy and the development of personal and social skills' (SCAA, 1996, p. 1), first by its very statement and by the omission of the names of other areas of learning and, secondly, by providing guidelines on later pages of the document which were intended to be a seamless web of connections between the early years curriculum and the National Curriculum – but these were only possible for literacy and numeracy and the personal and social links were made into the National Curriculum Orders for children aged from 6 to 16 years in English, maths, science, physical and religious education. The curriculum model for English early childhood then clearly accorded with the 'elementary' model as preparation for later schooling and work.

Meanwhile an umbrella group of early years organisations had come together to become the Early Childhood Education Forum and, as their first initiative, they instigated a curriculum project, *Quality in Diversity*, which was to encompass the ideas of as many early childhood educators and parents as possible throughout the country to develop curriculum guidelines for children from birth to 7 years (ECEF, 1998). The idea had been inspired by the New Zealand model – *Te Whariki* (see Carr and May, 2000) – which had sought to be culturally, philosophically and developmentally meaningful.

Four main principles underpin Te Whariki's aims and goals:

(1) *Whakamana (empowerment)*: the early childhood curriculum empowers the child to learn and grow.
(2) *Kotahitanga (holistic development)*: the early childhood curriculum reflects the holistic way children learn and grow.
(3) *Whânau tangata (family and community)*: the wider world of family and community is an integral part of the early childhood curriculum.
(4) Ngâ hononga (relationships): children learn through responsive and reciprocal relationships with people, places and things (Carr and May, 2000, p. 56).

In their account of the New Zealand curriculum's development, Carr and May (*ibid.*, p. 58) continue: 'The conceptualization of the early childhood curriculum therefore took a very different approach to either the subject based framework of the school curriculum, or the more traditional developmental curriculum map of physical, intellectual, emotional and social skills.'

Instead, they took as strands *well-being, belonging, contributing, communicating* and *exploring* and although the document was initially resisted by the Minister of Education because it did not look like a curriculum document, the Te Whariki received wide support among preschool providers.

While using the Te Whariki as a model, with similar strands which were called *foundations*, the UK's *Quality in Diversity* project adopted the principles of the Early Childhood Education Forum, many having echoes of New Zealand's principles (above) but, as a result of the historical legacy, these also include statements about learning beginning at birth; the inseparable nature of care and education; careful observation as the key to helping children learn; the importance of a proactive anti-bias approach; and the need for well trained educators. However, the UK publication, based on extensive work with practitioners and representatives of early childhood organisations, is defined as a 'framework to enable early childhood practitioners to think about, understand, support and extend the learning of young children from birth to the age of eight' (ECEF, 1998, p. 1). It is said to be a framework of 'Foundations... Goals... and Children's Entitlements' – not 'a curriculum'.

THE NEW MILLENNIUM ENGLISH MODEL

In September 2000 the new early learning goals (QCA, 1999a) were to be implemented in settings for children aged between 3 years and to the end of the reception year in primary school, and this phase was called the Foundation stage. Subsequently, guidance was issued to 'help practitioners plan to meet the diverse needs of all children so that most will achieve and some, where appropriate, will go beyond the early learning goals by the end of the foundation stage' (QCA, 2000a, p. 5). The curriculum framework is still, like the Desirable Outcomes (SCAA, 1996) it supersedes, based on six areas of learning – personal, social and emotional development; communication, language and literacy; mathematical development; knowledge and understanding of the world; physical development; and creative development – but it is made clear that children's learning is holistic, so the areas of learning are not to be treated like school subjects but as a way of thinking about aspects of learning embedded within children's real and relevant experiences. Furthermore, it is emphasised that 'play is a key way in which children learn' (QCA, 2000a, p. 25).

The new framework and the guidelines have been seen as more acceptable to early years practitioners partly as a result of this recognition for play, partly because the Foundation stage covers the reception year in primary school, thus addressing practitioners' anxieties about the increasing formalisation of provision for 4-year-olds in school. Additionally, the guidance (QCA, 2000a) uses the idea of 'stepping stones' to impress upon readers the uniqueness of each child's dispositions and earlier experience – and thus response to what is on offer in a nursery setting. So although the delineation of learning goals and some of the underlying aims may not have changed – such as early literacy development being a priority reminiscent of an elementary or social imperatives egalitarian model of curriculum – there are nods in the direction of the progressive and the developmental models of curriculum.

The early learning goals are to be thought of as achievable by the end of the reception year of primary school, so the start of the National Curriculum and the National Literacy and Numeracy Strategies are to be left until Year 1 – again events welcomed by early years practitioners. Some, however, express fears that teachers of Years 1 and 2 will feel they are under even greater pressure as a result because there will be only two years to cover a great deal of Key Stage 1 National Curriculum content. The counter to this view reflects that of several other European countries, where there is a belief that the laying of real foundations in the years before 6, through appropriate, meaningful learning experiences, will help children actually to achieve more than they would when taught inappropriately and formally during this early stage.

PLAY AND LEARNING

Although not claiming play as the exclusive mode of learning in early childhood, there is much research evidence to demonstrate that child-directed, playful experiences are important because they allow children to co-construct knowledge with other children and with adults who scaffold their experiences (see, for example, Weinberger, 1996; Bennett *et al.*, 1997; David *et al.*, 2000). The potential for subversion inherent in playful activities places children in powerful positions (Grainger and Goouch, 1999). Hilary Strandell (2000) argues that many play situations are not related to real life and that we should perhaps see play as a '(communicative) *resource for participation in everyday life*', that there is in any case no one 'reality' and that 'Doing reality, then, is a kind of *negotiation on meaning*' (Strandell, 2000, pp. 148–49). Children are, during this phase of life, exploring and experimenting with social relations and who they themselves are. Play provides a means for such explorations.

However, while it seems important to promote the adoption of play approaches to learning and teaching in the early years, it must also be recognised that many early years practitioners have limited training, and the imposition of learning goals and inspection regimes can often lead to a retreat into more formal methods owing to a lack of confidence in practitioners' own abilities (David *et al.*, 2000). A similar effect was found in New Zealand (Cullen, 1996).

CURRICULUM AND INVESTMENT IN EARLY CHILDHOOD

The early learning goals and the emphasis on learning through play have been broadly welcomed as the framework for curricula developed in English early years settings for the Foundation stage. However, there remain some who question any curricula that set defined outcomes for children's learning. My own view is that few, if any, societies have no expectations of young children and the adults from whom they learn.

This means the success of the early years curriculum will depend upon the understandings and practices of staff – in other words, levels of training. There is also recent evidence that the quality of premises impacts on children's achievements (Sylva *et al.*, 1999). Staff training, the availability of equipment and standard of premises are themselves dependent upon funding.

The former government minister responsible for early years provision, Margaret Hodge, has argued that all children should have access to the kinds of opportunities for learning afforded by affluent families. The constant reminders that the UK education system is failing our children always seem to omit the fact that we do not, as a society, pay enough attention to the very earliest years. It may also be worth noting the government is constantly reminding us our education system must do better in order that we may *compete* on the world stage – whereas surely we have reached a point in history where we wish to have an education system which is second to none in order that our citizens may *co-operate* with other nations to promote health, well-being and peace? Opening up discussion on such issues would highlight the fact that they impinge upon the curriculum, that all curricula are based upon sets of values. One area that has received little attention is that of young children's spiritual development. The OFSTED RgNIs (Registered Nursery Inspectors) were required to judge whether staff in a setting did or did not provide for this (OFSTED, 1998), but there has been little debate among inspectors, practitioners or parents about how this might be interpreted. The danger is that spirituality, morality and religiosity are often confused.

Thus, we perhaps need to debate those aspects of the curriculum which make it truly holistic – such as care and community, and attention to the 'needs' and rhythms of young children (David, 1996). In an age when some parents may have plenty of time but no resources and others no time and a sufficiency of resources (Handy, 1994), we need to debate the issues of working hours and other aspects of social justice as they impact upon children, who do not leave their home experiences at the door of the nursery. As a result, these factors too have implications for the QCA's (2000a, p. 1) definition of curriculum as 'everything children do, see, hear or feel in their setting, both planned and unplanned'.

Points for discussion

(1) Using the early learning goals (QCA, 1999a), explore the extent to which the values underpinning the aims and 'common features of good practice' (pp. 9–11) are evident in the learning goals for each of the six curriculum areas (pp. 23, 27, 31, 35, 39 and 43).

(2) Write your own set of aims for an early years curriculum and then interrogate them to explore the values with which you have underpinned your curriculum.

Further reading

Cousins, J. (1999) *Listening to Four-Year-Olds*. London: NEYN.

Miller, L. (2000) Play as a foundation for learning. In Drury, R., Miller, L. and Campbell, R. (eds.) *Looking at Early Years Education and Care*. London: David Fulton, pp. 7–16.

Pollard, A. with Filer, A. (1996) *The Social World of Children's Learning: Case Studies of Pupils from Four to Seven*. London: Cassell (especially Chapter 9).

Scott, W. (1996) Choices in learning. In Nutbrown, C. (ed.) *Respectful Educators – Capable Learners*. London: Paul Chapman Publishing, pp. 34–43.

Siraj-Blatchford, I. (ed.) (1998) *A Curriculum Development Handbook for Early Childhood Educators*. Stoke-on-Trent: Trentham Books.

5

WATCHING AND LEARNING: THE TOOLS OF ASSESSMENT

Cathy Nutbrown

This chapter focuses on how early childhood educators can understand the capabilities of the children they teach. It begins by asking *why* assessment is important, discussing why educators need a broad picture of children's capabilities, and considers *observation* as one of the best 'tools of the trade'.

After a brief overview of the recent history of baseline assessment in England and Wales, the chapter asks whether this form of assessment identifies, for educators, the capabilities of the young children with whom they work. Finding many baseline assessment instruments, and the National Framework for Baseline Assessment wanting, the chapter concludes with suggestions for improved policy and practice in early assessment of young children's learning.

WHY ASSESS YOUNG CHILDREN'S LEARNING?

To ask 'Why assess children's learning?' is to question one of the most fundamental components of teaching young children. Children's learning is so complex, rich, fascinating, varied and variable, surprising, enthusiastic and stimulating, that to see it taking place, every day, before one's very eyes is one of the greatest privileges of any early childhood educator. The very process of observing and assessing children's learning is, in a sense, its own justification. Watching children learn can open our eyes to the astonishing capacity of young children to learn, and shows us the crucial importance of these first few years in children's lives. But there is much more to say about assessing children's learning. There is much more to be gained from watching children learn than to make us marvel at children's powers to think, do, communicate and create, for there is an important piece of work for educators to do to help them to understand – really understand – what they see.

The legacy of some of the pioneers of early education (such as Froebel, Piaget, Vygotsky and Isaacs) and of those whose work in the latter half of the twentieth century has illuminated children's learning (such as Donaldson, 1983; Athey, 1990; Abbott and Rodger, 1994a) helps educators to consider their own observations of children in the light of a rich literature which opens up the meaning of children's words, representations and actions. Educators' personal experiences of individual children's learning can help them to see more clearly the general principles that other researchers and educators have established as characteristic of that learning. For example, those who work with babies and children under 3 years of age can draw on the work of Rouse (1991), Goldschmied and Jackson (1994) and Abbott and Moylett (1997) in order to embellish their own understanding of the children with whom they work. When early childhood educators hold up the work of others as a mirror to their own, they can see the essential points of their own work reflected more clearly.

Some of the pioneers of early childhood education learnt about children's learning by watching and learning themselves, by observing children and thinking about what they saw. Those published observations can be useful to educators now as tools for reflection on children's processes of learning and as a means of moving from the specifics of personal experiences to general understandings about children's thinking. Susan Isaacs, for example, ran an experimental school, The Malting House, in Cambridge from 1924 to 1927. Her compelling accounts of the day-to-day doings of the children in the school show clearly how her analysis of children's intellectual development is the product of a mass of detailed anecdotal insights. For example, she describes the development of the basic concepts of biology, change, growth, life and death, illustrating this process with a wealth of evidence:

18.6.25
The children let the rabbit out to run about the garden for the first time, to their great delight. They followed him about, stroked him and talked about his fur, his shape and his ways.

13.7.25
Some of the children called out that the rabbit was dying. They found it in the summerhouse, hardly able to move. They were very sorry and talked much about it. They shut it up in the hutch and gave it warm milk.

14.7.25

The rabbit had died in the night. Dan found it and said: 'It's dead – its tummy does not move up and down now.' Paul said, 'My daddy says that if we put it into water it will get alive again.' Mrs I said 'shall we do so and see?' They put it into a bath of water. Some of them said, 'It is alive.' Duncan said, 'If it floats, it's dead, and if it sinks, it's alive.' It floated on the surface. One of them said, 'It's alive, because it's moving.' This was a circular motion, due to the currents in the water. Mrs I therefore put in a small stick which also moved round and round, and they agreed that the stick was not alive. They then suggested that they should bury the rabbit, and all helped to dig a hole and bury it.

15.7.25

Frank and Duncan talked of digging the rabbit up – but Frank said, 'It's not there – it's gone up to the sky.' They began to dig, but tired of it and ran off to something else. Later they came back and dug again. Duncan, however, said, 'Don't bother – it's gone – it's up in the sky' and gave up digging. Mrs I therefore said, 'Shall we see if it's there?' and also dug. They found the rabbit, and were very interested to see it still there.

The diary entries by Isaacs and her colleagues were more than entertaining anecdotes: they formed the basis for her analysis of children's scientific thinking. Isaacs was able to learn about learning by intently studying her own detailed observations. Thus, assessment of children's learning through the tools of observation is not at all new, though for some who have not have the opportunities to continue to practise their skills of observing and reflecting upon their observations, those tools may well have become somewhat rusty. However, many have followed Isaacs' observational practice; indeed, much of my own earlier work on children's learning has been informed by my diary jottings (made whilst teaching) of children's words, actions and graphic representations (Nutbrown, 1999). Similarly, the pioneering practice of Reggio Emilia in northern Italy is developed largely through careful observation, documentation and reflection upon the children's work (Filippini and Vecchi, 1996 Abbot and Nutbrown 2001).

The importance of close observation is also illustrated by Goldschmied's work with babies under 2 years of age (1987). Observations of babies playing with the Treasure Basket can give the watching adult valuable insights into the children's learning and into their interactions with one another. Other reasons for observing and assessing concern the adults' part in providing care and education. Young children's awesome capacity for learning imposes a potentially overwhelming responsibility on early years practitioners to support, enrich and extend that learning. When educators understand more about children's learning they must then assume an even greater obligation to do whatever they can to foster and develop that learning: the extent to which educators achieve quality in day care and education services is a measure of the extent to which they succeed in providing appropriate environments and interactions in which young children can learn and develop.

The 1990s saw a proliferation of criteria for high-quality provision for young children's learning. Such statements represented attempts to identify and specify necessary conditions for this learning and development but, as Woodhead (1996) illustrates, quality is often culture and community specific and it is difficult to agree universal statements of quality. What might suit the discussion of quality in the UK may well be quite unsuitable in, say, the Caribbean. That said, it is true that – whatever their setting and whatever their international location – where educators observe children and use their observations to generate understandings of their learning and their needs, they are contributing to the development of a quality environment in which those children might thrive. Where educators observe young children they are using a tool that plays an important part in achieving high-quality preschool experiences, shaping present, daily learning experiences of young children whatever type of setting they attend. The evaluative purpose of assessment is central for early childhood educators, for they cannot know if the environments they create and the support they provide for children as they work are effective unless they watch and learn from what they see.

Observation can provide starting points for reviewing the effectiveness of provision, and such observational assessments of children's learning can be used to identify strengths, weaknesses, gaps and inconsistencies in the curriculum provided for all children.

Assessment can be used to plan and review the provision and teaching as well as to identify those significant moments in each child's learning educators which can build upon to shape a curriculum that matches each child's pressing cognitive and affective concerns.

Observation and assessment can illuminate the future, as well as provide information with which to improve the quality of the present. This forward-looking dimension of assessment is the means by which early childhood educators can explore the possible outcomes of the provision they offer; the curriculum, pedagogy, interactions and relationships. Increasingly, formal assessments are being used to diagnose children's abilities. Some of the many baseline assessment instruments attempt to assess, too young, what young children can do in particular (and often limited) aspects of curriculum, and there is a danger that formal assessment of 4-year-olds on entry to school limits the opportunities they are offered rather than opening up a broad canvas of learning. It is important, however, to use the active process of assessment to identify for each individual the next teaching steps so that learning opportunities in the immediate future are well matched to the children they are designed for.

This focus on the *next steps* in teaching (and learning) takes us into the area of development Vygotsky called 'the zone of proximal development'. He used this concept to argue passionately that assessment does not end with a description of a pupil's present state of knowing, but only begins there. He wrote: 'I do not terminate my study at this point, but only begin it' (Vygotsky, 1978, p. 85). Effective assessment is dynamic, not static, and can identify for the educator what the learner's next steps might be; assessment reveals learning potential as well as learning achievements. Vygotsky's arguments show how 'learning which is oriented toward developmental levels that have already been reached is ineffective from the viewpoint of a child's overall development. It does not aim for a new stage of the developmental process but rather lags behind this process' (*ibid.*, p. 89). *Observation and assessment are the essential tools of watching and learning by which we can both establish the progress that has already been made and explore the future – the learning that is still embryonic*. The role of the adult in paying careful and informed attention to children's learning and reflecting upon it is crucial to the enhancement of children's future learning.

VALUES AND VISION

Whilst the learning and development of all children can be enhanced through careful and respectful assessment, the focus of any specific act of assessment is most often an individual child, whose uniqueness is revealed and reinforced in the process. Yet assessment is not *just* about revealing uniqueness; it is important to identify significant milestones that are important for all children. Taken for granted at the heart of many statements about children's individuality is a set of (often unquestioned and unarticulated) assumptions about the concept of a 'child'; and taken for granted at the heart of many assessment policies and practices there often lie the same assumptions. Until the imposition of the National Framework for Baseline Assessment in September 1998 (SCAA, 1997a), it was possible to suggest that the ways in which early childhood educators assessed children's learning, and the purposes for which they did so, were based on an implicit (and often personal) value system, built up of beliefs about children, about their nature, their behaviours, their feelings, their approach to living and learning. Whenever educators set about observing, assessing and evaluating young children's learning, they bring to that task some cherished beliefs about what they are looking for, what they *expect* to see, how they *anticipate* children might behave. It must be said that the proliferation of baseline assessment instruments in the late 1990s (QCA, 1998) suggested that there was a variety of assumptions about children and how they *should* behave and what they *should* learn. It might also be the case that national policy-makers built the National Framework for Baseline Assessment upon certain assumptions about children, childhood and their learning which do not embrace the values of individuality, difference and personal distinctive achievements, but rather assert the importance of common (and narrowly constructed) goals (SCAA, 1997b). The language of policy documents in the late 1990s suggested it was the case that 'childhood' had been reconstructed for policy (or perhaps *through* policy) with very young 'children' becoming 'pupils' and 'experiences' giving way to 'outcomes' (Nutbrown, 1998). The year 2000 promised the re-emergence of a more appropriate language of early education with talk of 'foundations', a re-endorsement of 'play' and discussion again of 'children'. But it remained the case that this re-emergence of values; of children as capable learners and of the importance of play, were still harnessed to an assessment strategy which seemed in discord with a notion of fluid development and creative, flexible teaching. Clearly an important task for early childhood policy-makers in the early 2000s was the unshackling of baseline assessment from the new, and hard fought-for, Foundation Stage.

Values underpin everything, and vision is a healthy catalyst for change. It is important early childhood educators are supported in the appreciation and articulation of their own personal vision of early experiences for children (how things might be) as such vision derives from the values they hold, their own constructions of 'childhood'. It is important, too, that early childhood educators do not adopt the policy language of the late 1990s without interrogation and scrutiny of the values that give rise to such language.

NATIONAL FRAMEWORK FOR BASELINE ASSESSMENT

There is nothing new about the practice of assessing the achievements of children in the preschool years. The best practice in early years education has always involved educators observing and recording children's learning and progress, sharing such observations with parents and using them as a basis for planning future teaching and learning opportunities. Burgess-Macey (1994, p. 48), commenting on the 1990s interest in 'Baseline Assessment', highlighted the change in purpose:

The current interest in baseline assessment in schools, however, arises from a different source. Schools feel the need to prove that they are teaching children effectively and that the learning that a child can demonstrate by the age of the Key Stage 1 tests of assessment has in fact been facilitated by the school. Without baseline assessment on entry to school the value-added component of a child's later performance cannot be calculated.

She stressed (*ibid.*) concern about purpose and practice:

Early years educators need to treat the issue of assessment very carefully. We need to be clear about which purposes of assessment we are working towards, and which models of the early years curriculum and of children's learning underpin our models of assessment. We cannot uncritically adopt a model handed down from the National Curriculum and assessment procedures.

In 1996 proposals to create and impose a *National Framework for Baseline Assessment* (SCAA, 1996b) carried with them the potential to restrict early assessment to narrow foci, as well as the risk of restricting innovative teaching practices. What is worthy of assessment invariably becomes quickly redefined as what is worthy of being taught, therefore influencing decisions about the learning that is valued. Decisions about how to assess the development of children before they are 5 years of age, as they enter compulsory schooling, are fundamental to future debate and decision-making about standards, teaching methods and children's achievements.

There is an important point to be made about centrally imposed terminology. The term *baseline assessment* is vague and carries with it a high level of inaccuracy. Though no single term can satisfy all meanings, it seems that *baseline screening* more accurately describes the 1997 government proposals and that the term *entry assessment* is a more appropriate way of describing the beginning of an assessment process undertake by teachers as part on ongoing school assessment processes. 'Entry' is surely preferable to 'baseline' as it implies 'entry' to the school system and does not imply (as does 'baseline') that this particular assessment marks the beginning of learning or of achievement. Important too is the distinction between initial or quick 'screening' and more long-term and in-depth 'assessment'.

National Baseline Assessment as required in September 1998 provided a form of *assessment for management*, which now enables schools and LEAs to plot their progress against other schools and the progress of their pupils year by year, cohort by cohort (for example, Strand, 1996). A minimal list of knowledge and skills in literacy, mathematics and some aspects of personal and social development is required to be assessed when children begin school (QCA, 1998). But teachers always need to base their teaching on the 'fine-meshed' assessments which they carry out in order to *teach* and which they subsequently use to complete *wide-meshed* assessments required for purposes *separate* from teaching.

The SCAA focused on two *purposes* for assessment: 1) teaching and learning; and 2) the 'value-added' by a school, endorsing the view that these *two* purposes were to be achieved within *one* instrument (SCAA, 1997b), but it is difficult (if it is possible at all) to satisfy both purposes without compromising either.

During 1997 as teachers began to prepare for the requirements of the National Framework for Baseline Assessment, they saw the status of their own more detailed assessments being diminished – at least so far as official recognition was concerned. Teaching young children will continue to improve so long as teachers' time is not wasted on completing the kinds of assessments which involve them in – sometimes – purposeless administration that undermines their belief in their own judgements which are born of professional knowledge and their relationships with the children they teach.

THE STATUS OF 'ASSESSMENT FOR TEACHING'

Good teaching depends on good assessment, but the status of *assessment for teaching* in the last decade had been eroded and, during the late 1990s, purposes of assessment in the early years became confused. There was a clear example of this confusion in the introductory phase of baseline assessment. To complete the required baseline assessments teachers had to draw on the *fine-meshed* assessments (for *teaching*) already carried out:

> In making your assessments, you will draw upon knowledge of the children that you have built up since they started school. You may have existing assessment records or informal notes to which you can refer. Some assessments you make will be based on what you have observed during the time children have been in school (SCAA, 1997b, p. 7).

Given that it was expected teachers should carry out their daily observations and reflections on children's work, two fundamental questions arose – and remain largely unanswered. First, how can such summative assessments be claimed to help teachers *plan* their teaching? And, secondly, why must teachers who already have more detailed information about children's achievements – derived from *fine-meshed* assessments for *teaching* – go on to make crude judgements according to *wide-meshed* assessment scales?

EARLY ASSESSMENT FOR THE FUTURE

Children's early learning and development are exciting. It is stimulating and rewarding for teachers (as well as children and their parents) to see a child taking new steps in learning. But the prevailing conditions for effective teaching must include *a fair breeze with a following wind.* Everything must be heading in the same direction – charting the same course, running the same race. It will not do for those who teach and those who are responsible for teachers and education in terms of policy to be in opposition – a team effort is what children need. The reinstatement of the status of *assessment for teaching* is essential to optimum early education experiences for young children. But there are other conditions that make up a *fair breeze* for early education: *time* for children (enough teachers to work with them), *time* for assessment, *confidence* in teachers' teaching and assessments, and *recognition* of the judgements teachers make about what they teach, how they teach and when. These together can make for teaching that enhances learning.

So what might the future hold for baseline assessment and the improvement of assessment for learning in the early years of education? There are three key action points. First, the elevation of the status of ongoing teacher assessment as the main tool for understanding children's learning needs and progress; second, professional development opportunities that challenge teachers and other early childhood educators to observe children's learning and understand what they see; and, finally, the termination of baseline assessment as a national requirement at the mid-point of the Foundation stage. With the introduction of the Foundation stage in 2000 ranging from 3 years to the end of the reception year (almost 6 years for some children), the early years of schooling were set to be the only Key Stage that was required to be assessed at the mid-point. Clearly, the only sensible move would be for baseline assessment in the early years of the 2000s to meet its demise, in favour of ongoing teacher assessment – fully supported by rich and challenging professional development.

In October 2000 it was reported that ministers were considering a number of changes to baseline assessment. These included four key factors:

(1) Moving baseline assessment to the *end* of the Foundation Stage (in which case it would presumably be renamed 'Foundation Stage Assessment').

(2) Amendment of the assessment criteria to include children's progress towards the early learning goals (in which case a further phase of development of assessment instruments would be required).

(3) A single baseline assessment scheme (thereby discouraging the use of

many and varied schemes and assisting the collection of national statistics).

(4) Making national comparisons using the data (this would produce the inevitable 'league tables' of the performance of the nation's 4-year-olds).

At the end of 2000 it was stated (QCA, 2000a) that changes would be implemented in September 2002, following consultation.

WITH DUE RESPECT...

In this chapter I have discussed why educators should observe and assess young children, the difficulties the imposed national framework for baseline assessment has caused and how those difficulties might be reduced, or better still, eradicated through the reinstatement of assessment for teaching, by teachers. Clearly, many questions remain, but the answers will depend upon the principles on which work with young children in general, and assessment in particular, is based. Above all, the principle of respect is crucial. Assessment must be carried out with proper respect for children, their parents, carers and their educators. Respectful assessment can be expressed through what is done, what is said, how relationships are conducted and the attitudes educators bring to their work. Those who watch young children, really watch and listen and reflect on their learning, will know it is time for revision of policy and practice. Future policies and pratice must support the full involvement of parents and educators towards respectful understandings of children's learning. It is time, too, that opportunities for professional development for educators is of a kind that is worthy of children's amazing capacity to learn and communicate. The 'one-stop' summaries of children's abilities according to predetermined lists (that miss the true riches of children's minds) is not professional development and does nothing to truly focus the minds of educators on children's learning.

Time for teaching and assessment, *confidence* in teachers' teaching and assessments, *recognition* of the judgements teachers make can create the important climate of *respectful* teaching. The concept of respect can underpin and inform the way adults work with children and the ways in which policies are developed and implemented, but the notion of respect in education can be misunderstood (Nutbrown, 1996; 1997). What do I mean when I speak of *respect* in education? 'When advocates of respect for children are accused of being "idealistic", of "romanticising early childhood" – their meaning is misunderstood. Respect is not about "being nice" – it is about being clear, honest, courteous, diligent and consistent' (Nutbrown, 1998).

Table 5.1. What is a respectful educator? What is respectful teaching? What is respectful assessment?

Respectful Approaches	Disrespectful Approaches
Taking account of the learner – 'children as participants'	Ignoring the learner – 'children as recipients'
Building on existing learning	Disregarding/unaware of existing learning
Based on tuning into learners' agendas	Based on predetermined curriculum
Responsive to learners' needs and interests	Unresponsive to learners' needs and interests
Informed by children's developmental needs	Informed by targets/key stages/ages
Curriculum based on children's identified needs	Curriculum based on external definitions of needs
Includes/embraces issues of children's rights	Ignores/disregards issues of children's rights
Clarity for learner	Lack of clarity for learner
Authentic assessment to inform teaching	Inauthentic assessment used to track progress of cohort
Challenge	No challenge
Opportunity for extension and diversity	Closed to extension
Holistic	Compartmentalised
Involves parents	Excludes parents
Evaluation	'It works' – no evaluation
Revision in the light of experience	Carrying on regardless
Recognises all achievements	Values achievement of specific prespecified goals
Purposeful	Lack of purpose
Knowledgeable teachers	Teachers with limited knowledge
Professional development for teachers and other educators	Lack of professional development for teachers and other educators
Teachers and other educators with appropriate initial training and qualification	Teachers and other educators with limited/inappropriate training qualifications
Each learner matters	The cohort/group/majority matter
Equality for all children	The 'same' for all
Includes all children	Excludes some children
Sufficient and appropriate equipment/resources	Insufficient and inappropriate equipment/resources
Appropriate ratio of adults to children	Too many children – too few adults
Sufficient/appropriate space and access to learning areas/experiences	Insufficient/inappropriate space and limited access to learning areas/experiences

The concept of respectful assessment and respectful teaching may still raise an eyebrow or two, and could be dismissed by some as an over-romanticising of work with and for young children. So the careful articulation of our terms is important, and it is worth examining here what the concept of respectfully working with children might include. Table 5.1 shows some aspects which I suggest might constitute respectful teaching, and it is worth noting that the opposite of respectful approaches is *dis*respectful (I doubt that anyone would endorse such a term!).

Teaching young children needs those qualities of clarity, honesty, courtesy, diligence and consistency. It means identifying what children *can* do, what they *might* do and what their teachers need next to teach. This is indeed a task that – despite repeated attempts to make it simple – can never be other than complex. Watching children as they learn and understanding the significance of those learning moments are complex tasks that make high demands on all who attempt them.

Points for discussion

Reflect on Figure 5.1 and make your own list of the features of respectful approaches to education, teaching and assessment. Consider, too, what you think would constitute disrespectful practice. If you share this activity as a staff team or with a group of early childhood educators, discuss your lists and revisit your assessment policies and practice in the light of your discussions.

Further reading

Desforges, M. and Lindsay, G. (1997) *Baseline Assessment: Problems and Possibilities*. London: Hodder & Stoughton.

Nutbrown, C. (1997) *Recognising Early Literacy Development – Assessing Children's Achievements*. London: Paul Chapman Publishing.

Nutbrown, C. (2000) Alex's story: literacy and literacy teaching in the earliest years. In Millard, E. (ed.) *Enquiring into Literacy: Papers from the Literacy Research Centre Sheffield. Sheffield Papers in Education*. Sheffield: University of Sheffield, School of Education.

6

BEING UNDER 3 YEARS OF AGE: ENHANCING QUALITY EXPERIENCES[1]

Dorothy Selleck

Children are born into different kinds of families where they work out how to be themselves. They are people under 3 years of age with feelings to communicate and ideas of their own.

> [The] child with her consuming interests, her inexhaustible questions, and insisting body. The child who is learning to make mistakes, figuring out how to become a person, through the curious combinations of word and gesture, and the gaps between them (Phillips, 1998a).

Parents have many demands on their time, not only for childrearing, but also to progress their own life-long learning, leisure and earning opportunities. In this chapter I present how practices in early years settings with professional staff may complement, and enhance, the care, play and learning of babies and toddlers that are happening with families at home.

A CONTEMPORARY OVERVIEW IN A CHANGING NATIONAL CONTEXT

In the London borough where I work, parents use services for their children under 3 years of age for many purposes. Parents may need

[1] This chapter includes examples of practice developed with staff teams at Randolph Beresford Early Years Centre and at Marshcroft Early Years Centre. Names of children and practitioners have been changed to preserve confidentiality.

childcare so as to work and support their families financially. Other parents will need to study, to learn skills to enter the workforce. Homeless, refugee and migrant families may want to retrain or learn British standards and law in order to take up work in a new country which they were qualified to do in a different society. Some parents choose services to complement home care with the opportunities for care, play and learning in groups. Wealthy families, as well as teenage mothers on low incomes and, indeed, all parents at times of stress, isolation or uncertainty are able to turn to professional staff for support. The wide social, economic and cultural diversity in the London Borough of Hammersmith and Fulham is a vignette of a national scene, though the balance may be different in more rural communities. Many of us in many different circumstances need or want services for the care, play and learning of children under 3 years of age.

Over last few years parents have used many kinds and combinations of childcare. A national survey of the demand for childcare (over four months in 1999) showed that 64% of 0–2-year-olds had been cared for by their grandparents, 37% received care from another relative or friend, 26% were cared for in nurseries and crèches, 20% in playgroups and babysitters were also used by 13%. Most parents looked to formal provision during the week, especially in the morning, while at other times the overwhelming majority of children were looked after by informal providers. Given a choice, parents of under-2s stated a preference for a nursery, 40%; a registered childminder, 12%; or for a daily nanny, 15% (La Valle *et al.*, 2000). Evidently there is a gap in affordable available services with specialised and trained staff for this age-group.

A collection of press cuttings about the dilemmas of working parents reveals the political, cultural and populist backdrop to this demand for more and better-quality childcare for this age-group (Robinson, 2000). That it is 'excruciatingly difficult to work and give children the care they need'; 'couples become alienated with no time for anything but work and childcare'; 'women are paying a heavy price on the work ladder for just being female'; 'breast feeding may be best for babies' ... but not for working mothers, and especially not if you are a member of Parliament! 'Baby bounty plans to woo women voters'; 'cash bonanzas for nurseries to break the cycle of poverty, so upping academic success and lowering the risk of children offending later in their teenage years' ... are all newspaper headline examples of incentives to increase services and up opportunities for children. This chapter aims to look at the possibilities for synergy rather than the potential political and ideological tensions between meeting children's needs and the needs of their parents. Is it possible to be 'good enough' in our services to complement *good enough parents* (Winnicott, 1965)?

Since the last edition of this book there have been many changes and developments. A Labour government, re-elected in June 2001, with new money to invest in early years services has presented us with myriad funding streams. Never before has there been such an opportunity to think about our aspirations for children as national strategies and standards, partnership plans and parent power all bombard as well as buoy up those of us who manage...so as to manage changes. The responsibilities of managers are to lead a newly recruited, minimally qualified additional workforce (DfEE, 2001) as well as to build on professional development, enhancing qualifications and life-long professional learning in a nationally accredited framework of qualifications (QCA, 1999b).

Early Years Development and Childcare Partnerships and Sure Start projects promise a more egalitarian representative forum for planning local services to meet local needs *with* families of young children. From bumps, to babies, to starting school, Sure Start programmes (DfEE, 2000a; 2000b) are building on local initiatives to reduce poverty and meet targets to improve children's health, enhance children's abilities as learners, as well as to strengthen families and communities. There are worthwhile schemes to support breast feeding; to help during post-natal depression; as well as developing play facilities for children under 3 years of age in crèches, drop-ins, parent link schemes, toy libraries; and many other ways of working to ensure all children have 'good quality' play and learning opportunities to help them to progress towards early learning goals (QCA/DfEE 2000). Never before has there been such a determined strategic national drive, combined with locally driven initiatives, to address the needs of parents (mostly mothers), with the job of nurturing babies' health, learning and well-being from the foetus to the 'foundation stage'. Hopefully, this Sure Start approach will develop to address the needs of all new mothers/parents, not only financially impoverished, but also the isolated, stressed and besotted, tired but 'happy' average parent! Many schemes, such as the Peers Early Education Project (PEEP, 1999) in Oxford, offer universal provision (not only targeted at 'needy families') to bring about significant improvement in educational achievement – especially in literacy – through their projects with books, rhymes and songs for parents *with* their babies.

As well as supporting parents *with* their babies, an expansion of services in the voluntary and private sectors, day care, co-ordinated early years centres and childminders' networks is burgeoning to support working and studying parents, all part of the political mission and momentum to enhance the life chances of babies and toddlers.

A CONTEMPORARY REVIEW OF RESEARCH
AND SPECIALIST LITERATURE

In reporting on new thinking in work with under-3s, it seems important to draw on research and practice with babies, parents (mostly mothers), families and the social context in which we all live. In the three crucial areas prioritised here I draw on expertise from pedagogy/education/cognitive psychology, sociology, practice consultants, child psychotherapists, clinical psychologists and brain scientists – to pick out a few. In the past these people with specialisms in this age-group but from different professional disciplines would not have been as likely to be connected to each other. Now, through national symposiums (e.g. Parent Child, 2000), media and publications (e.g. *Tuning in to Children*, BBC Radio 4, 1999), it is more possible to enable and encourage us to listen and learn from each other.

Babies' brain powers! Adults observing

There is an abundance of development in children's brains at this age phase. Physiologically, much has been explained by ingenious clinical experiments and sophisticated recording equipment that may trace the thinking activity and physical changes and growth inside babies' heads. Neuroscience has presented stunning new evidence to show parents and practitioners there is much to wonder at in the powerful learning capacities of children under 3 years of age (e.g. Bates, Plunkett, Greenough, Huttenlocher and others in Purves and Selleck, 1999).

Other specialists help us to manage the significance of these wonders and the impact on practice of this phase. What must practitioners do when synapses connect neurons (synaptogenises), when there may be 'critical periods' in the development of sensory and motor systems? Do we need to do anything crucial to ensure a rich environment for children to learn so they do not miss out? There is no doubt children (as well as rats) respond to play opportunities and fail to thrive when deprived of touch, holding and playful companionship (love?) (as, for example, in Romanian children's homes in the 1990s). But it seems that the other extreme – over stimulation, bombarding babies with objects, colour or even unremitting attention – can be just as unhelpful (Goldschmied and Jackson, 1994; Trevarthen, 1999; Bruer, 2000).

The main message from scientists seems to be that children need spontaneous playful interactions rather than any kind of preplanned or formal responses:

The best way to talk to babies is to know nothing about it, you do it because you are human . . . it is clear from the beginning that children have a driving motivation to become part of a meaningful world . . . the most important creators of a curriculum are children, they are the ones who create the interest (Trevarthen, 1999).

Children are immensely curious and engaging. They are willing participants in the games, songs and musical dances of childhood, of their families and culture. When we can follow the children's lead, respond to their cues of gaze, gesture and 'baby talk'/tonal vocalisations, when we may match the pace, rhythm/musicality and direction of children's interests, then that is the milieu in which little ones learn best.

If children are the creators of curriculum, then the adults who work with them need to be observers who describe their subjects as real multi-dimensional people responding to all the events of human life around them. Practitioners need to be able to engage with very young children. This means that practitioners must be recruited, trained and supported who are in touch with their own emotions and inner states of mind (Solity, 1995; Rustin, 1997).

Attachment

Pauline . . . 'Work is OK . . . I was off for a year after he was born, but I didn't want to go back even then. I wanted to be with my baby. I was enjoying it. But I knew I had to, financially . . . I can't even think about it, my not being with him. It would give me a nervous breakdown!' Pauline was not sad but her story was sad . . . we deny these feelings at our peril . . . (Benn, 1998).

[In] the beginning every child is an only child. The child is not possessive of the mother because he already possesses her . . . Everyone begins their life belonging to someone else . . . being separate, or having to share leaves one in shock . . . as everyone who is in love (or in mourning) knows, what is politely referred to as separation is mutilation . . . (Phillips, 1998b).

These two quotations, one from a mother and one from a psychotherapist advocating for a child's feelings, hint at a body of literature on the attachment, or bonding together, of babies and the main people who care for them, play with them and take up their cues for attention. The significance of this special relationship in developing healthy relationships later on, and in becoming confident learners, is well documented (Rutter, 1995; Elfer, 1997).

There is a growing body of literature that emphasises the importance of a continuing attachment relationship between key persons/key practitioners who care for, play with and educate children in settings outside their homes in close association with children's significant attachment figures from home. I return to this below.

There is also growing documentation on the consequences of damaged lives when children are not supported to form secure attachments in infancy. Parents, and later, nursery staff, by attending to infants' psychological, and biological and learning needs, can provide children with a secure attachment that will enable them to develop fruitful long-term relationships and a sense of being valued and loveable. Unfortunately, according to some, the reverse is also true. By failing to respond in a consistent and sensitive way, psychological damage or trauma may be inflicted on a child's attachment system, wounding his or her self-esteem and his or her capacity to tune into others later on (de Zulueta, 1993; Robertson and Robertson, 1999; Balbernie, 2000; Bruner, 2000).

Continuity, reciprocity, identity

In the beginning, only the presence of a parent (or committed regular key person in the nursery) can provide the continuity, attention and sensuous pleasure the baby needs to make sense of all his or her experiences and set in motion the processes of mental development. Familiarity, pattern and predictability give older babies a sense of being themselves. Continuity of attention from key people who know children well, who are interpreting and responding to their gestures and cues enable children to attend to their inclinations and to play freely. From the sustained continuity of regular contact with a few familiar people, toddlers may enjoy an increasing range of relationships and activities (Shuttleworth in Rustin *et al.*, 1997).

By the time babies are a few months old they may instigate as well as follow quite complex games with their familiar people. There is synchrony of pitch and voice, a communicative musicality in their narratives. Expressive melodramas not unlike the improvisation of jazz performers may be 'conversations' that pass to and from little children. When there are opportunities to be in continuous relationships with adults, sustained over time, babies seem to be absorbed and involved in another's mind (Trevarthen, 1999).

Children start to become aware they belong to a culture as well as to a family. Children growing up in multicultural and multilingual environments can learn many languages and pick up the cues of engagement appropriate to their own and other children's families. We know that children of a few weeks old can be engrossed in mutual interactions with another baby, and that toddlers develop close and interdependent relationships when there are regular opportunities for them to be together (Whaley and Rubenstein, 1994; Goldschmied and Selleck, 1996). Research shows that children may learn to treat everyone differently but with equal concern or they may, at an early age, learn negative attitudes of discrimination, prejudice or racism (Lane, 1999).

The messages from this research seem clear. Children above all else need continuity of experiences with significant close adults who stay alongside children and engage with them in these three years. Adults who have the capacities and support for attachments, intimacy and involvement with children, their families and their friends will support their well-being and learning best (Goldschmied and Jackson, 1994; Elfer, 1996). Quality services must be planned to enable such continuity for the under-3s.

PRACTICE DEVELOPMENT

Introduction to the processes and practices for evolving quality practice

Early years managers lead teams with varying degrees of commitment and with a broad spectrum of capacities and potential. Working with babies is a vocation for some, a considered career choice, a decision to engage with a stage of a child's learning that is powerful, significant and enjoyable. For others it may be the best fit with their lack of formal qualifications and, for others, an alternative in their locality for other low-paid work. So team leaders of services to babies and toddlers have to take account of this uneven mixture of qualities of the personnel in each group.

Three areas of professional practice are of particular significance to baby/toddler practitioners.

Professional involvement

Work with babies and toddlers is physically demanding, emotionally draining, as well as intellectually challenging. It needs very observant and astute people to tune into babies from other people's families. If this work goes unsupported, unsupervised, undervalued and lowly in pay and status, it may inevitably result in practitioners offering 'burn-out, automatic-pilot performance'. They may be pleasant and benign . . . but is this adequate?

Intellectual curiosity: a culture of ongoing professional development

Work with babies may be seen by some as needing a nurturing motherliness that precludes intellectual curiosity and ongoing study. While the first quality is undoubtedly an asset, for practitioners to sustain vitality and a capacity for reflection, analysis and creativity in their work with children and families, an ongoing involvement in training, reading and professional team talk is essential.

Harmonious, interactive teamwork

People who work with under-3s are part of a team. Their work with parents is just as important as their responses to children. Many workers are in organisations where there are shifts and rotas for leave and training, as well as liaison with other professionals. It is inappropriate in work with the youngest children to have an attitude of 'keeping your head down and doing your own thing as best as you can'. Quality experiences for babies are best planned in a culture of equal concern and attention for each and every practitioner's thoughts and feelings in an atmosphere of challenge, trust and co-construction.

So what really makes a difference to quality for babies and toddlers? How best are staff kept up to date with research and the implications for practice? How do they work harmoniously together to observe children, develop a key practitioner approach and design their curriculum for babies?

There are many initiatives developed in Early Years Development and Childcare Partnerships (EYDCPs). These may include a good resource library, a running programme of courses and visits matched to a training needs analysis, regular in-house staff team sessions for planning and evaluation, localised home-grown and -owned curricula and networks and cluster groups of support and professional discourse.

Paramount is attention to the following *processes* and *practices* of quality: a journey of change, over time, observation, a key person approach and curriculum. I will take these in turn.

Observation: tuning into children

[To] be a good observer... This requires a space in the mind where thoughts can begin to take shape and where confused experiences can be held in an inchoate form until their meaning becomes clearer. This kind of mental functioning requires a capacity to tolerate anxiety, uncertainty, discomfort, helplessness, a sense of bombardment

(Rustin, 1997).

Observation is taking time to hear and see what a child seems to be doing, feeling or thinking. A practitioner observes, then 'documents' (Dahlberg *et al.*, 1999) the experience of being alongside the child, in the child's shoes. The observation . . . spoken or written . . . is communicated through personal expressions as distinctive as any thumb print. This subjective expression reflects what each practitioner knows from studying, and then how she or he relates that knowledge to his or her own experiences in an effort to understand what may be going on for a child. Observation opens up possibilities of empathy.

Rigorous, reflective observation of babies and toddlers involves psychological and pedagogical states of uncertainty. That is, a capacity to hold back on first thoughts, resisting projecting personal ideas or feelings of our own on to the baby so as to leave time for supposing, time to imagine what other feelings might be in a child's heart and mind. That is a psychological state of uncertainty.

It is also important to reflect on a child's meanings or intentions before taking action, before planning an activity, or deciding on a method, or an approach to supporting the child's learning. That is a state of pedagogical uncertainty.

Tuning into children through observation involves the adult's capacity to tolerate the anxiety associated with uncertainty about the meaning or implication of what the adult takes in – in his or her mind and eye. That means not rushing into a response to a child without careful listening and thoughtfulness. This thinking process, rather than an instant 'common sense' response, is important if we are to enhance the quality of our interactions with a child who is learning to manage his or her own feelings, or moving on at his or her own pace to the next zone of his or her own thinking (Berk and Winser, 1995; Rustin *et al.*, 1997; Elfer and Selleck, 1999).

These processes are exemplified from documented case study material from the London Borough of Hammersmith and Fulham (LBH&F) EYDCP. These examples come from an area of London that provides services for families from diverse economic, social and cultural communities (LBH&F EYDCP, Annex 5 of the plan, 1999). In the following excerpts practitioners have used their preferred methodology. Some observations are scribed from conversations, some are excerpts from a diary between a pair of key workers/practitioners, and others are small pieces from the 'learning stories' written by a key worker practitioner to be shared with the child's parents and the staff team. (There were also video observations that are not accessible here.) These examples are part of the documentation of a project with two staff teams over many weeks of observations in their own settings. The significance of the qualities of the observer and his or her potential for recognising as well as enhancing the quality of children's experiences is dynamic.

Ibrahim, 26 months: a spoken observation in a staff team
'Ibrahim grabbed at the fruit, I told him he had to share, the last piece was
for Rose-May. I wondered how Ibrahim felt when he had to share the fruit?
Was he being greedy? Was he hungry and should he have the right to help
himself? Is it socially acceptable to take food in a group? If Ibrahim had
helped himself there would not be enough pieces for everyone to have
some, but he was hungry...?

'Are we preparing children to belong in the group in nursery...should we also
be supporting them to belong to their own families and communities? Can we
do both? Are manners different in groups? Maybe at home you can help
yourself when you are hungry, at nursery you have to take one piece only? Are
we denying children's home cultures at a formative time in their identities?

'Ibrahim threw a piece of jigsaw at my forehead, it really hurt me when I
was helping the children with the pieces. I felt upset with all the children
scrabbling and pulling. Ibrahim was upset too.'

Different responses were offered as possibilities/opinions of working with
Ibrahim. They included the following suggestions of how a practitioner
should respond when he hurt Rose-May. Say:

'Stop crying, it's all right.'
or
'I am not cross with you, but with what you have done.'
or
'I am cross with you, that hurt me.'
or
'No! Don't do that. It is wrong.'

Managing a child's behaviour that is difficult for adults or other children
The group then explored the different values and attitudes to children and
childrearing raised by this issue and how they perceived their role in
supporting and responding to Ibrahim's learning:

- As educators?
- As social trainers in acceptable etiquette?
- As carers matching their responses to children's needs, e.g. hunger;
  love; to be powerful and in control...?
- As adults who set limits on children's behaviour to teach them right
  from wrong?
- Or what?

The group said:
Responding to children depends on their age, what is going on in their
life... it must be an individual response to a unique child. Ibrahim is
having a hard time at the moment, you know your key children...that
makes a difference. He does need telling off sometimes, he can hurt other
children. As his key practitioner I can tell him off in a way that really
affects him, he looks really sad, we sort of understand each other.

'Settling in'

Jack, 18 months: a spoken observation

He just wants to go to you, to be on you, to suck his thumb.
He is a baby, he wants to be held, to have his finger in your ear. If you
were at home he would be on your hip while you did the hoovering!
Jack was over the moon to see his granny when she returned after a
shorter session.

---

*Oumou, 20 months; six-week review form and spoken observation to the
team*

She used to cling on to me, I used to carry her around a lot, she knew how
I was special for her... but now she doesn't need me in that way she is
confident and goes off with others. It was good when I had done that
work well so that she was ready to move on.

Omara, 17 months: learning story (narrative observation)

Day 1: Joe (father) brought Omara in for a visit. She appeared happy
and stayed close to him at all times, she made no other contact with
other children in the nursery.

1st week: At the beginning she clung to her father and held her drinking
bottle very tight. When I approached her she seemed to become
unhappy.

2nd week: Omara cried, I picked her up and carried her round with me, I
comforted her and provided her with company, I took her with me as I
went about my duties in the nursery.

2nd key practitioner (job share): Omara cried all day. I carried her round
and gave her water in her bottle, this did not help much. She cried for
most of the day. I let her have her drinking bottle and she walked
around with it to comfort her. She did not eat lunch or pudding but was
able to sleep with her bottle.

3rd week: She began talking more, she ate well at lunchtime and played
with the dough and the sand.

4th week: Omara came with me for a trip on the tube train. She pointed
to trains at the station, laughing and shouting. She seemd very relaxed
and was chasing the squirrels. She rolled on the grass with the other
children and seemed to be having fun. She is able to say goodbye and
wave to her father and sometimes watches him go. She will then return
to her activity.

This team included staff with a range of expertise. Some are highly qualified academically and practically, whereas others were newer to work with children, or to this age-group, or recently and minimally qualified. Some staff were keen to work to preset professional guidelines – a professional job engaged in with pride and predictability. Other staff were able to approach their work in a more fluid style of involvement, open to pedagogical and psychological states of uncertainty (see above).

The quality of these observations of Jack, Ibrahim, Oumou and Omara opens up issues for practitioners, trainers and managers that are distinctive to services to children under 3 and their families, and these may be generalised to other settings.

In many pages of documentation in this project, it was possible to find many rich and significant reflective discussions about children's learning. However, comparatively few of these discussions focused on a child rather than the group; on the unique particulars of an individual child's experiences in the play spaces rather than the planned play environment for all the children, or on the received rather than the planned curriculum. It is a tribute to the sophisticated work of the team in this early years centre that there were processes and structures in place to attend to observations of children's learning (reviews, diaries, notebooks, written and video 'learning stories'). In other settings where there are no such structures there are even fewer examples of observations of individual children and their learning. What are the possible reasons for this and does it matter in the development of quality practice for babies and toddlers?

First, it seems it is hard really to look, to be in a child' shoes. It may also be painful to imagine how it might be to tune in to the parents' feelings while containing the child's desolation at separation and 'settling in' times (Omara weeping pitifully all day long, refusing food and clinging on to her new carer for comfort). It can be uncomfortable to empathise with a child who is feeling thwarted or vengeful so that his or her impulse is to hit and hurt (Ibrahim throwing the jigsaw). Yet it was because the team were able to bear it that they were capable of containing rather than denying Ibrahim's anger. They were able to bear with Omara the painful transition of settling in rather than jollying her out of it, or denying the sadness and tension of those early days in the nursery for everyone. By being able to come alongside each child's feelings in attuned observations, this team was able to evolve responsive criteria of good practice.

Secondly, our national training for practitioners working with babies and toddlers has focused on 'developmental milestones' and competency-based assessment. This culture of tidy quality rather than the complexity and diversity of babies' experiences makes it difficult to match up to each child's own interests. Practitioners have, in the past, been under pressure to 'teach' rather than to look at learning. There has been more emphasis on the 'preparation of the room' rather than on observing the learning of the children in it. This has sometimes resulted in a mismatch of curriculum for babies and toddlers. Observation of what children are really interested in and an emphasis on the *received* curriculum (through observation) rather than the planned curriculum (based on developmental stages) do seem to make a difference to children's enjoyment and involvement in their play.

For instance, Ibrahim left his repetitive play in the pushchair – pacing round the garden when Joan observed his interest in a patch of soil. She fetched a selection of spades so he could 'dig for worms'. Ibrahim initiated this new but unplanned garden activity.

Oumou chose to press the buttons of the photocopier as Sita copied letters to the parents, rather than to play in the activity set up for the group. Oumou chose to be alongside Sita. If Joan and Sita had stuck with the planned curriculum, rather than been influenced by the toddlers' preoccupations, the quality of the child's play and learning is likely to have been 'lower level' (DfEE, 2001).

Watching and listening to a child make a difference. Each child is likely to be more involved in meaningful activities when the curriculum is matched to his or her interests and when he or she is engaged in a shared purpose with others. Ibrahim didn't find a worm but pocketed his own buried coin; Oumou was delighted with the clean printed sheets she produced for Sita!

Thirdly, talking together about a child's learning needs detail, not generalities. Key practitioners who know a baby and his or her family well need to relate their curriculum to particular episodes of observed children's behaviour and play. Monica could plan for and follow up Omara's interest in the squirrels in the park. Only Monica's shared experience with Omara and her shared observations with the other staff could match Omara's personal and particular squirrel-roly-poly-grass pleasures to the team's plans and choices for play materials, songs and books to match her zone of thinking. If Monica's observation had been general ('the children had a good time in the park') rather than specific and from Omara's point of view ('Omara was relaxed and chased the squirrels, rolling on the grass'), the potential for meaningful and responsive curriculum planning might have been diminished.

More emphasis on training and professional development of observation methodology, and time to practise observation skills, is urgently needed. This is crucial if little children are not just to 'settle in' and morph into no-protest institutionalised babes where there are largely adult-led plans out of synch with an infant's moods and meanings. If babies and toddlers are to be innovators and instigators in the social synchrony of learning, the child must come before the chart, observation before responding and planning (Elfer and Selleck, 1999; Trevarthen, 1999; Bruner, 2000).

Adults learn in a social context too. Staff teams need time to think together about their observations, to work together on the *task* of developing their practice, as well as to engage in the *process* of reflecting on the impact of their own part and contribution to their staff team.

The key person approach for children, families, staff and the nursery as a whole

Studies have helped us to understand that babies are born with a built-in readiness to make a special relationship with first one and then a small circle of adults who will protect them and meet their physical needs. Such a relationship is an 'attachment' (Rutter, 1995). Babies and young children show attachment behaviour when they make sure their special adult remains nearby, crying for them, smiling when close, moving towards them when anxious and moving away and exploring when they feel safe and connected into the people who support their thinking and feelings.

Young children rely on their special adults to meet their emotional needs as well as their physical needs. Most adults most of the time are not overwhelmed by anxiety or terror or loneliness when they are away from people with whom they have close emotional ties. However, babies are easily overwhelmed by intense feelings, especially of separation from the people who have become attached: 'Ultimately the child needs to abrogate his omnipotence – abjure his magic – and learn to wait' (Phillips, 1998a).

This is an elegant description of developing separateness, or independence, using the language of psychoanalysis. One- and two-year-olds begin to be able to wait a little longer than a baby can and are not so completely dependent, but they may still easily become overwhelmed. Babies and young children need a special adult on whom they can rely, someone who will meet their emotional needs as well as their physical needs. Such adults will keep them 'in mind', helping them to feel safe, understanding their expressions of love and attachment, and responding with appropriate holding, touch, movement and talk.

At home it is parents who act as these key adults and with whom the baby or young child has his or her main attachments. Key practitioners in nursery settings must take on that aspect of the parents' role during the hours they are apart. This is offering an attachment relationship, the purpose of which is to ensure the emotional and physical needs of the baby or young child are met sensitively and reliably by mainly one or two adults.

In other respects, though, relationships within the nursery are not like those at home. There is a community of people in the nursery, with a rich diversity of cultural and ethnic backgrounds, that is quite different from the family group and that offers the baby or young child special opportunities for relationships, exploration and learning not available at home. This rich network of relationships is very valuable but it complements and is dependent on the baby or young child having an attachment relationship with mainly one or two members of staff and is not an alternative to this. Very young children have not reached sufficient emotional independence to cope for other than short amounts of time without someone reliable to think about them and comfort them. With the security of this special attachment relationship, they can draw on the other relationships available in nursery settings. Without this attachment relationship, other relationships will feel bewildering and overwhelming (Shropshire and Telford EYDCP, 2000; Elfer *et al.*, 2001).

The diary of Omara's first few weeks recorded by her key practitioners (see above) signifies the crucial role of key practitioners in supporting children under 3 years of age and their families. In the context of carefully devised 'criteria for good practice' for 'settling in', children may have a healthy emotional start with someone in particular. In the new and stimulating nursery setting a child may then go on to learn to belong to, and become part of, the nursery community group.

An approach where practitioners may develop a pattern of trust and continuity of care with their key children and their families is crucial to a child's security. It will be necessary to manage changes in settings where children have been passed from room to room, and from key worker to key worker over their 36 months of development in one or more settings. 'Hiring teachers with a style that favours forming relationships and committing to two or three year' is a model developed in some settings (Raikes, 1996). In some innovative early years centres it is now possible for children to stay with their key practitioner and to remain with their key group of peers as they progress from babyhood into the 'foundation stage' (Pascal *et al.*, 1999; West, 2000).

This commitment to constancy and continuity in relationships within settings is likely to be the most significant factor in the quality experiences for children under 3 years of age.

Developmentally distinctive curriculum

The following three observations of different children in different settings are picked out in order to consider what may be a distinctive curriculum for the under-3s. In the stages from birth and on to connect into the Foundation stage, these three children are making their own choices, following their own schema, using the spaces, materials and resources available to them. They are making sense of what is of interest to them.

Samir, 20 months, with Tyrese, 18 months

After a tearful and tense start to the morning, Samir settles with a group at the water trough. He selects two plastic cars from the boxes of toys. He places them at opposite corners on the rim of the water trough and then drives them together and crashes them with accompanying crash noises. He selects another car and offers it to Tyrese in a gesture that invites him to join in. Tyrese copies Samir and runs the car across the opposite side of the trough. 'I got car,' calls Samir as he follows the rim of the trough. Samir drives the cars round the corners and finally crashes again. 'I got car,' he calls each time to Tyrese as he seems to celebrate the drive round the edge and the crashing crescendo.

Ibrahim, 26 months

He wakes from his afternoon nap, gathers his bedding, and hands it to an adult. Then while he is waiting for help with his shoes, he takes a small toy truck and wheels it round the perimeter of the rug. He carefully follows the border of the rug and precisely 'drives' it round each of the corners. As soon as he is dressed he chooses a trike from the garden and drives it round the perimeter path.

Hermione, 30 months, and Jayanthi, 26 months, with Mandy (practitioner)

Hermione sucks on her bottle lying in the home corner after her nanny leaves her in her playgroup. Mandy offers pillows, occasionally passing, sometimes talking with her in an unhurried manner over 25 minutes. Hermione is sucking and rocking dreamily. Once or twice she stands up and looks about the room, adjusts the enclosure she has made for herself, pushing the home corner furniture closer together, creating a set of boundaries for the space she was in alone.

After the bottle was finished she stood and watched all the activities in turn, sand, clay, an adult making Christmas chains, the climbing frame, the sand. Hermione inspected each activity, looking at what was on offer, talking to the children and adults briefly and briefly connecting with each group, making a circuit of the room.

Then she rushed out to the garden and the trikes as the outside doors were opened. Hermione called to Jayanthi and they made a number of circuits of the whole garden rushing from one side to the other and back again. Then Hermione instigated a number of stops, the fences, the bump in the grass, the pillar. Each time stopping to talk to Jayanthi, to call her to stop too, and to plan with her where to cycle next, and where they would stop next, she called to Jayanthi: 'Turn at the fence; stop by Mandy; over the bumbbety bump...'

These three children are learning in so many ways but, for the purposes of this chapter, we will think about just one area of learning...mathematical development. These three children are learning the foundations for mathematics. Hermione (with Jayanthi) and Samir (with Tyrese) are being active mathematicians, expressing mathematical ideas and making mathematical discoveries with a companion. The children call to one another as they trace the boundaries. Ibrahim and Hermione are exploring the garden space on the tricycle, feeling the extremities of the pathways. Each child is repeatedly 'measuring' the length of the path, and mapping the route and its landmarks, the pillar, the bump over the grass, the end at the fence, turning corners. Three toddlers expressing with their active bodies their thinking, imagining and understanding of mathematical concepts and ideas (ECEF, 1998).

Hermione, at 30 months, has progressed to developing her own mathematical ideas and methods to solve practical problems. She is able to play at, as well as talk about, position, direction and movement in her trike riding. She was able to give instructions to other children about movement and direction: '*round* the pillar, *over* the bump, *turn* at the fence, and *stop* at the bench by Mandy.' All these calculations and transactions are accomplishments that match the end-of-year outcomes for reception class children set out in the National Numeracy Strategy and in the curriculum for the Foundation stage (QCA, 2000a). Samir and Ibrahim sustained an interest for a length of time on a construction they each decided to work on (driving round the boundary of the rug and the water trough). They describe the simple journey with their own imaginative vocalisations about force and direction, 'stepping stones' of progress as detailed in the curriculum guidelines (QCA, 2000a, p. 80).

What is distinctive about the learning powers of this age-group and the practitioners who need to develop their practice to support that learning? Pedagogues from different cultures and theoretical perspectives have documented the significance of children in the spaces of their environment. Athey (1990) and Nutbrown (1994, pp. 10–15) assert it is not sufficient simply to identify a child's interest or his or her pattern of repeatable behaviour into which experiences are assimilated and gradually co-ordinated. If observation seems to indicate that Samir, Ibrahim and Hermione are preoccupied with the early action 'schema' of 'going round a boundary' then each child needs to be provided with a range of interesting and stimulating experiences (including but not exclusively mathematical ones) which extend thinking along that particular path.

Italian practitioners, on the other hand, in their lavish dissertation of Reggio children in the nursery environment, urge a curriculum of possibilities, attention to beauty, fluidity and dialogue in planning the spaces for children to explore and transform (Ceppi and Zini, 1999).

We may match our observations to our chosen frameworks or theories (e.g. Montessori, High/Scope, national guidelines for day care or an approach of observing children's schema). We may also be bound by our own constructions and cultures of childhood. (A powerful child or an obedient child? An innocent child or a little terror? A child growing towards independence and omnipotence or dependent and democratic?) These debates must be the backdrop to each setting's own preferred curriculum.

So there should be no certainty or absolute in advocating curriculum for, or with, this age-group. What seem most important, bearing in mind contemporary research and diverse family and community contexts, are the following:

- *Following a child's inclinations*, curiosities, schema and then as adults we may wonder, reflect and enjoy the children's capacities, imaginations and creations, found by themselves, and engaged in for themselves.

- *Being energetic and responsive* in turn to offer the most aesthetically pleasing, multi-sensory spaces, places and objects to engage with a child's powers to think, to express and explore, to represent, construct and reconstruct according to each child's own logic, pace and pattern.

- *Embracing each baby into a community* of conviviality, passionate and compassionate feelings, lively reciprocity of conversation-like exchanges within the shared cultural values of each of our multifaceted communities, a social culture that may be modified and flexible in the interests of the people in it – people under 3 years of age too!

Babies being seen and heard.

Issues for discussion

(1) In what ways may you become more skilful at 'being in a child's shoes'? What kinds of observation enable you to see more clearly, and follow more nearly?

(2) When do you take time to talk? How do you assess the quality of your work on the *task* of developing quality as well as reflecting on the *process* of how your group is able to work together?

(3) How do you plan for the children to be in small groups, in key relationships, where there are opportunities for continuity with other children and adults?

(4) Is your curriculum one of 'environments' or of 'didactic learning goals'? Is your curriculum more focused on observation of the received curriculum, or are you leading and 'teaching' to adult social and cultural 'norms'?

7

DIVERSITY AND LEARNING IN THE EARLY YEARS

Iram Siraj-Blatchford

INTRODUCTION

In modern, diverse societies, it is essential children learn social competence to respect other groups and individuals, regardless of difference. This learning must begin in the earliest years of a child's education. In this chapter I identify the groups which are often disadvantaged due to the poor understanding that some early years staff have of them. There is a need to challenge the hidden assumptions that oppress particular individuals and groups. While most early childhood settings appear to be calm and friendly places on the surface, I argue there may be a great deal of underlying inequality. This may occur through differential policies, interactions or displays, or through variations (or lack of variation) in the planning, curriculum or programme the staff offer to some individuals or groups. These are important issues to be considered because they concern the early socialisation of all children. In the early years children are very vulnerable and every adult, and other children as well, has the power to affect each child's behaviour, actions, intentions, learning outcomes and beliefs.

I aim to explore the ways in which children can be disadvantaged on the grounds of diversity in ethnic background, language, gender and socio-economic class in both intentional and in unintentional ways. Sheila Wolfendale in Chapter 8 looks in more detail at children with special needs, and this too is an important area of equity education. The structures through which inequality can be perpetuated or measured are related to societal aspects such as employment, housing or education. For instance, we know women earn less than men, as a group, and that working-class people live in poorer homes, have relatively poor nutrition, health and education; hence the recent Sure Start programme (see Chapter 6 on the under-3s).

Although I am concerned with the structural inequalities which create an over-representation of some groups in disadvantaged conditions, I have cautioned elsewhere (Siraj-Blatchford, 1996) against the assumption that all members of a structurally oppressed group (e.g. all females) are necessarily oppressed by those members of a structurally dominant group (e.g. all males). Because of the interplay between social class, gender, ethnicity and dis/ability, identities are multifaceted. I therefore argue that children can hold contradictory individual positions with respect to the structural position their 'group' holds in society. Interactional contexts are also often highly significant.

Later in the chapter I attempt to identify the salient features of effective practice in promoting respect and learning in children, for parents and for staff in early child care and education settings (Siraj-Blatchford and Clarke, 2000).

MULTIPLE IDENTITIES

Identity formation is a complex process that is never completed. The effects of gender, class and other formative categories overlap, in often very complicated ways, to shape an individual's identity. While I do not attempt to discuss this complexity in detail in this chapter, it is important for practitioners to be aware of the nature of shifting and changing identities. Because no group of children or any individual should be treated as having a homogeneous experience with others of their 'type', Roberts (1998) argues the process by which all children develop their self-esteem and identity rests heavily upon the type of interactions and relationships people form with young children.

A number of publications related to the development of children's personal, social and emotional education provide very useful strategies for supporting the positive development of children's personal identities (Lang, 1995; Roberts, 1998), yet few writers relate this work specifically to ethnicity, language, gender or class.

There is now a great deal of research evidence of racial, gender and class inequality at a structural level in education (MacPherson, 1999). Concerning racial identity, culture and 'agency' (the interactions between individuals and groups), there is only an emerging literature, and most of this is about adolescent schoolchildren (Gillborn, 1990). This is particularly interesting because issues of gender and class identities have received more attention over the years, but again with regard to older children (Willis, 1977; Mahony, 1985).

Working-class and minority ethnic children's poor academic performance has been well documented (Swann Report, DES, 1985; Bernstein, 1992) as has girls' performance in particular subjects (Lloyd, 1987). The link between racism, sexism, class prejudice and underachievement has been thoroughly argued. However, if those who work with young children are able to undermine children's self-esteem (however unintentional this might be) through negative beliefs about children's ability due to their gender, religion, socioeconomic status, language or ethnicity, then we have to evaluate these actions very carefully.

A child may be classed, gendered or 'racialised' (language status is also important here) in more than one way. Stuart Hall (1992), for example, discusses not only the discourses of identity but also those of difference *within* ethnic groups. In the very act of identifying ourselves as one thing, we simultaneously distance ourselves from something else. In terms of race and ethnicity, Hall argues there are often contradictions within these categories as well as between these and other categories, such as sexuality, class, dis/ability. The way we perceive identities is very much shaped by how they are produced and taken up through the *practices* of representation (Grossberg, 1994).

Making use of the metaphor of a kaleidoscope in understanding identity based on a range of inequalities, Hall (1992) argues there will be individual differences within any identity-forming category, such as race, language, gender and social class. For instance, in Britain, a Pakistani woman who is a first-generation immigrant, and working class, will have a different identity from her daughter who is second-generation British-Pakistani and has become a teacher. Their experience will vary because of how others perceive the combination of ethnic background in relation to their gender, socioeconomic status, dress, language, even age and so forth. Mother and daughter will certainly not be treated by others in the same way but they might have some shared experiences.

Staff also need to find resources and a shared language with which to work with dual-heritage children and their parents to support a strong identity. But it would be even better if staff worked with all children to make them aware they *all* have an ethnic/racial identity and that they all have a linguistic, gendered, cultural and diverse identity. Surely this is the way forward? In being sure of one's own identity as multifaceted, it must be easier for children to accept that others are exactly the same – even when the combinations are different!

The sexism, racism and other inequalities in our society can explain why, at a structural level, certain groups of people have less power while others have more. But at the level of interaction and agency we should be critically aware of the danger of stereotyping and should focus on individuals. This is not to suggest we should ignore structure – far from it. We need to engage in developing the awareness of children and staff through policies and practices that explain and counter group inequalities. I will turn to the point of practice later. What I am suggesting is that educators need to work from a number of standpoints fully to empower the children in their care. Children need to be educated to deal confidently and fairly with each other and with others in an unjust society (Siraj-Blatchford and Siraj-Blatchford, 1999; Siraj-Blatchford and Clarke, 2000).

The experiences of children can come from parents' views, media images and the child's own perceptions of the way people in his or her own image are seen and treated. In the absence of strong and positive role models, children may be left with a negative or a positive perception of people like themselves. This bias can start from birth. In the 'Effective Provision for Pre-school Education' project, the largest project on early years education in the UK, we have found some marked differences in equity issues. For instance, we know most providers create a poor environment for children in terms of diversity (Sylva *et al.*, 1999) with the exception of combined centres and some nursery schools. In addition, our study also suggests that minority ethnic workers are better represented in social services-type day-care and combined centres and very few are employed in other sectors (Taggart *et al.*, 2000). Managers and staff in settings need to be challenged by such data and think about how this has come about and indeed how it might be changed.

Many parents and staff conclude from children's behaviour that they are naturally different, without considering their own contribution to the children's socialisation or considering the impact of role-modelling. Difference, therefore, is also a matter of social learning, as well as physiology. This has implications for practice and the kinds of activities we should make sure all children have access to, regardless of their gendered or other previous experiences.

Early years educators are beginning to understand the knowledge and practices on how children take on these biases, and about how to deal with these matters.

DIVERSITY AND ACHIEVEMENT

Cultural identity should be seen as a significant area of concern for curriculum development (Siraj-Blatchford, 1996). All children and adults identify with classed, gendered and racialised groups (as well as other groups) but what is especially significant is that some cultural identities are seen as less 'academic' than others (often by the staff and children). We know children can hold views about their 'masterful' or 'helpless' attributes as learners (Dweck and Leggett, 1988). Dweck and Leggett (*ibid.*) therefore emphasise the importance of developing 'mastery' learning dispositions in children. There is evidence children who experience education through taking some responsibility for their actions and learning become more effective learners. They are learning not only the content of the curriculum but also the processes by which learning takes place (Siraj-Blatchford and Clarke, 2000). Roberts (1998) argues that the important area of personal and social education should be treated as a curriculum area worthy of separate activities, planning and assessment.

The 'helpless' views adopted by some children can be related to particular areas of learning and can lead to underachievement in a particular area of the curriculum. Children construct their identities in association with their perceived cultural heritage. Recently we have heard a good deal in educational debates about (working-class) boys' under-achievement. The results from the school league-tables suggest some boys do underachieve in terms of basic literacy, but it is important to note this is only certain groups of boys and not all boys. In the UK, working-class white boys and African-Caribbean boys are particularly vulnerable (Siraj-Blatchford, 1998). Similarly, children from some minority ethnic groups perform poorly in significant areas of the curriculum while other minority ethnic groups achieve particularly highly (Gillborn and Gipps, 1997).

It is apparent that certain confounding identities, for instance, white/working class/male, can lead to lower outcomes because of expectations held by the children and adults. In asserting their masculinity, white working-class boys might choose gross-motor construction activities over reading or pre-reading activities. Similarly, some girls may identify more strongly with home-corner play and favour nurturing activities over construction choices. Class, gender and ethnicity are all complicit here and the permutations are not simple but they do exist and do lead to underachievement. The answer is to avoid stereotyping children's identities, but it also requires educators to take an active role in planning for, supporting and developing individual children's identities as masterful learners of a broad and balanced curriculum (Siraj-Blatchford, 1998).

As previously suggested, in the active construction of their identities, children distance themselves from 'others' (Siraj-Blatchford and Siraj-Blatchford, 1999). As one little boy was overheard in a playgroup saying to another boy: 'Why do you just sit reading? Girls read, boys play football!' The issue is therefore to show children they are mistaken in associating these 'others' with particular areas of learning. We have to extend children's identity as learners and break down the stereotypes. Boys need to disassociate literacy from 'girls' stuff, and be presented with strong male role models that value literacy. Work with fathers is particularly relevant here.

DIVERSITY AND LEARNING

Children need to be in a state of emotional well-being, secure and to have a positive self-identity and self-esteem. The curriculum must be social/ interactional and instructive and children need to be cognitively engaged (Siraj-Blatchford and Clarke, 2000).

It is widely recognised that an integrated, holistic and developmental approach is needed to learning, teaching and care with children from birth to 7 years of age. They learn not only from what we intend to teach but also from all their experiences. For example, if girls and boys or children from traveller families are treated differently or in a particular manner from other people, children will learn about the difference as part of their world-view. To deny this effect is to deny children are influenced by their socialisation. The need for emotional, social, physical, moral, aesthetic and mental well-being all go hand in hand.

The early years curriculum should therefore incorporate work on children's awareness of similarities and differences, and help them to see this as 'normal'. Some children can be limited in their development by their view that there are people around them who do not value them because of who they are. This would suggest that early years staff need to offer *all* children guidance and support in developing positive attitudes towards all people. A focus on similarities is as important as dealing with human differences (see Siraj-Blatchford and Siraj-Blatchford, 1999). The early years are an appropriate time to develop this work with young children.

The most common form of prejudice young children experience is through name-calling or through negative references by other children (or adults) to their gender, dress, appearance, skin colour, language or culture. Educators may hear some of these remarks and it is vital these are dealt with appropriately as they arise. The following childlike remarks have deep consequences for the children who utter them, and for those receiving them:

- 'You're dark so you're dirty.'
- 'Don't be a girly.'
- 'She's got disgusting clothes.'

Grugeon and Woods' (1990) ethnographic study of primary schools identified a number of the effects of racism upon the self-images of South Asian children. Children were seen colouring themselves pink, describing themselves as having blue eyes and fair hair, they refused to go out into the sun in case they became brown(er), and avoided participation in minority ethnic festivals.

A number of studies have also drawn attention to the verbal abuse directed at minority ethnic children by other minority ethnic children. While Grudgeon and Woods call for further research to study what they consider 'minorities among minorities', I would argue along with Troyna and Hatcher (1991) that these cases actually provide evidence of children simply 'trading' on commonly held and expressed racist ideologies without necessarily believing in them. Educating through talk and activity is essential, rather than condemnation and punitive action. We could argue from this evidence that children might also be trading insults across gender and class boundaries in the same way.

Children in all types of early childhood settings might have similar experiences. Students, teachers, childminders and playgroup workers have often asked how they can deal with class, gender and ethnic prejudice. It would be a great mistake to assume this is only a 'problem' in largely multi-ethnic settings. Strategies that allow children to discuss, understand and deal with oppressive behaviour aimed at particular groups such as minority ethnic children, girls, the disabled and younger children are essential in all settings. I suggest that educators should always make opportunities for stressing similarities as well as differences.

PROMOTING POSITIVE SELF-ESTEEM

Early childhood educators have an instrumental role to play in this development. Staff need to help children learn to take increasing responsibility for their own behaviour in a way that shows respect and caring for themselves, other children and adults, and their immediate and outside environment. Values education goes hand in hand with good behaviour management practices. The way adults and children relate to each other in any setting is an indication of the ethos of that setting. To create a positive ethos for equity practices, staff in every setting will need to explore what the ethos in their setting feels like to the users (e.g. parents, children and staff). Staff need to explore what behaviours, procedures and structures create the ethos; what aspects of the existing provision is positive and which is negative; and who is responsible for change.

Children need help from the adults around them in learning how to care for each other and to share things. To help the children in this respect, the educator must have the trust of the children and their parents. Young children's capacity to reflect and see things from another person's point of view is not fully developed. Most small children find it difficult to see another person's view as equally important. Children need a lot of adult guidance to appreciate the views and feelings of others. This can be learnt from a very early age. In her research on the relationship between mothers and their babies, and relationships between very young siblings, Judy Dunn

(1987, p. 38) suggests that mothers who talk to their children about 'feeling states' have children who themselves 'become particularly articulate about and interested in feeling states'. Consideration for others has to be learnt.

Of course educators cannot expect children to behave in this way if they do not practise the same behaviour themselves. If children see us showing kindness, patience, love, empathy, respect and care for others they are more likely to want to emulate such behaviour. For many educators the experience of working actively with children in this way may be underdeveloped, especially when it comes to dealing with incidents of sexism or racism. Each setting, as part of its equity policy, will need to discuss the issue of harassment and devise procedures for dealing with it. In earlier writings I have shown how staff can take some of the following actions in dealing with incidents of name-calling.

Short-term action:

- If you hear sexist, racist or other remarks against another person because of ethnicity, class or disability you should not ignore it or you will be condoning the behaviour and therefore complying with the remarks.

- As a 'significant' other in the child's life, he or she is likely to learn from your value position. Explain clearly why the remarks made were wrong and hurtful or offensive, and ask the abused child how he or she felt so that both children can begin to think actively about the incident.

- Do not attack the child who has made the offending remarks in a personal manner or imply the child as a person is wrong, only what was said is wrong.

- Explain in appropriate terms to the abuser why the comment was wrong, and give both children the correct information.

- Support and physically comfort the abused child, making sure he or she knows you support his or her identity and that of his or her group and spend some time working with him or her on the activity he or she is engaged with.

- At some point during the same day, work with the child who made the offending remarks to ensure he or she knows you continue to value him or her as a person.

Long-term action:

- Target the parents of children who make offensive discriminatory comments to ensure they understand your policy for equality, and that you will not accept abuse against any child. Point out how this damages their child.

- Develop topics and read stories that raise issues of similarities and differences in language, gender and ethnicity and encourage the children to talk about their understandings and feelings.

- Create the kind of ethos that promotes and values diverse images and contributions to society.

- Involve parents and children (depending on the age of the children) in decision-making processes, particularly during the development of a policy on equality.

- Talk through your equality policy with all parents as and when children enter the setting, along with the other information parents need.

- Develop appropriate teaching and learning strategies for children who are acquiring English so they do not get bored, frustrated and driven to poor behaviour patterns (adapted from Siraj-Blatchford, 1994).

A positive self-concept is necessary for healthy development and learning and includes feelings about gender, race, ability, culture and language. Positive self-esteem depends on whether children feel others accept them and see them as competent and worth while.

SOCIAL COMPETENCE

One of the most important challenges for early childhood workers is to help children develop the skills to interact with others. Developing the social skills that assist children to get along with their peers and adults will have a significant impact on their lives. Even at this level, language is a major tool. Social skills involve the strategies we use when interacting with others. They cover awareness of feelings of others. Social skills are used to enter and maintain interactions, to engage others in conversation, to maintain friendships and to cope with conflict. Non-verbal skills involve smiling, nodding, eye contact and the development of listening skills. All these non-verbal strategies form foundations for language interactions.

All babies and toddlers in childcare and nursery settings need opportunities for warm interactions with adults. Young children need consistency in the care provided, and those children who come from language backgrounds other than English need support from staff who speak their first or home languages on a consistent basis. The children need to receive messages that say they are important to their caregivers. They need to develop a feeling of trust in their new environment. Staff need to respect all the children in their care. This means taking particular care to understand and acknowledge the different cultural and socioeconomic backgrounds of the children and making special efforts to work with families to assist the children to settle in to a new environment (Siraj-Blatchford and Clarke, 2000).

Boys and girls can have different language experiences within the same household. Dunn (1987, p. 37) studied the relationship between mothers' conversation styles with their children aged 18–24 months. She states:

> The analysis also showed marked and consistent differences in the frequency of such conversations in families with girls and with boys. Mothers talked more to 18-month-old daughters about feeling states than they did to their 18-month-old sons. By 24 months the daughters themselves talked more about feeling states than did the sons.

In multicultural or diverse societies there is a great variety of family values and traditions and it is important children are brought up to balance the tensions and handle the adjustments of being reared in one way and being educated in another. Children need to become socialised into the new practices and society. Early childhood staff need to be patient, caring, tolerant, flexible and need to be able to communicate effectively with parents and other staff about their work.

Effective early childhood curriculum and programmes provide children with a range of first-hand experiences that promote interactive learning, foster children's self-esteem and support individual children in their construction of knowledge. They also recognise the key role of play in young children's development and learning. Central to this is the role of the early childhood staff in establishing the learning environment, structuring interactions and supporting learners in their development.

Young, developing children do not compartmentalise their learning, so an integrated environment suitable for the development of cognitive, social, emotional, aesthetic, linguistic/communicative and physical dimensions needs to be created. So the approaches highlighted in this chapter must go across the early learning goals (QCA, 1999a) – all of them.

All children have the right to an early childhood curriculum that supports and affirms their gender, cultural and linguistic identities and backgrounds. From an early age, young children are beginning to construct their identity and self-concept and this early development is influenced by the way others view them and respond to them and their family. Within today's society, the prejudice and racist attitudes displayed towards children and families can influence their attitudes towards themselves and others (MacPherson, 1999). Early childhood educators need to examine their own attitudes and prejudices and learn to deal with them in positive ways.

All early childhood programmes should reflect multicultural and equity perspectives regardless of whether they are developed for exclusively English-speaking children or for children from a range of diverse backgrounds and languages. A culturally responsive curriculum and staff who understand and respect the cultural and linguistic backgrounds of the children in their care can make a difference. Children can grow up with the ability to retain their home language and culture, and to have pride in their gender and class identity as well as adapting to the new cultures and languages of any early childhood setting they enter.

Curriculum for children in the early years should:

- foster children's self-esteem

- acknowledge the cultural and linguistic backgrounds of all children

- actively maintain and develop the children's first or home languages

- promote the learning of English as an additional language

- value bilingualism as an asset

- value what boys and girls can do equally

- support families in their efforts to maintain their languages and culture

- foster an awareness of diversity in class, gender, ability and culture

- promote respect for similarity and difference

- challenge bias and prejudice

- promote a sense of fairness

- promote principles of inclusion and equity

- support the participation of the parents in the children's learning (Siraj-Blatchford and Clarke, 2000).

All those working with young children need to learn about the family and community lives of the children they teach. They can keep contact with the families, with community centres, with ethnic associations and community-based organisations. They can discuss with parents and community members issues that concern both parents and staff. The following list covers some of the aspects of family and community life that should be explored and so should enhance understanding:

- family history

- religious beliefs and practices (including important cultural events)

- children's everyday lives at home

- language practices
- parents' theories about learning
- parents' views on schooling and early education
- community events and contacts.

INVOLVING PARENTS

Research on preschool education in five countries evaluated by Sylva and Siraj-Blatchford (1995) for UNESCO considers the links between home and school. The authors report the importance of involving parents and the local community in the construction and implementation of the curriculum. When they begin school or early childhood education, children and their parents 'bring to the school a wealth of cultural, linguistic and economic experience which the school can call upon' (*ibid.*, p. 37).

Sylva and Siraj-Blatchford (*ibid.*) conclude that 'It therefore becomes the responsibility of the teacher to localise the curriculum and to enlist the support of the local community and families in framing school policy and practice and making the school and educational materials familiar and relevant to the children's experience'.

Parents need to be given information about the curriculum and learning outcomes and about the achievement of their children. Sharing information of this kind demands a shared understanding of what children are learning. Early years practitioners will need to establish a dialogue with parents that is meaningful to them. Observations of children can be exchanged between staff and parents in an informal way, and showing any assessments that have been done as part of the routine record-keeping processes can provide a more formal means of developing mutual understandings (Moriarty and Siraj-Blatchford, 1998). To achieve true inclusiveness, everyone has to be part of the process of education and care.

Points for discussion

(1) When was the last time an audit of equity issues (SEN, gender and racial equality, etc.) was conducted in your setting and what were the outcomes?

(2) How can the Curriculum Guidance for the Foundation Stage be truly inclusive to all children – and their parents?

(3) How are parents involved in informing your inclusive practice and how do they remain partners in its implementation?

Further reading

Roberts, R. (1998) Thinking about me and them: personal and social development. In Siraj-Blatchford, I. (ed.) *A Curriculum Development Handbook for Early Childhood Educators*. Stoke-on-Trent: Trentham Books (pp. 155-74).

Siraj-Blatchford, I. and Clarke, P. (2000) *Supporting Identity, Diversity and Language in the Early Years*. Buckingham: Open University Press.

Wardle, F. (1999) *Tomorrow's Children: Meeting the Needs of Multiracial and Multiethnic Children at Home, in Early Childhood Programs and at School*. Colorado: Center for the Study of Biracial Children.

8

MEETING SPECIAL NEEDS
IN THE EARLY YEARS

Sheila Wolfendale

INTRODUCTION

This chapter provides a review of recent developments in special needs in the early years. A number of concepts, principles and values are examined that are put into the context of special needs legislation and policy evolution, and a number of issues are explored.

VALUES AND PRINCIPLES

It is a mixed blessing that, in a book devoted to a diverse range of perspectives on the early years, there should be a chapter on special needs. The dilemma for early years/special needs workers is encapsulated by the presence of such a chapter, integral to the book but with a title that potentially marginalises 'special needs' into being an adjunct to mainstream day care and early education.

Aware of the paradox, I feel readers might wish to know the chapter stance at the outset. I plan to acknowledge and celebrate achievements in special needs/early years, commensurate with early years issues becoming higher on the education agenda. So a number of notable developments will be chronicled. At the same time I want to demonstrate a broad responsibility on the part of all early years practitioners towards the distinctive learning and developmental needs of all children, in creating opportunities for them to flourish.

RIGHTS AND OPPORTUNITIES

It is a fairly recent phenomenon that special needs and disability areas were perceived to come within the orbit of equal opportunities, belatedly joining 'race, sex and class' as the major educational and social issues. The language of the Warnock Report (1978), the Education Act 1981 and its accompanying Circular 1/83 was not couched in equal opportunities terms but these in part paved the way for the perspective propagated within the Education Reform Act 1988 that pupils with special educational needs have a fundamental, inalienable entitlement to the National Curriculum. These rights to access to all available curriculum and educational opportunities became a bedrock principle permeating educational thinking, including those working in preschool and multidisciplinary settings (Cameron and Sturge-Moore, 1990).

The broadest universal context for these developments was the moral imperative provided in the International Convention on the Rights of the Child (Newell, 1991). This convention, adopted by the United Nations General Assembly in 1989, has been signed by the majority of countries. It is a set of international standards and measures that recognises the particular vulnerability of children, bringing together in one comprehensive code the benefits and protection for children scattered in scores of other agreements and adding new rights never before recognised. Once the convention was signed and ratified by 20 countries (and this was attained), it had the force of international law.

This will and should have implications at every level of policy, decision-making, provision and practice of children from birth if the fundamental premise is to protect and guarantee children's rights. A number of articles within the convention are explicitly geared towards special needs and disability.

Definitions and terminology

The debate on the meaning, purpose and adequacy of the terms 'special needs', 'special education needs' and disability has often recurred. These were terms that started out, pre-Warnock in actual fact, as intended to be benign and advantaging towards children perceived to be vulnerable and educationally at risk but which became contentious. At its worst, 'special needs' has been perceived as being a separate area, with its own panoply of procedure and personnel and, in education, 'SEN' is too often used as a shorthand label that does indeed encapsulate this view (see Norwich, 1990).

The Children Act 1989 had its own definition of 'need', relating particularly to the early years. Woodhead (1991) challenged a number of 'givens' that he says have informed policy-making in the early years and beyond. His thesis is that it behoves early years workers to 'recognise the plurality of pathways to maturity within that perspective' (*ibid.*, p. 50).

Such social and cultural imperatives need to inform our practice as an influential backcloth to the need to provide for a range of 'conditions' listed by Cameron and Sturge-Moore (1990) in their definition of 'special needs' and their justifications for using the term within early years contexts.

For the purposes of the chapter, 'early years' go up to school entry at 5 years and the first couple of years in school, that is the 0–8 years spectrum.

THE PLACING OF SPECIAL NEEDS IN THE EARLY YEARS ON THE AGENDA

Significant developments to 1996

The public and legislative agenda: focus on education

The Warnock Report in 1978 gave under-5s and special needs a higher profile than that area had hitherto had by recommending it as a priority area in terms of teacher training and increased provision. Emphasis was given to the proven effectiveness of intervention programmes, including Portage, partly to justify this call for increased investment in the early years as both a preventive and 'remedial' measure. Equally, the Court Report published a little earlier (Committee on Child Health Services, 1976) had focused attention on health and development in the early years and had recommended implementation of local early screening and surveillance systems to detect developmental delay and early-appearing disability.

Other government reports on early years included the Select Committee on Educational Provision for the Under Fives (House of Commons, 1989) and the Rumbold Report (DES, 1990), which included brief mention of special needs.

The Warnock Report paved the way for the legislation that amended existing law on special education, namely the Education Act 1981 (implemented from 1 April 1983), which conferred new duties on local education and health authorities in respect of identifying and assessing young children with possible special needs. The accompanying circular to the Education Act 1981, updated in 1989 (Circular 22/89) to take account of the Education Reform Act 1988 as well as recent developments, had a whole section on under-5s with special needs, doubtless influenced by the (1987) Select Committee criticisms into this phase of education and provision.

The Education Reform Act 1988, whilst not statutorily covering preschool, nevertheless had implications for the education of 4-year-olds in infant schools (Dowling, 1995) and for the applicability of the National Curriculum for young children with special educational needs.

A subsequent and significant legislative landmark was the Education Act 1993, Part 3 of which referred exclusively to special educational needs. This part of the Act repealed the Education Act 1981, retaining core principles and formal assessment procedures, but strengthening a number of parental rights and clarifying the processes. The 1993 Education Act was subsequently subsumed along with other education Acts of the past 15–18 years into the consolidated Education Act 1996.

Schools are now required by law to have written accountable SEN policies. The 1994 Code of Practice constituted a set of guidelines to which LEAs and schools must have 'due regard' in the planning and delivery of SEN services. It adopted a five-stage model of identifying and assessing children with special educational needs (summarised in Figure 8.1).

Figure 8.1. The stage model of the 1994 Code of Practice

Stage 1 – Gathering information and increased differentiation of child's normal classroom work.

Review:
- Focusing on progress made by child.
- Effectiveness of special help given
- Future action

▼

Stage 2 – Production of an Individual Education Plan. The special needs co-ordinator is responsible for co-ordinating the child's special educational provision and working with those who work directly with the child.

▼

Stage 3 – Involvement of specialists from outside the school. The special needs co-ordinator continues to take a leading role, again working closely with the child's teachers.

▼

Stage 4 – Consideration of whether the LEA will carry out a statutory assessment.

▼

Stage 5 – Statutory assessment.

The Code of Practice acknowledged the importance of partnership between LEAs, child health and social services in working together to meet the needs of children under 5 years of age with SEN. Parents of children under 5 with SEN were able to express a preference for a particular maintained school to be named in their child's statement.

The Education Act 1993 also introduced the Special Educational Needs Tribunal (SENT) for parents who seek redress against decisions over their children's SEN with which they disagree. There is plenty of evidence, for example, from OFSTED reports that schools, progressively from 1994–95 were indeed having 'due regard' to the Code of Practice. From nursery stage upwards, children perceived to have SEN and/or to be of concern were placed on the SEN Register, and the role of SENCOS (teachers who are designated SEN co-ordinators) has assumed increasing significance.

The chart in Figure 8.2 represents and illustrates a whole range of SEN responsibilities on the part of schools, early years settings, practitioners, policy-makers and parents in the immediate post-Code of Practice era. It illustrates interconnections as well as individual and collective responsibilities in the area of SEN.

The period around the mid-1990s also saw increased manifestation of inter-agency co-operation, as witnessed by the introduction of Children's Services Plans, which require local agencies to dovetail and co-ordinate their provision for children with special needs and disabilities (see Roffey, 1999, for elaboration of the SEN legal contexts and special needs roles and responsibilities).

The parents' agenda

The various Acts have enshrined and latterly strengthened a number of parental rights. Many parents themselves have translated rhetoric and principles into a number of realities and practical action, which include:

- Finding a collective voice: a number of local, regional and national parents' groups emerged, and parents of children with SEN have begun to share their views and concerns more widely (Gascoigne, 1995; Wolfendale, 1997a).

- Empowerment, via the emergence of parent advocacy, representation, self-help and parent–professional coalitions (Armstrong, 1995; Garner and Sandow, 1995; Hornby, 1995).

- Participating in assessment processes (Wolfendale, 1993).

- Parents as educators, as in Portage and other home-based early learning schemes.

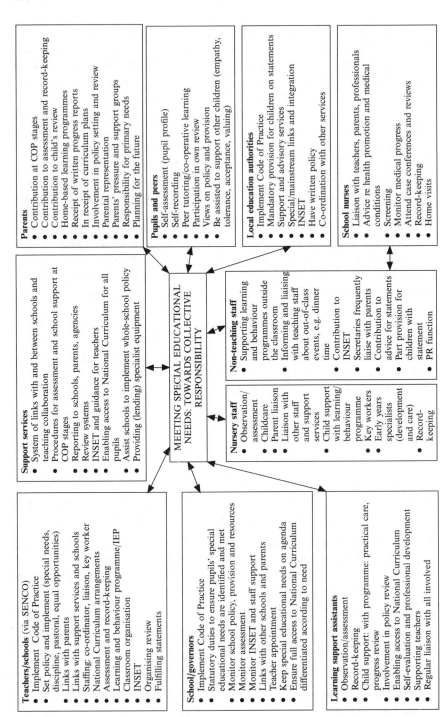

Figure 8.2. Collective responsibility for SEN

The Code of Practice set out a number of key principles for establishing and facilitating parent–professional partnership and illustrated how this can be effected throughout the stages of the Code. The 'message' was further reinforced via the existence of Department for Education and Employment grants (GEST) from 1994 to 1997 to LEAs and schools to set up and maintain Parent Partnership Schemes.

SIGNIFICANT DEVELOPMENTS IN EARLY YEARS AND SPECIAL NEEDS FROM 1997

This section of the chapter comprises its main part, as there has been a burgeoning of policy and practice initiatives in these areas.

A political and policy-driven educational agenda for special needs, with reference to early years

Several months after the Labour government came to power in 1997, it published a green paper (DfEE, 1997) which signalled an intention to reframe SEN policy and practice. On the basis of this 'manifesto' and responses to consultation, a year later the SEN 'Programme of Action' was published (DfEE, 1998). This landmark publication heralded a number of significant changes, chief amongst which were: revision of the 1994 SEN Code of Practice; revision of the SEN Tribunal procedures; enhancement of parent partnership; and investment in early years. The timetable on pages 4–7 summarises proposed action during the period 1998–2000. The guiding principles include 'promoting the inclusion of children with SEN within mainstream schooling wherever possible...' (*ibid.*, p. 8).

Of especial relevance to early years providers and practitioners is the cross-reference to Early Years Development and Childcare Plans and Partnerships and to the advent of Sure Start, both of which are discussed later in this chapter, as are several other areas mentioned in the programmes of action, such as parents, multi-agency working and the revised Code of Practice, which is examined in the next section.

The Green Paper and Programme of Action are, of course, manifestations of a 'top down' approach, yet much of the substance of these documents reflects existing 'on the ground' practice, so there is consonance between public policy and local execution. Indeed, the documents were welcomed by local SEN policy-makers and practitioners.

Revision of the 1994 SEN Code of Practice

The twofold rationale for revising the Code of Practice is that: 1) procedures, especially the five-stage model, were thought to need improving and streamlining; and 2) many post-code SEN and related developments and initiatives need to be incorporated into a revised Code of Practice.

A draft revised SEN Code of Practice was published in July 2000 for consultation, and with the intention that the final version, i.e. a 'new' Code of Practice, will be issued during 2001, for implementation in September 2001. Description of the revised code in this chapter is based on the draft consultation version (DfEE, 2000). As before, the draft revised code deals with principles, partnership with parents, identification, assessment, review and provision across all age-phases, and multi-agency work. There is a whole new section on 'Pupil Participation' (see below).

Chapter Four deals with Identification, Assessment and Provision in Early Education Settings.

Early years workers will welcome incorporation of and cross-reference to Early Years Development and Childcare Partnerships; to the newly designated (since 1999) Foundation stage of education for children aged 3–5 years and associated QCA curriculum guidance (QCA 2000a, and see below); and on entry to school baseline assessment, mandatory since September 1998.

The draft revised Code of Practice does away with the staged approach described earlier in this chapter and replaces it with two clear stages, 'School Action' and 'School Action Plus'. For early years, these are designated 'Early Years Action' and 'Early Years Action Plus'. This approach is described as 'a model of graduated action and intervention within both early education and school settings' (*ibid.*, s. 4.3, p.19), and 'once practitioners have identified that a child has SEN ..., the provider should intervene through Early Years Action' (*ibid.*) and if further advice and support are needed, then Early Years Action Plus is triggered, leading to statutory assessment.

Since, at the time of writing, we only have the *draft* revised code to hand, it is not appropriate to dissect these plans since they may change as a consequence of consultation. However, one may conclude, from the proposed amendments that, in respect of early years SEN, the emphasis upon inclusivity and interdepartmental cross-referencing is to be welcomed.

An agenda for the early years

This section contextualises the preceding SEN discussion by drawing the reader's attention to the broader early years terrain, of which SEN is a part.

After the Labour government took office in May 1997, it set out its National Childcare Strategy, of which increased childcare provision is a major plank, and proceeded to set up local Early Years Development and Childcare Partnerships, which bring together maintained, private and voluntary sector providers with local education authorities, social services departments, health services and parent representatives in the planning and provision of services in the early education sector, including delivery of services to meet SEN.

All early years government-funded providers must 1) have regard to the SEN Code of Practice and 2) have a written SEN policy. Also, one of the criteria by which Early Excellence Centres are thus designated is that of meeting and providing for special needs (DfEE, 2000b).

Radical changes to assessment are also changing the early years landscape. Mandated by the government, the Qualifications and Curriculum Authority (QCA) created a Foundation stage from 3 to 5 years and developed and trialled a set of early learning goals comprising six areas of learning: personal, social and emotional development; communication, language and literacy; mathematical development; knowledge and understanding of the world; physical development; and creative development. These early learning goals were applied within all nursery/early years settings from September 2000 and the QCA issued a pack of curriculum guidance for the Foundation stage (QCA, 2000a) to support practitioners in supporting children to work towards and attain the early learning goals. A page-long section in the guidance (pp. 18–19) is devoted to discussion as to how practitioners can meet additional, extra needs of some young children. This advice is sensible but couched in general terms and unfortunately made no cross-reference to the existing, soon-to-be-implemented revised SEN Code of Practice (see above) to assist early years workers through procedures for identifying and assessing SEN.

As mentioned above, the draft revised Code of Practice refers to on-entry to school baseline assessment, and another key area of early years assessment. The inclusion of a special needs dimension into baseline assessment schemes (QCA, 1997) is one of the key accreditation criteria baseline assessment schemes have to meet to be accepted and accredited by the QCA. That is, scheme providers (mostly LEAs) must be able to demonstrate their assessment schemes are sensitive enough to identify early-appearing learning or behaviour difficulties and areas of concern to do with learning and adjustment (Wolfendale, 2000b).

A cornerstone of the present government's drive to tackle child poverty and social inclusion is the ambitious, long-term Sure Start programme (Russell, 2000). The government has invested £1.46 billion to set up 500

Sure Start projects across England by 2004. The programme aims are to improve the health, well-being and therefore life-chances of children before and after birth, offering services such as family support, advice on parenting, increased/better access to health care and so on.

Each programme has to make a clear statement on special needs and developing ways of working with families that complement existing services. There is also a clear commitment to the early identification of special educational needs and social inclusion. Each programme has to set out:

- the different provision and services available to young children with special education needs and their families;

- arrangements made by existing service providers for early identification, assessment and support for young children with special educational needs; and

- details of specialist provision and services.

(Evaluation of Sure Start is referred to later in this chapter, and see also Chapter 6 of this book.)

We can see there is a whole mosaic of early childhood developments and policies and a significant number of local initiatives, some of which, although related to the theme of this chapter, are outside its scope and parameters, due to a limit on chapter length. For example, the reader is referred to Wade and Moore (2000) for a description of Bookstart, an early years family literacy approach, and to Mortimer (2000) for models and ideas for developing individual behaviour plans in the early years, and Wolfendale (2000a) for discussion on intervention and for accounts of providing for young children with special needs and disabilities, some in inclusive settings.

Promoting partnership with parents in SEN

The 'parents' agenda was introduced earlier in the chapter, along with a brief résumé of notable earlier developments. Contributors to a book examining the impact of the (1994) SEN Code of Practice upon parent partnership (Wolfendale, 1997a) felt that, although much had been achieved in parent/professional, home/school co-operation, there was still a long way to go.

There is now further accumulating evidence of progress towards a working partnership that is in the best interests of children with SEN. Two research reports, both commissioned by the DfEE, provided considerable data on the service delivery of the burgeoning LEA-based Parent Partnership Services (PPS).

Wolfendale and Cook (1997) and Vernon (1999) describe a wide range of activities by PPS staff, which include provision of information about SEN to parents (leaflets, resources, handbooks), direct casework, advocacy, conciliation and oversight of Named Persons Schemes (typically volunteers who work with and support parents whose children are going through statutory assessment and beyond).

The provision of PPSs within LEAs has been seen by governments (pre and post-1997) as an effective vehicle to provide parent-focused services, which at best epitomise partnership (see Wolfendale and Cook, 1997, for discussion on partnership criteria) and at the least offer information, support and sympathy.

The present government is committed to extending PPS and, via legislation, the Special Educational Needs and Disability Act 2001 (SENDA) ensures that all LEAs will have these, as well as a system for independent parental support (replacing Named Persons) and conciliation or dispute resolution arrangements. The draft revised Code of Practice sets out a helpful table summarising the roles and responsibilities of LEAs, schools, independent parental supporters and voluntary groups in promoting partnership with parents (DfEE, 2000d).

As far as nurseries' and schools' responsibilities are concerned, the draft revised Code cross-refers to other parent-focused initiatives, such as Home–School Agreements, which educational institutions are now expected to have.

In fact, a government-driven ideological commitment to enhancing and supporting the parental contribution to all child-focused services is pervasive across services and agencies, with an especial emphasis upon the early years. Parents/carers must be represented on local Early Years Development and Childcare Partnerships; Sure Start is essentially family-focused; and the government is equally committed to expansion of parenting education and support programmes (Wolfendale and Einzig, 1999) and, in 1999, created the National Family and Parenting Institute (address in references), which has a remit to be a voice for families, raise awareness of the importance of parenting and family relationships, and to undertake a range of activities to realise these and other aims.

Listening and responding to the views of young children

Chapter 3 of this book explores children's rights; this section examines the contribution children can make to the organisation and delivery of education and other services, with especial focus on the early years and SEN.

Elsewhere (Wolfendale, 2000a) I offer a rationale and justification for consulting children on both equal opportunities and educational and psychological grounds. We have accumulating evidence that children from nursery age upwards can graphically articulate their views (Miller, 1996; Daycare Trust, 1999), can productively be involved in decision-making of direct relevance and concern to them, and can participate in profiling their own developmental progress (Wolfendale, 1998).

Alderson (2000) explores the nature of sharing decisions and responsibility and conceptualises levels of the children being consulted, which are:

(1) being informed
(2) expressing a view
(3) influencing the decision-making
(4) being the main decider.

Of course each of these levels is not mutually exclusive but rather shades into the others in given real-life problem-solving situations and settings, wherein factors affecting any child – such as medical, psychological and educational welfare – are considerations to take account of.

Lewis and Lindsay (2000) give due attention to the many ethical issues inherent in researching *on* and *with* children (see Chapter 1 in particular) and discuss a number of methodological considerations. They say: 'The challenges to obtaining children's views are considerable but . . . need to be addressed in developing innovative research practice' (*ibid.*, p. 197). Ethical issues include informed consent, confidentiality, how not to exploit children, adequacy of the research instruments and their age, gender, ethnicity and setting appropriateness.

The existing (1994) SEN Code of Practice advocated listening to children but the draft revised code goes further. Chapter 3 (DfEE, 2000d) is entitled 'Pupil Participation' and it covers involving pupils in assessment and decision-making; pupil participation in schools and other settings; and LEA responsibilities in promoting pupil participation. A couple of paragraphs are devoted to the rhetoric and practicalities of consulting and involving young children.

TOWARDS A SYSTEMIC AND EQUITABLE APPROACH TO MEETING SPECIAL NEEDS IN THE EARLY YEARS

This book and certainly this chapter epitomise an ethical, principled philosophy that investment in services for young children and their families pays longer-term dividends for society. The final section of the chapter explores a number of concerted efforts towards realising these aspirations, as exemplified by an inclusion ideology, policy frameworks, quality assurance mechanisms and moves towards evidence-based practice (and see Wolfendale, 2000a, Chap. 1, for discussion around the nature of investment and dividends in the early years).

Inclusion

The inclusion ideology is now subscribed to by government departments, local agencies and an increasing number of schools (Sebba and Sachdev, 1997; Abbott and Alderson, 1999), although definitions and models of inclusion still do vary (Widdows, 1997).

Practical handbooks aimed at supporting early years workers to implement inclusive policies include the Pre-School Learning Alliance publication (1999) and Dickens and Denziloe (1998), who provide a myriad of practical proposals as to how to operate inclusive practice. From an overarching strategy framework for implementing inclusive practice the reader is referred to the CSIE *Index for Inclusion* as a comprehensive resource (CSIE, 2000). The SEN and Disability Act reinforces the commitment towards inclusive practice. However, it remains the case that notwithstanding increased commitment to this principle, there has to be commensurate matched funding to support the introduction of physical and other human resources that are needed to change long-standing separatist practices.

Sharing responsibility for meeting SEN in the early years

The Early Years Development and Childcare Partnerships alluded to earlier have responsibilities towards SEN and these are the appropriate vehicles for corporate delivery of services. A number of parallel initiatives cross-refer and inter-relate, several of which have already been referred to, such as Sure Start, family literacy and parent partnership initiatives. There is also Quality Protects, the social services-based project that aims to improve children's services (see Khan and Russell, 1999; Department of Health, 2000b). The government has recently announced the creation of a Children's Fund, which will allocate money to voluntary, charitable and community organisations that offer support to children of primary school age and families at risk and will expect them to work preventively.

As with the existing (1994) SEN Code of Practice, the draft revised version (DfEE, 2000d) contains a chapter on working in partnership with other agencies – see Russell (2000) for views on a comprehensive and integrated approach to early years services for children with SEN.

Early years and SEN policy dimensions

There is much on policy that pervades this chapter: the SEN Code of Practice codifies policy, and expectations upon educational institutions and Early Years Development and Childcare Partnerships presuppose these have to have written, accountable policies, which set out principles, values, aims and objectives through which special educational needs will be provided for.

An encompassing policy document is that of NASEN (1999), which has formulated lists of responsibilities for LEAs, health, social services, schools and central government. The NASEN policy is predicated upon a number of key principles which include: early identification, priority of access, equal opportunities, individual needs, parental involvement, provision, training and support, and shared responsibility. This policy framework is to be welcomed, coming at a time when the plethora of early years and SEN initiatives could have the opposite effect of what is intended, i.e. practice could fragment beneath the weight of new projects, instead of 'joining up' and co-ordinating.

Judging quality and effectiveness of provision for young children with SEN and their families

Service providers nowadays expect to be assessed and judged as to the quality and effectiveness of what they offer. The system that has applied for several years is that of OFSTED, which has now unified its early years inspection regimes under the jurisdiction of its Early Years Directorate, which will be responsible for the registration and inspection of about 80,000 childminders and 25,000 early years settings from September 2001. A number of early years quality assurance models have been proposed (see Wolfendale, 1997b, for a brief review) and what all these signify is that a principled approach to early years provision must include transparency and accountability procedures.

A performance and evidence-based approach to service delivery and evaluation is increasingly taking hold (*NCB Highlight* 170, 1999): 'Children and their families have a right to expect that our interventions in their lives will be based on the best available knowledge' (Macdonald and Roberts, 1995, p. 3). Provision that comes under the aegis of local Early Years Development and Childcare Partnerships is expected to conform to providing evidence of effectiveness and thus to build in suitable monitoring and evaluation procedures. The ambitious Sure Start programme (see earlier) has a number of aims, targets and objectives, the realisation or not of which will be key planks of the national and local evaluation strategy.

To support Sure Start workers, the Sure Start Unit produced a handbook, *A Guide to Evidence-Based Practice* (Sure Start, 1999b), which provides a description and review of around 20 early intervention programmes, and commentary on the research and evidence base of each. The Preface (*ibid.*, p. 4) states: 'Evaluation is necessary to know whether services are succeeding in their objectives and to discover which aspects of the way they function are contributing to, or detracting from, that success.' A handbook that uses a similar formula but which includes a greater number and range of services is Utting (1999).

To summarise: we have witnessed and many readers are participating in radical changes and development which impact directly upon the lives, learning and well-being of all young children, including those deemed to have special needs. To those of us who are committed to equality of opportunity, we can only hope these changes are now irreversible, and that they will provide the building blocks for further improvements and innovations in provision and services for young children.

Further reading and points for discussion

These areas are suggested as being amenable for discussion and lively debate between practitioners, policy-makers, researchers and students:

- inclusive education;
- ensuring quality early years/SEN services;
- equality and equal opportunities;
- effective means of recognising, identifying and assessing SEN;
- skills needed to work with early years and SEN;
- providing accountable evidence-based services; and
- best practice in working with families.

Additionally, these books are recommended to stimulate thinking and practice in the area of working with young children with special needs:

Sayeed, Z. and Guerin, E. (2000). This book provides a description and analysis of play and its use in helping young children to reach their potential. It is for professionals working with young children with SEN and from a range of cultural and linguistic backgrounds. Included in the authors' model of play-based assessment is a framework that can be used to assess and mediate children's learning and development.

Webster-Stratton (1999). For teachers and colleagues of children aged 4–8 years, this book shows how practitioners can work with parents in addressing children's educational and emotional needs. A range of practical strategies is offered, based on empirically validated programmes (Wilson, 1998). See also Chapter 11 of this book.

Wilson (1998). This text offers a holistic approach, focusing on the young child with SEN as an active learner. Case-study methods are used to illustrate different methods of intervention and to relate theory and research to practice.

9

WORKING AS A TEAM

Margy Whalley

The feeling of power and confidence achieved by powerless groups
who challenge their ascribed position in society by acting collectively
(Dominelli, 1990, p. 126).

INTRODUCTION

In this chapter I want to outline the belief system that underpins the way
we have worked at Pen Green since it opened in 1983. I want to look at the
structural and pedagogic implications of adopting a community development model. I want to show how we evaluate our work and ensure what we
are offering is a quality service that can respond to constantly changing
community needs. I want to describe how we work with parents, volunteers
and workers from other agencies and to look in some detail at our staff
development programme and our inservice training. Above all I want to
celebrate the many mistakes we made, mostly with good intentions, and to
be clear that making mistakes has become a very important part of our
learning process. Making mistakes implies we have taken risks; taking risks
assumes staff have the self-confidence and the ability to make decisions and
to take on personal responsibility. I want to encourage children, parents
and under-5s workers to believe in themselves and to congratulate them on
taking risks and taking charge of their own lives.

I am aware that being a strong, assertive, challenging child or parent, or
under-5s worker, may not make for an easy life. The children who leave
our community nursery have been described by one local teacher as having

'the Pen Green Syndrome'. This is an interesting psycho-social disorder which presents in 4-year-olds going up to big school – children who are not interested in what their infant teacher has decided to put out for them, assertively or subversively (depending on your viewpoint) put it away and take out activities they really want to do, maybe even something they had planned to do on the way to school. The Pen Green Syndrome manifests itself in parents who boycott or protest at governors meetings called at inconvenient times, or at parents meetings that have no crèche facilities, or where they are asked to sit on little chairs. It manifests itself in staff who challenge the assumption they can plan and develop quality work for children and families without the non-contact time professional colleagues with older children assume.

In the final section I want to consider the impact of the last five years on teamwork at Pen Green. The period from 1996, when this chapter was first written, to 2001 and the production of the third edition has been marked by radical changes in politics, policy and practice in the early years. Most of these changes have been described in previous chapters. Services at Pen Green during this period evolved and expanded considerably. Having a flexible and responsive team approach has helped us to cope with and benefit from the changes in our external environment. Our approach in the twenty-first century is underpinned by the same principles that informed out way of working in the early 1980s. Like Eden Charles (1994, p. 137) we believe 'the macho-competitive approach to being in organisations and society is so powerful and destructive. It wastes human life and ignores the deeper levels of experiencing feelings.' In the 1980s we were committed to finding more humane and effective ways of working as a team and this is still a central concern for all the staff at Pen Green.

THE BACKGROUND:
A SEARCH FOR A CONCEPTUAL FRAMEWORK

The Pen Green Centre for Under Fives and Families was set up in 1983 in an empty comprehensive school on a 1930s estate. The Pen Green Estate is made up of 13 streets backing on to the now defunct steelworks. The houses were only separated from the blast furnaces by a railway and a 60-foot strip of land.

The 'bad news' for those of us who set the centre up in those early days was that the closure of the local comprehensive school had been much resented by the local community. The proposed new 'preschool centre' was viewed with a great deal of hostility by both local people and other professionals. The most active voluntary group locally was a Community Action Group that had strongly protested at the lack of consultation between local community and county council.

The two lead departments were social services and education and neither had a clear understanding of how the centre would work in practice. The education department described it as an extended-day, year-round nursery school with some parental involvement; social services saw it as a day nursery for referred children. Corby then and now has no local authority day nursery provision. The two departments had no shared conceptual framework or language and geographically Corby was very isolated from the administration in Northampton. The district health authority, which had contributed to the capital costs of the new centre, became immersed in a reorganisation and was unable to contribute to running costs, but retained its policy and management role.

The 'good news' outweighed the bad and still does for those of us working in Corby. There was strong local political support for the new project and the steering group that had been set up had strong councillor support. The steering group was truly multidisciplinary, having representation from the LEA, social services, the health authority and voluntary groups in the community. This steering group visited a well established combined centre in London, read the limited amount of research available on joint provision, and resolved to put all staff on the same conditions of service, since differentials in holidays and hours of work appeared to be a real block to a creative partnership.

Social services locally were organised on a patch basis and local social workers were working as community development workers in the local community association. They influenced the decision to make it a local community resource rather than a town-wide service. Since the closure of the steelworks, male unemployment in this patch was as high as 43% and there was a good working relationship between agency workers and the local community group – a 'partnership in adversity'. Many of those parents involved in the action group against the centre had already been involved in local housing campaigns and were very ready to express their concerns about the nature of the proposed centre for under-5s. They were clear they did not want it to be a 'dumping ground' for problem families'. This action group was critical to the development of the Pen Green Centre for Under Fives and Families. Several of its members became vociferous spokespeople *for* the new centre and used it on a daily basis. Parents, staff, children and community groups were all brought on board; 'parental involvement' was *not* an optional extra – it was integral to the way we worked.

Most significantly, some of these parents were involved in the initial recruitment of staff and these staff, as a consequence, felt directly accountable to them. All newly appointed staff then had between two and six months to work together while the alterations to the building were completed. Much of this time was spent walking the streets, getting to know local people and local resources and visiting other centres. Parents and staff remember that blissful period when everything was open to negotiation; when we had an empty nursery waiting to be filled. People were invited in and started using the centre whilst the concrete was still wet and rooms undesignated. Staff who remember that period are thankful that time was spent in finding out what was needed rather than imposing a predetermined 'neat and tidy' plan. In the life of an establishment it is rare to get that kind of quality time.

RECRUITMENT AND STAFF DEVELOPMENT

What we started with in 1983 was a commitment-based, multidisciplinary centre. The brief included offering year-round nursery and day-care facilities with provision for an extended day, a service for supporting families and a health 'resource'. Contextually we were working in a socioeconomically depressed community with an active and critical community group, and some very creative professional colleagues well accustomed to working co-operatively in adversity. Some of the structural obstacles to a creative team approach had been removed, such as differentials in conditions of service, but some still remained. Chief among these were the grossly differentiated pay-scales between care workers and teachers or field social workers; and the inappropriate pay-scales for key workers like secretaries, cooks and other support staff (mostly women).

Most of the research on combined provision emphasises the difficulties experienced when integrating staff who have always focused on the needs of children in a care capacity and those who see themselves as educators. Our experience was very different. In the first place we were recruiting staff from many different sectors, not only from education and day care but also from social work, health and the voluntary sector. They had a vast range of different qualifications including CQSW, BTech, NVQ (Level 3) and PLA courses, PGCE, BEd, NNEB, SRN, and they were accustomed to different styles of working and different models of supervision and support. The varied backgrounds of many of the staff (some qualified in more than one discipline, some with no formal qualifications but enormous amounts of experience in the private or voluntary sectors) meant there was no simplistic polarisation between education and care. All their different experiences informed our practice and made it possible for us to set up an appropriately flexible management structure and support system for staff working in a challenging and innovative way. We tried to take the best from all the different models of supervision and support.

The critical difference between our centre and those that had been modified from already existing schools, day nurseries or children's centres was we could be clear at interview about what the job involved. Even our adverts were 'different' and usually required major debates and sanctions from whichever personnel department was handling them. One department found them so idiosyncratic they refused to handle any of the process and left it entirely up to us.

Parents who have been involved in interviewing, over the years, have found it to be a fulfilling and challenging process. Some parents have even been motivated to make career decisions on the basis of interviewing others! Parents were not 'preselected' for interviewing so that applicants met many different members of the community: some shy, some assertive and some negative. A tradition was soon established that meant when there was a vacancy, parents would interview for the member of staff who would subsequently be working directly with their child. It became clear that parents who had appointed staff continued to root for their chosen candidate throughout their time at the centre and quickly introduced the new member of staff to other parents in their 'family group'. Interviews were always informal and candidates were told this would be the case. On some occasions interview panels were very unwieldy. My own interview was conducted by the two chairmen of the social services and education committee and 12 other officers, employees and members of the community.

All posts are advertised as 'family worker' posts, a generic title that embraces those primarily working with children and those who are chiefly concerned with adults. Some posts are more senior than others but we do attempt to distribute the unpleasant and mundane jobs fairly evenly.

All family workers in the nursery have a responsibility for up to ten families and they are the key workers for those families. They home visit 'their families' and keep developmental records on 'their' children. With some families, family workers liaise with the statutory social worker, attend case conferences and attend court. No new member of staff undertakes this sort of work without support and/or training. They need to feel both confident and competent. The important point is that staff are encouraged to take on that level of responsibility where they are involved as the key worker. Family workers in the nursery are also given the opportunity to work directly with parents by each offering one session a week as part of a group work programme – again with appropriate training and always with a co-worker. Other family workers recruited to work primarily with parents are asked to spend time in the nursery, to home visit families and to spend time with the children at lunchtime.

There was no assumption a teaching or NNEB qualification implied any differentiation in the core family worker role. Teachers appointed to family worker posts needed to be prepared to take on additional responsibilities commensurate with their substantially higher salary and different training. The responsibility an individual was able to take on had to be negotiated on the basis of what skills and experience they brought with them. Clearly a probationary teacher, leaving a one-year PGCE course, would only have a very limited experience of curriculum planning and development; he or she might, however, have a strong specialism such as dance or music or other life experience he or she wanted to offer.

All staff when appointed are given some time to get to know the different aspects of the centre's work. In the early years, staff had an enormous amount of freedom to visit other centres all over England. Such visits are still encouraged and most staff, including ancillary and support staff and many parents, will have been to a variety of different types of centre within their first few years in the job. Over the years staff have visited early years provision in Italy, Denmark and Madrid. Most staff have been involved in what has now become a rich exchange programme. All the nursery staff and several parents have had these opportunities, and so have support staff, such as our cook and administrative assistant.

It soon became apparent that, since the majority of new staff came from a teaching or nursery nurse background, most had a vast range of experience with young children but felt less confident in working with adults. Having said this, all three senior staff in 1983 had either PGCE and CQSW or PGCE and extensive community work experience. Overall, staff tended not to come from either mainstream education or social services but rather from residential/special schools, child and family guidance or community nurseries.

We quickly realised no single qualification could provide all the skills and knowledge needed for working in this new way. We had an enormous skills bank to call on for our own inservice training but we also needed a comprehensive inservice rolling programme staff could opt into on the basis of their level of confidence and competence. Some key areas of work had not been addressed in any initial training course and these were management and team-building skills and budgetry control. Some training needed to be ongoing, some addressed current issues (such as the AIDS awareness programme in the mid-1980s). Table 9.1 gives a rough outline of our staff development programme.

We do not view staff development as an optional extra. It enables us to provide a quality service. As Professor Tomlinson said in an open lecture (1986), what we need are 'confident and secure professionals well trained in their own service who can co-operate and see the part to be played by other services'. Centres for early childhood education with care should be 'learning organisations'. Because we are committed to staff development, we currently have staff studying and writing assignments for the Advanced Diploma in Nursery Nursing; BTEC course in social care; the Adult

Table 9.1. Staff development programme

Timing	Content	Geared to
Stage 1 (during the first 18 months)	Listening skills Counselling Family dynamics Home visiting Working with parents	Most relevant for NNEB, teaching staff and support staff volunteers
Stage 2	Assertiveness Group work Marital counselling Boundaries with co-workers	For all staff colleagues from other agencies working with adult groups
Annual programmes	Gender issues Race issues Violence First aid	All staff
Child focused (ongoing)	Child psychology and child development Early years curriculum Working with troubled children Assessment Record-keeping – an educational model Record-keeping – a social work model Child abuse/child protection	As part of planned individual programmes/all nursery staff
Responding to new legislation (when it comes out)	NHS white papers (*Promoting Better Health, Working for Patients*) National Curriculum Children Act	As appropriate
Training relating to co-operative working (ongoing)	Working with other agencies Working with volunteers Management, team-building Supervision/appraisal	All staff

Education Teachers Certificate; advanced counselling courses; contemporary dance; NVQs in working with children and families; GSCE maths and English; an MA in Early Childhood Studies; an MA in Action Research; a PhD in Management Studies and so much more! Of course there is some reduction in the quality of services when staff are attending courses or taking time back for courses they have attended in their own time but we inconvenience parents and children as little as possible. In the long term, staff are enabled, through training, to feel confident in and to challenge their own practice. They have no need to put up a front of so-called 'professionalism'. Senior staff spend a great deal of time in supervision and support, encouraging staff and setting up in-house training courses. Training is the carrot that keeps us all motivated. When we feel out of our depth we can reassure and revitalise ourselves by attending a course or a study day and understand a little more. Training is also one concrete way of showing low-paid workers and volunteers they are valued and that they too have choices and career prospects. We rejected the traditional model of training whereby emotionally fraught teachers or burnt-out social workers were sent off on expensive secondments. We believe staff have the right to a properly structured staff development programme that involves training, supervision and support, the majority of which should take place in work time.

MANAGING SERVICES

What I have tried to do is give an impression of an environment where:

(1) Decisions are made as a response to the expressed needs of the local community and not their *assumed* needs. When we have set up groups or activities because, as a staff group, we thought they were 'a good idea', they rarely took off. Our rather self-conscious health food pantry was a disaster!

(2) Staff were given time to get to know the local neighbourhood and parents were invited in from the word go. Parents helped to make the decisions about room allocation, use of space and what equipment we needed to buy.

(3) Parents were on the interview panels for all staff appointments – not only the parents who might have had the confidence to fight for a seat on the school governing body, but also parents who were too afraid even to attend parent evenings in mainstream school.

(4) Staff needs are seen as central and staff working in a different way need a whole range of training courses and a lot of personal support.

All staff are involved in team-building, and 'all staff' includes ancillary support staff whenever possible. They also need to be given time in lieu when they have given up weekends or evenings on training courses.

(5) Everyone is learning – children, staff and parents.

The staff we appointed were committed to ongoing training and development. They didn't believe their initial qualifications meant they had 'arrived'.

To enable all this to happen whilst maintaining an extended-day, year-round provision for up to 70 families in the community nursery and 300-plus families in the 'drop in', parents' groups and health facilities involves a lot of organisation and a healthy and committed staff who enjoy shared responsibility. When I was first appointed I misread the advert and thought when it stated all staff would be on the 'same conditions of service' it meant we would all have the same pay! My naïvety must be attributed to having worked overseas on multidisciplinary pre-5s projects for over six years and having earned 'local wages'.

Clearly the pay structure at Pen Green implies some sort of hierarchy with teachers' salaries being the most advantageous. Whilst it is obvious differentials in salary do affect how people perceive their role, it is even more important people feel valued for what they are doing. Staff also believed that what they were doing was important and that their personal contribution made a difference. It is fair to say most of the staff had already experienced hierarchical work settings. They were attracted to posts at Pen Green because they wanted to take on more responsibility and wanted to see rigid inter-agency role definitions relaxed.

The management structure we established involved a co-operative approach. In our first naïve attempts to work together we sometimes skirted uncomfortably around issues involving those who earned more and those who were willing to take on more; sometimes we confused democracy and accountability. 'Teamwork' and 'collegiality' seemed to imply no management at all. We also at times avoided dealing with the 80:20 factor that our management consultant highlighted for us, i.e. 20% of the people in most organisations end up doing 80% of the work! Once or twice we did recruit staff who, like many in the caring professions, hoped to 'find themselves' through helping others, who were ungrounded and demanded too much personal support; usually they did not stay long. Very occasionally we recruited staff who, despite the extensive interview process, really did not understand how hard (emotionally and physically) the work was and who found the job just did not give enough back. The majority of staff we recruited have managed to balance their personal and professional lives. Perhaps in the early days when we were struggling to empower traditionally passive low-paid under-5s workers and families who felt deskilled, we underestimated the need for senior staff to have time together to reflect on how they were working, set targets and review progress on a regular basis.

Instead of a hierarchy we established a 'side-archy' (Whitacker 1997) that allows staff to focus on their strengths. Even in the early days we saw conflict as healthy, and felt anger and resentment were better expressed than stored. Staff who work with young children and families almost always see themselves (and are defined by others) as 'nurturers', but that does not mean they have to be 'nice' all the time; consensus was not always the most desirable outcome. We have also learnt to recognise the fact there is a manipulative and controlling part in all of us.

Staff meetings

In practice, then, we spent time in pairs or small groups visiting other centres and seeing how they worked, bringing back ideas and arguing over 'good practice'. Staff quickly realised that, with the wide range of views and experience we had amassed, we needed to continue to carve out time for ourselves as a staff group even when the centre was fully operational. We had seen many different models in practice from hurried after-school staff meetings and lunchtime meetings in educational settings, to interminable and unfocused team meetings in social services establishments.

We decided a mid-week break was the answer and this has been the pattern for eight years. Nursery education, day care and family work take place on Monday, Tuesday, Thursday and Friday, and Wednesday became a community morning. This meant we could offer a session to any family on the waiting list and to foster parents and childminders. Wednesday afternoon was set aside for staff development, team-building and sometimes training events. It was the one time in the week when staff could work together without interruption, with clear heads and lots of energy. Professional colleagues from the LEA and other local authority day nurseries looked on it with some suspicion. Some felt we were 'neglecting' the children's needs. In fact, nursery children were getting far more time and continuity in the nursery sessions we did offer, which gave them the opportunity for extended uninterrupted play. Children and parents accept the weekend break and just as easily learnt to accept the Wednesday afternoon break and welcomed the choices and flexibility we could offer them at other times.

Having fought for it, how did we use the time? Our initial staff group of six permanent staff (plus four support staff) met in one group for the whole afternoon. When numbers increased to around 16 permanent staff, it became important to split the time available so staff could work in small groups, meeting as a whole group for a relatively short period for an information exchange, diary dates and general business session. Staff spend most of the time in two groups: those primarily concerned with the nursery children and those mainly working with adults. Senior staff try to move between groups but the head of nursery spends all her time with the 'nursery group' since they are planning and exploring the nursery curriculum. This is a fairly crude division of staff since all have concerns for and are involved in working with both adults and children. Both groups use part of the session to focus on 'people' issues like problematic staff relationships, people's feelings about their work and sometimes personal issues. The rest of the session is task orientated, sometimes with an agenda that has come from personal support sessions or management meetings, sometimes coming from individuals within the group.

Meetings are informal with a rotating 'chair' and a minute-taker. Minutes are essential both to remind us of what we committed ourselves to, and for sharing information between groups and for staff who are on leave or attending courses. Over the years chairing the meeting has been a real issue and the structure of the meeting has changed many times. Recently staff decided to vote for five or six staff who could run the meetings most effectively and this worked well for a time. We also recognised the fact that seniority in terms of length of experience or formal qualifications did not necessarily imply greater competence in running an effective staff meeting with a large staff group. There is always a real tension between getting tasks completed and giving time to individual members of staff who need to share difficult work situations. Sometimes the balance is wrong and we go round in circles or become self-indulgent; when it is working well a great deal gets achieved. Whatever happens it is almost always the most demanding and stressful session of the week! Because we were often working with large numbers of staff (up to 28 at one time, including our community service volunteers and social work students) and because it seemed important to increase our awareness of each other's different workloads, we set up a tradition of 'Not the staff meeting staff meetings'. The main agenda of these meetings, which were planned by small groups of staff who did not usually get the chance to work together, was team-building and fun and the learning was kept light.

Feedback from colleagues and trainers who have taken part in staff meetings has been amazement at the energy and diversity of views, and the assertiveness of even fairly new staff when working in small groups. We realise this is quality non-contact time and we do not see it as a privilege but as an essential part of our staff development plan. One vital lesson we learnt within the first few months was that parents did resent the closure, for one afternoon a week, of their new play facility. They also welcomed the opportunity, when the space was handed over to them, and some staff support was offered, to set up their own playgroup one afternoon a week. Parents who used the service the rest of the week became service providers on Wednesdays; they went on courses and from 1985 set up two playgroups offering sessions in the next-door building, five days a week for about 60 children.

Staff meetings have been discussed in some detail because that is where most ideas are generated or debated, where policies are revised and where staff share knowledge and give each other support. Nursery staff also meet from 4.30 to 6.00 pm every Monday night. This time was spent in the early years of the life of the centre in making the environment attractive and welcoming to parents and children. We were in an old, poorly maintained building that seemed to be falling down around us! We set up wonderful displays which disguised the unfortunate state of the plasterwork. Over the years the building has been renovated and made more attractive; formal displays were largely overtaken by attractively mounted photographs of the children's learning process. Monday nights are now spent sharing our observations of children, writing formative and summarative assessments of the progress and planning a rich early years curriculum and allocating responsibility for putting it into effect. Other aspects of our organisational structure are shown in Figure 9.1.

Parents meetings

Parents in the first two years were encouraged to attend the part of the main staff meetings where general issues were discussed. Some did attend and brought a friend along. It seemed important, however, that staff should have their own time.

It also seemed important for parents to have a meeting, preferably chaired by a parent, where they could give critical feedback, exchange views about what was going on in the centre and share information with staff. Access to the group, which runs in the evening, was made easier by the centre covering the cost of babysitting fees and by staff offering transport on winter nights. The meetings were always informal with coffee and wine. One regular attender would always arrive half an hour late and the meeting would have to stop for a five-minute summary of *Eastenders* before business could be resumed. Recently an evening crèche is on offer for, in the current climate of anxiety over child abuse, many parents are reluctant to leave young children with babysitters even when babysitters are available.

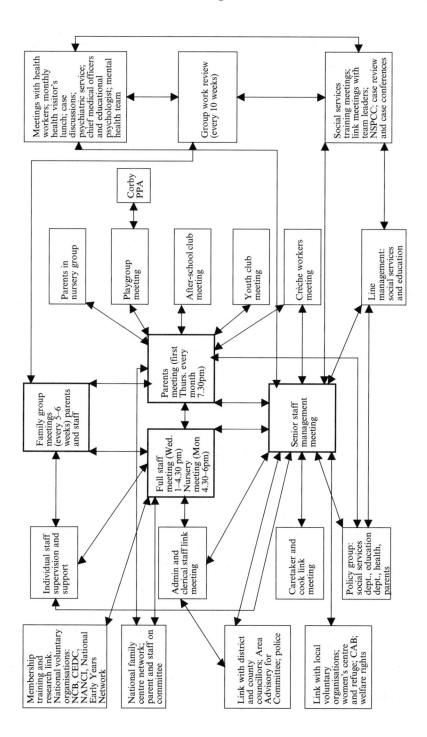

Figure 9.1. Towards communication, co-operation and collaboration: a management 'side-archy' and communication network.

Both because of the change in employment patterns and because some parents said they would find it easier to bring criticisms and share information in smaller family group meetings, these have now been set up during the day with a crèche. This gives parents an opportunity to discuss issues about their own child's education and care with other parents who share the same family worker. The family worker running the meeting is supported by a senior member of staff so they can listen and get support during and afterwards, if the discussion has been difficult or painful. These meetings give parents a real opportunity both to understand how the centre works internally and how it is managed by the two lead departments and the policy group. Parents nominate representatives to go from the family group meeting to the month parents meeting. Two parents who attend this parents meeting are then elected to represent all users on the policy group and in this way have a voice in the overall policy-making and management of the centre. The parents meeting is primarily concerned with day-to-day events, staff appointments, training, social events, budgets, fundraising and suggestions for the group work programmes.

Sometimes it deals with more contentious issues. On two occasions the parents meeting has formed itself into a community action group to protest at cuts in services and the possible closure of the adjacent building. On these occasions parents have become vociferous campaigners and have made many representations to the county council. Interestingly, parents who have been actively involved in the centre have moved on to become governors in the three local schools.

Staff support and supervision

At the same time as setting up staff groups and parents' groups to discuss central issues, we also looked around for the best possible model of supervision and support for individual members of staff. It would not have been possible for staff to remain open to criticism and to appraise their own work critically if they had not received consistent professional support. We set up a system where most staff receive supervision/support every three weeks from a senior member of staff. Senior staff then receive support from the Head of Centre who in turn has a monthly consultancy session with an external consultant (a lecturer in the university social work department). This level of supervision is essential for staff working in centres for under-5s and families which combine a social work and educative role. Clearly the LEA inspectorate can offer curriculum advice, and senior officers from both lead departments fulfil the line management function, but what is needed additionally is a structure that addresses personal and professional issues. Problem areas, such as leadership styles and personality clashes, need to be discussed freely and confidentially. Time needs to be taken to give staff positive feedback, information on training and careers advice. Supervision and support sessions need to be regular and uninterrupted. Ideas and problems that come up in supervision need to be appropriately fed back to management meetings and/or staff meetings. Staff have a right to this kind of support and it becomes a mechanism of quality control because it involves target-setting, goals and reviews. Staff may also need specialist support or outside consultants for particular pieces of work.

We have also adopted the social work model of taking time out for team-building and we spend two days each year away on a university campus with a trainer who has worked with us for some years. This is an important annual event and very hard work; the residential component was requested by staff so they could combine self-development and team-building with a relaxing evening away from family and other pressures! Recently senior staff spent a weekend away on a management training weekend which proved to be very challenging and the management consultant was invited back to work with the staff team to great effect. Staff made the request this should also be an annual event roughly at the beginning of each school year and this has considerably enhanced our review process.

It may appear staff spend a lot of time in meetings discussing what they do! At Pen Green we have adopted a community development model of working with parents and children that involves planning, taking action and reflection at all stages and that aims at empowering not deskilling. To work in this way we need:

> to be prepared to work with contradictions and confusions. It is not a field for people who like to be clear-cut, precise and polished ... it is a field for compromise, negotiation, flexibility, sharing and a balance of conflicting interests. (Jordan, 1987, p. 36).

To achieve this we also need to work closely with other professional colleagues from other disciplines so we can develop a common philosophy and provide an effective service. To make this possible we share much of our in-house training with colleagues from health and social services, and with parent volunteers. (We pay for supply cover so the playgroup staff can attend training sessions and meetings.) We try to avoid stereotyping and 'blaming' other agencies and we have gained an understanding of each other's management structures and the constraints that other agency workers experience through a programme of working lunches, reviews and seminars.

WHO BENEFITS?

Working as a team is a process not a technique. It is rooted in an ideology of empowerment, encouraging adults (whether parents or staff) to take control of their own lives and giving children permission to do the same.

Working as we do with parents and staff implies a different way of working with children and they are the beneficiaries both directly and indirectly. Instead of a fragmented service where children can be developmentally assessed twice in one day by different (well meaning) professionals, where children's health, educational and social/welfare needs are kept separate, professionals and parents plan and work co-operatively. Instead of 20 different workers being 'involved' in the case of abused or neglected children and few making any impact, families can seek support from one or two people they self-select and they can get it within their own community. In this way they are not pathologised. Instead of a perceived dichotomy between the needs of parents and the needs of children, where both end up fighting for recognition, there is an acceptance they are equally important.

HOW DO WE KNOW WE HAVE
ACHIEVED A QUALITY SERVICE?

I have outlined the forums we have set up for parents to express their views, and our own staff meetings and group work reviews give us a great deal of critical information on the service we provide. Parents evaluate all the groups they attend and staff who are well trained and properly supervised have learnt how to take criticism and constantly review their own practice. Part of our initial vision was to provide a high-quality and developmentally appropriate curriculum to all the children who come into the centre. Parents help us to evaluate how successfully we have achieved this goal.

Quality in the curriculum means
parents and staff need to work together

Nursery staff spend many hours each week planning the nursery activities and assessing children's development. We believe it is critical that what we do is shared with parents and that parents have a great deal of the information that informs that process. Parents have always been encouraged to get involved in curriculum development, either through attendance at staff meetings, courses where parent volunteers and parent supply staff participate, or through study groups. Several years ago staff were introduced to the concept of 'schemas' (Athey, 1990) and have spent a great deal of their inservice training on increasing their understanding of the patterns in children's play. We had always based our curriculum on observations of children's interests and preoccupations but with the help of Chris Athey and Tina Bruce we developed an intellectual framework and a helpful language to describe what we saw. Parents were involved in 'schema' training and 'schema spotting' from the start, and were equally fascinated with the way we could all now reconcile bits of children's behaviour that had seemed random, or even counter-productive, with a cognitive structure. We were all equally impressed with how persistently children returned to *their* primary concerns (at home and at nursery) despite well meaning staff trying to encourage them into more teacher-led activities. Staff and parents both gained from making videos at home and in the nursery and looking in some detail at their own children's behaviour. Staff and parents then analysed their observations with the help of our very supportive early years consultant, Tina Bruce, who has worked with us since 1989. We feel we have created a most successful pedagogue/practitioner partnership. Parents began to record observations on children at home and these observations were shared with staff and became the basis for planning for children in the nursery. Parents were encouraged to make audio tapes of their observations if they weren't confident writing things down (Arnold, 1996).

Now all new parents are encouraged to make observations after the initial home visit and are introduced to our ideas about curriculum development. The children's open files, which always contained records of work, home visits and staff observations, have been transformed into rather splendid folders emblazoned with 'A record of my achievement'. These folders contain material from home and nursery. In our experience all parents, even where there has been child neglect or child abuse, care passionately about their children's development and are keen to collaborate.

Parents are encouraged to become deeply involved in their children's learning and staff offer many different 'ways in' to make this programme accessible to all parents. The models for engaging parents that staff currently offer include:

- Key concept sessions offered to all new parents on child development theory and how it relates in practice in the nursery and at home.

- Long-term study groups offered to parents in the morning, afternoon and evening to fit in with Corby's shiftwork patterns.

- Home/nursery books and videos describing or illustrating children's development in their play in nursery.

- The loan of camcorders to parents so they can record what fascinates their children at home.

- Interactive workshops in the evenings on IT, maths, etc.

- Trips to the Science Museum in London where parents and staff take their children to the discovery area every term.

More than 84% of nursery families have taken part, and parental involvement in their children's learning has been sustained and documented over a 3–4 year period (Whalley and the Pen Green Team, 1997, 2000). Parents understand that staff genuinely recognise their critical contribution to their own child's development and their key role as their child's first educator. Parents constantly reminded us their children only had 'one shot' at being 2 and 3 and 4 years of age and that they valued an early years curriculum which supports a child's cognitive development and their respective needs.

EVALUATING SERVICES

We have survived vandalism and fires, cuts in services and enormous changes in legislation by constantly going back to the community users and asking what is most important to them; and by asking ourselves, 'is what we are doing "good enough"?'

We had a two-day closure and review of services one year when staff offered all-day crèche facilities so that as wide a representation as possible of our 300-plus users could come in at different times. The aim was to discuss what we could hold on to with a cut in staff and what had to go. All the sessions were very well attended. We recorded all the passionate arguments that were made by parents, each fighting to maintain the corner of the service that was most relevant to him or her! Some were concerned with maintaining maximum flexibility in the nursery, others with retaining after-school provision for 5–11-year-olds, or groups for parents. Symbolically, at the end of each session, parents and staff were given gas-filled balloons on which they wrote messages. Some gave the balloons to staff to keep, some sent them off with angry or poignant messages. This review marked an ending but was also a celebration of the future. It was also enormously helpful for your staff learning curve. The temptation for staff had been to try to be paternalistic and protect parents and children from the reality of the cuts and this was not helpful. Parents who use a service, value it and feel some ownership of it will probably want to fight for it when times are hard. With the kind of framework I have described it is possible for staff, parents and children to take risks and to take responsibility for services. This chapter started with a quotation from Lena Dominelli about powerless groups challenging their position in society. Parents (principally women) and children, are, I believe, undervalued and often feel powerless. Working collectively with staff there is nothing they cannot achieve.

A changing world

Corby continues to be an exciting and challenging town in which to deliver services to children and families. The streets around the centre that once backed on to the blast furnaces still bear the names of great engineers and scientists – Stevenson's Way, James Watt Avenue and Telford Way. The former 1930s comprehensive school building in which we work has been transformed with funding from the Labour government Early Excellence Programme and we now have architecture that can be described as pedagogically responsive. The environment is now much more aesthetically appealing, safe and secure, and it challenges and stimulates the children. We continue to visit the Science Museum but we also have our own science discovery area which is used constantly by the children. At Pen Green we still provide:

- early years education with extended hours and extended years provision to support families;
- inclusive flexible education with care for children in need and children with special education needs;
- adult community education and family support services; and
- a focus for voluntary work and community regeneration.

Additionally, we now offer a comprehensive programme of training and support to early years practitioners and we have a research and development base, the first of its kind in the UK.

The challenges for the staff team over this five-year period, which has been marked by expansion and new initiatives such as the EYDCPs, the Early Excellence Programme, Sure Start and neighbourhood nurseries, has been to keep the community on board. Corby is still an area characterised by poverty and has benefited enormously from the plethora of government initiatives, not only those already mentioned that relate directly to early years but also an Education Action Zone, a health improvement programme and the Single Regeneration Programme. However, families in Corby do express anxieties about these targeted programmes and 'zone fatigue' is a phenomenon we have to guard against. Staff at Pen Green by the 1990s were working with over 500 families. In 2001, working in partnership with the new Corby Sure Start, we are responding to the needs of over 1,000 families. Developing a shared vision with a staff group that has expanded over 18 years from 6 to 78 is a huge task. Having a shared philosophy that underpins our team approach has never been more important. With the expansion of the early years programme there has also been increased external accountability and staff have had to develop their skills as advocates for children and families, ethical entrepreneurs and reflective practitioners, with the ability to articulate their achievements and critique their own practice.

Non-contact time remains a critical issue and the need for high-level supervision/support and consultancy time for senior staff is still a priority. We have continued our policy of taking time out of the increasingly heavy demands that are made on us and still spend two days together every year working with an external consultant who supports our team approach and helps us to work together more effectively. Risk-taking is still encouraged and the Pen Green culture is one in which making mistakes is seen as an inevitable part of the learning process. All staff are excited by their own learning and this generates excitement and enthusiasm among the children, parents and the wider community. We feel less defensive now about our approach to leadership and management since others now seem to recognise the importance of 'relationality', affiliation, intuition and consensus and see the benefits of an enabling approach where all staff can become leaders.

Further reading and points for discussion

Vision and values

Does your centre or school have a clear vision and explicitly stated values? If so, who was involved in writing them? Did all the stakeholders' views get heard? How often do you go back to your vision and values and review and revise what you wrote? How do you evaluate your achievements?

Roles and relationships

How do you feel about the 80:20 theory, i.e. does 20% of the staff do 80% of the work most of the time?

What motivates you and the other members of your team? What are the intrinsic rewards and the extrinsic rewards for the important job you are doing? Does every member of staff receive support, supervision and consultation. How do you establish training priorities?

Further reading

Allman, P. (1983) *The Nature and Process of Adult Development*, Buckingham: Open University Press.

Boot, J., Lawrence, J., and Morris, J. (eds.) (1994) *Managing the Unknown by Creating New Futures*. London: McGraw Hill.

Dalhberg, G. and Asen, G. (1994) Evaluation and regulation: a question of empowerment. In Moss, P. and Pence, H. (eds). *Valuing Quality in Early Childhood Services. New Approaches to Defining Quality*. London: Paul Chapman Publishing.

Edgington, M. (1991) *The Nursery Teacher in Action*. London: Paul Chapman Publishing.

Marshall, J., (1994) Re-visioning organisations by developing female values in J. Boot *et al.* (eds.) (1994) op cit.

Rodd, G. (1994) *Leadership in Early Childhood*. Buckingham: Open University Press (2nd edn 1998).

Stacey, M. (1991) *Parents and Teachers Together*. Buckingham: Open University Press.

Whalley, M. (1999) Women leaders in early childhood settings: a dialogue in the 1990s. Unpublished Ph.D thesis, University of Wolverhampton.

Whalley, M. and the Pen Green Team (2000) *Involving Parents in their Children's Learning*. London: Paul Chapman Publishing.

10

WORKING WITH PARENTS

Lucy Draper and Bernadette Duffy

INTRODUCTION

Parents are children's first and most enduring educators. When parents and practitioners work together in early year's settings, the results have a positive impact on the child's development and learning. Therefore, each setting should seek to develop an effective partnership with parents (QCA, 2000a).

In this chapter we draw on our work at Thomas Coram Early Excellence Centre and address the issue of working in partnership with parents in response to the following questions:

- Why should we work in partnership with parents?

- What are the benefits and challenges of working together?

We then describe our work at Thomas Coram and some of the lessons we have learnt about specific groups of parents and what partnership means to them. While using our own centre as an example, we hope this chapter will have relevance to practitioners working in a wide range of settings.

When we use the term 'parents' we are referring to all those who take on this role in children's lives, whether or not they are the child's biological parents. When we use the term 'practitioner' we are referring to the wide range of adults who support children's learning and development, whether paid or unpaid.

Families are changing, as they always have done. Nor are parents a homogeneous group, their views and beliefs will be diverse. Our views about what constitutes a family and the roles those different individuals take need to reflect this. This, in turn, will influence the way in which we work with parents.

WHY SHOULD WE WORK IN PARTNERSHIP?

There is long tradition of working with parents in early childhood settings. At the beginning of the last century, Margaret Macmillan included lectures for parents and parent groups as part of the nursery schools she established. However, by the 1960s, parent involvement programmes tended to focus on parents whose children's achievements seemed low, and parental involvement was seen as a way of compensating for the limitations of home. In recent years models of parental involvement have moved from being largely compensatory to participatory (Whalley and the Pen Green Centre, 1997).

Today, working in partnership with parents is interpreted in a number of ways. These can include parents working with staff in settings, practitioners visiting families in their own homes, parents as governors or on management committees, parents attending workshops and courses, and parents running services such as toy libraries.

Government legislation and guidance strongly encourage working in partnership with parents. For example, the Education Reform Act 1988 emphasised schools' accountability to parents and parental choice, whilst the Children Act 1989 stressed the importance of parental responsibility and the s. 19 reviews of local needs required consultation with parents. More recently, the Code of Practice on the identification and assessment of children with special educational needs (currently under review – see Chapter 8) includes partnership as a fundamental principle: 'If effective provision is to be made for children with special educational needs it is essential that schools, LEAs, the health service, social services, voluntary organisations and other agencies work very closely together and that all work closely with parents' (DfEE, 1994).

Children's services and community care plans call for consultation with parents about the way in which services for children are developed, organised and delivered (Ball, 1997). Sure Start guidance (2000) on providing good-quality childcare and early learning states: 'It is vital to include families in experiences offered for children . . . Mothers, fathers and extended family all have a role to play.' Curriculum guidance for the Foundation stage reinforces these views, emphasising that effective practice involves using the knowledge and expertise of parents and other family adults (QCA, 2000a).

Messages from research reinforce this emphasis. There is growing evidence of the long-term benefits of preventive work with parents and young children within mainstream open access services (Pugh, 1999). In America, the 'Perry Preschool High Scope' project found that high levels of parental involvement were one of the keys to a successful early years programme (Schweinhart *et al.*, 1993). Projects such as PEEP (Peers Early

Education Partnership) in Oxford demonstrate the significant and lasting benefits of working with parents and children from babyhood onwards (PEEP, 1999). Services for parents must be delivered in ways that are non-stigmatising, across agency, accessible and affordable. Initial findings from the evaluation of the Early Excellence Centre programme indicate the success of this approach, especially for the most vulnerable families (DfEE, 2000e). The 'Effective Provision of Pre-school Education' project is identifying the key role of the home learning environment in children's achievements (Sammons *et al* 1999). Home learning has a powerful impact and it is essential practitioners recognise this, build on it and encourage greater links between home and setting.

WHAT ARE THE BENEFITS AND CHALLENGES OF WORKING IN PARTNERSHIP?

Benefits for children

As Athey (1990) puts it: 'Parents and professionals can help children separately or they can work together to the greater benefit of the child.' Sure Start guidance (2000) stresses the importance of consistency for the child: 'A strong relationship with parents encourages continuity for the child, good communication, participation and ownership.' It is important to children that the adults in their lives share an understanding of who they are, what matters most to them and what they are capable of. They mind very much about whether the adults they care about – first their parents and later in their lives their nursery workers – seem to like and respect each other. Continuity between home and setting benefits children's learning. Parents and staff who are focusing together on the child's learning are able to share insights and to understand the child more fully. By understanding more about the child, the adults are better able to promote learning and development. This involves practitioners going to some degree of trouble to get to know the family and in showing an interest (without being off-puttingly intrusive) in a child's home circumstances and life history to date, in their interests and achievements, hopes and fears, likes and dislikes. It will also entail staff sharing with parents the details of a child's life in the nursery, and the sometimes familiar and sometimes entirely new facets of a child's personality that reveal themselves in the early years setting.

Benefits for parents

Parents are ultimately responsible for their children. Bringing up children is a rewarding but often challenging experience and many parents welcome the support of practitioners who have a broader and less intense perspective than their own (Katz, 1980). When staff see themselves as facilitators and ensure the level of parental involvement is under the control of parents and that there is no coercion, parents are free to make their own choices. Parents need opportunities to develop themselves as individuals and the opportunity to work together can often release untapped potential in parents. Many early years practitioners have started out by getting involved in their own child's setting. Other parents have got involved in courses, which have led on to further and higher education. Involvement in management committees and governing bodies empowers parents and gives them a voice in their community. Programmes designed to bring practitioners and parents together also bring parents together. This helps to build support networks in the centre and wider community.

Benefits for practitioners

Parents and practitioners need each other and have useful differences in their approach that can complement each other. Parents are experts on their own individual child, and practitioners offer expertise in this stage of children's development and learning. By combining these, the best opportunities can be provided for each child. By working together they bring together the two halves of the child's world (Henry, 1996). Parents have known their child from birth and wise practitioners look to learn from the parents of the children they are trying to help. For many staff the opportunity to work in partnership adds a new dimension to their work. Practitioners can assume their experience of family life is the way it is and working with parents from diverse communities widens their views on families and family life. There is a wide range of equally valid childrearing practices and patterns of family life. Differences can be shared, respected and explored. Home life provides many opportunities for learning the setting can build on.

At Thomas Coram, we have tried to make our partnership focus include all these elements and thus benefit children, parents *and* practitioners. We believe that, though there are different roles and responsibilities, there is not such a great separation between staff and parents. Many practitioners *are* parents and all have been children. Everybody shares a concern for the welfare of the children, and this is also true of the wider community.

The challenges of partnership

However, working in partnership with parents is not always easy and partnerships are not necessarily equal. At Thomas Coram, we recognise parents and practitioners may both have anxieties about working together. For example, if practitioners have a view of themselves as the expert on children's learning they may find it difficult to value the parents' views. Often practitioners who feel confident in their work with children feel less confident in their work with parents. On the other hand, parents may have negative memories of school and reflect these in their relationship with early years practitioners. The needs of parents for whom English is an additional language can also be neglected. Family circumstances (for example, pressures of work, no transport to the setting and the circumstances of the setting, such as no crèche facilities) can make it difficult for parents to participate in programmes settings establish. Lack of opportunity to meet can also be a problem. In settings where children are transported long distances to attend practitioners and parents may see little of each other and when there is a rapid turnover of children, opportunities to build relationships can be limited. Such situations do not make partnership easy. However, none of these problems is insurmountable and, in the following section, we will be describing some of the ways in which we have tried to put partnership into action at Thomas Coram.

THOMAS CORAM EARLY EXCELLENCE CENTRE

The centre is situated in the Kings Cross area of London and is a partnership between Camden Local Authority and Coram Family, a well established charity. It is part of Coram Community Campus, which houses a wide range of providers from the maintained and voluntary sectors (see Figure 1.1 in Chapter 1). It consists of an Early Childhood Centre – often referred to as 'the nursery', which provides 108 places for children from 6 months to 5 years – and – adjoining it in the same building – a Parents Centre which provides support and training for parents from the nursery and the wider community, as well as a drop-in centre, crèches and out-of-school childcare. The activities in the Parents Centre are accessible to both the parents of children attending the nursery and to families in the wider community. The centre as a whole also offers a training and dissemination programme. Potentially, therefore, a family can have a connection with the whole centre for many years and spanning the child's transition from home to nursery to school.

When we are thinking about partnership with parents we need to think about what we wish to achieve in our particular setting. What are the characteristics and needs of the community we serve and how will we reflect this in what we offer? At Thomas Coram we have been very conscious of ensuring we are not assuming our agenda for partnership is shared by parents (Henry, 1996).

We believe that for successful partnerships the following are essential:

- trust
- sharing information
- sharing decision-making
- sharing responsibility
- accountability.

A successful partnership involves a two-way flow of information, and flexibility and responsiveness have been found to be key factors in successful partnerships (*ibid.*). We want to create a centre that reflects our ethos that everyone is welcome, that parents can express their views and feelings, that diversity is valued and that the centre is seen as part of the wider community. In the following section we will be giving examples that highlight different aspects of our work with parents:

- working with parents around children's learning
- support for parents
- access to further training
- parental involvement in management.

Working with parents around children's learning

In any early years setting, the 'settling-in' process is a crucial arena for the establishment of a good partnership between parents and practitioners. We know from attachment theory that the child who feels securely attached to a parent or carer will also have the confidence to be able to learn from new experiences. The Parents Centre gives the opportunity for parents and children to 'practise' small amounts of separation, without the stress that is sometimes felt when a child is starting a nursery full time and a parent perhaps needs to get back to work. In the drop-in, which parents and children attend together, a child may start by taking a few small steps away from his or her parent or, sitting on their lap, simply start to show an interest in an activity in which other children are involved. Later, parents may choose to attend groups or classes, while the children stay in the crèche for an hour or two. In the nursery, our first contact with many families is during Wednesday's visitors morning when prospective families come to look at the centre. Once children are offered a place the family is invited to join our induction programme, which consists of visits to the centre, home visits and a settling period. During this time we get to know the family and they get to know us. Part of this process is a detailed parent conference during which parents tell us about their child in a semi-structured interview .The information we get from this covers all areas of the child's development and learning and provides the foundation for our planning for the individual child.

In our experience arrival and collection times are very important in developing our relationships with parents. We organise the sessions to ensure that staff, especially key workers, are free at these important times of day to welcome families and exchange information. Key workers in each base room hold meetings with the parents to discuss what is going on in the room and possible new developments. As well as daily informal contacts there are regular times for parent and key worker to meet and review individual children's progress. As part of this review, parents and key workers jointly decide the next priorities for learning and how they can work together to support the child.

A large number of the parents who use the nursery are working or studying and we have tried to develop ways of ensuring these families are offered accessible ways to be involved. One method has been the use of home/centre books where parents and key workers enter into a dialogue by recording observations of the child's experience at home and at the centre. Another has been the use of regular newsletters and information sheets about the current work of the centre. At the moment we are developing a web site, which will contain a wide range of information about the centre and opportunities for parents to get involved in current projects. The toy and book libraries also provide opportunities to bring centre and home life together.

There are also opportunities for parents to get involved in specific programmes. Peters and Kostelnik (1981) point out that practitioners often present irrelevant and ineffective materials because they have neglected to find out the strengths and needs parents bring to the programmes in the process. We have tried to ensure we consider this in the programme we offer. In the groups there is a strong focus on the children's learning and development. Many draw on our in-house skills and this is particularly important in ensuring we reflect the cultural and linguistic diversity of the community we serve. Our training co-ordinator runs a group for staff wishing to develop their skills as trainers and part of this involves observing them as they work in groups with parents and offering feedback. One group, which is facilitated by our training co-ordinator, is called 'Why does my child do that?' In this group staff and parents look at videos of the children at home and centre and analyse their significance. The discussion that has resulted has been rich and offered parents and staff new insights on the children. Another group, facilitated by staff across the centre, has focused on different aspects of the curriculum and involved parents, staff and children exploring the potential of resources and materials together. The parent volunteer group offers support and training for parents who wish to volunteer to work alongside staff in the centre.

Support for parents

Our work rests on an acknowledgement of the importance of parents and carers in their children's lives, and of the rewards – as well as the challenges and difficulties – involved in the parenting task. (In a recent survey, joy was named as the emotion felt most often by 87% of parents, followed by pride (77%), frustration (27%) and despair (9%) (Barnardo's, 1998a).) The staff are privileged to have come to know an enormous amount about families' lives – in the relatively informal setting of the drop-in, we have watched babies grow and develop, eat and sleep and, both literally and metaphorically, take their first steps. We have listened to their parents' worries and concerns, heard about their pregnancy and childbirth experiences, been part of workshops where they have shared a wide range of cultural expertise concerning children and childcare, and music sessions where songs and lullabies from many different languages are shared and learnt. Sometimes we have heard about difficulties with housing or money or immigration status and at times, hopefully, have been able to give useful advice in these areas. It is also not unusual for parents to share their worries about conflict with partners or other family members.

There are very wide variations in beliefs (held by both practitioners and parents) about what is 'good for children'. The example that follows illustrates how we explored one of these differences of opinion:

We were asked by a local family centre to come and talk to a group of parents, whose children were having difficulty in settling in to the crèche there. Staff described the parents as always leaving their children at the door to the crèche and 'running away', consistently refusing – despite repeated requests from childcare staff – to spend any time with their children in the crèche.

These parents were all recently arrived in the UK from Albania, living in bed-and-breakfast accommodation, and struggling to get used to a new country, a new language and a strange climate. None of them spoke much English.

Through an interpreter, we began by asking them what experiences they had of leaving their children with others in their home country. They spoke eagerly and explained that back home all the children went to full-time nursery, provided free by the state, from the age of 9 months, when mothers would return to work. Nursery staff had explained to them they must always say goodbye to their children at the door to the nursery, that if they waited around it would upset and confuse the children, who would then be unable to learn. We asked them how they felt about this and they replied: 'Often it broke our hearts, but we knew that the teachers were professionals who understood children and who taught them very well.' They believed it was their task as responsible parents to support their children by ignoring their distress and encouraging them to say goodbye quickly. They were very confused by the different approach in the UK and, though too polite to say so, clearly felt that childcare staff here were less knowledgeable about what was best for children.

Bringing the crèche staff into the group, we were then able to have a discussion along the lines of 'Look, here are two different ways of looking at what's good for children. We want you to think together about what would work best for each individual child.' The crèche staff, given the new information, stopped seeing the parents as obstructive, unreasonable and uncaring of their children. The parents gained respect for the crèche staff and were given new confidence in feeling free to trust their own judgements and knowledge of their children.

Two mornings a week a clinical psychologist is available to see parents who have particular concerns about their children. Parents who have worries about their children's behaviour often find it very hard to seek help, and may worry they will be blamed for these difficulties or 'reported' to social services. The service has worked very well and proved to be helpful to parents with a variety of concerns about their children's sleeping, eating or behaviour. It seems that because the service, though specialised, is based in a community setting, parents find it much easier and less threatening to use. Some 93% of parents attend their first appointments, compared with 68% who are referred to psychologists in clinical settings.

There may be two reasons for this. One is that the psychologist is a familiar face to parents ordinarily attending the centre, and in many ways seems like just another member of the staff team, who makes a cup of tea in the kitchen and answers the door to families arriving. Another is that a long process may have taken place *before* the parent makes an appointment to see the psychologist – parents may have had discussions with nursery or Parents Centre staff or with other parents about their concerns and they know the psychology service is available, but it is up to them when or if to make an appointment.

A number of child protection concerns *have* arisen in this process, and referrals to social services have been made, but always in the context of general support for the family, and no parent has ever stopped attending as the result of a referral. The psychologist also co-facilitated groups with staff for parents who are concerned about their children's behaviour using the Webster-Stratton approach (see Chapter 11).

We run a support group for parents whose children have special needs. A parent who has a child with special needs, or one who is beginning to be concerned his or her child is not 'the same' as other children, will have all the usual range of preoccupations of any parent, but may also feel very different and isolated from the general community of parents, who are sharing their pleasures in watching their children learn and develop. In this group parents often express a huge relief in finally meeting others who understand their situation. Discussion in the group may revolve around standard preoccupations with money, housing or relationships, but will also often turn to concerns with finding their children a nursery or school, and with how (when they do) staff will respond to their children's particular needs. One mother – who has three children under 3 years of age, one with severe developmental delay – described a daily routine in which she has to get up three hours before the children are due at nursery in order to get them washed, dressed, fed and ready on time. She is grateful when she has an especially difficult morning, and they arrive late at nursery (often with her feeling close to the end of her tether), that the staff do not criticise her for the lateness but are sympathetic and welcoming. Not all the parents in the group have had this experience.

A recent discussion in the group about how it feels to be stared at (or looked away from) in the street when you have a child with special needs led to one mother writing an article for a national newspaper explaining what this feels like and what responses would be more positive. Members of the group are now planning to collect their experiences in relation to schools and to write a similar article aimed at teachers.

Thomas Coram is situated in a culturally very diverse neighbourhood, and families attending the centre speak 48 different languages. Working in effective partnership with parents from different ethnic backgrounds requires both knowledge of and respect for these differences, and a commitment to provide a service of equal quality to all their children. Parents who were not themselves educated in the UK may be unfamiliar with the British education system and possibly unconfident it will serve their children well:

I went to school until I was seven in the Caribbean and I don't remember sensing that parents showed an interest. It was accepted that all of the teachers had the interests of the children at heart. What's happened in this country is that black people have come to realise that they are at a disadvantage which society is not going to address for them, therefore we have to take it upon ourselves to solve this problem. As a consequence of that we are going to ask 'How did you get on in school today?' The only way we are going to move forward is through education. We have got to take it on board, we cannot afford to leave it in the hands of teachers (Lloyd, 1999a).

Again, having information and knowledge about parents' point of view is crucial. At a series of 'International Parenting' workshops, groups of parents made presentations about their home cultures, particularly in relation to pregnancy, childbirth and childrearing. Childcare practitioners who attended these workshops found them particularly valuable, and we are hoping to gather the material together to publish.

Research in the UK has shown that black and minority ethnic parents are less likely to attend family centres or 'parenting skills' classes than white parents, even though they have similar needs for support (Butt and Box, 1998). We have looked for particular models of parenting support that would meet the needs of all parents and have recently been running a programme called 'Strengthening Families: Strengthening Communities' (Steele *et al.*, 2000) that has had particular success in the USA with families from many different cultural backgrounds. This programme has many things in common with better-known models, but two features of it are unique. One is that it emphasises the strengths in a family's cultural history and looks at ways in which parents can pass these on to their children (rather than focusing on problems). The other is that it includes discussion of a 'spiritual' component in parenting, which can mean a variety of things from formal religious teaching to creating a moral framework for children's lives.

This has been eagerly welcomed by parents, which bears out the findings of a Moyenda research project *Black Families Talking*, which summarised the main features of South Asian, African and African-Caribbean family survival strategies (Hylton, 1997). These included spirituality, religion, holding alternative world views and maintaining the concept of 'family' as being all-blood relatives.

Partnership with parents has in practice more often meant partnership with mothers than with fathers. We commissioned a research project (Lloyd, 1999b) to interview fathers and male carers (including specifically reaching out to Bangladeshi fathers), and to make recommendations for future work based on the findings. Some of the results were predictable: for working fathers it was hard to be involved in daytime centre activities, and they said they would welcome evening and weekend activities. Though they said staff were very welcoming, they felt other parents were less so, and they also felt the centre's activities targeted at parents were not of great interest to them (except computer skills training).

Common issues raised by fathers were 'how do you stimulate your child' and a concern they and their children 'play properly'. Bangladeshi fathers were particularly concerned about how to educate their children and found the school system (particularly procedures and tests) hard to understand. There were concerns raised by many of the fathers about maintaining discipline and communication with their children. For the Bangladeshi fathers, the dilemma between 'being seen to be able to discipline' clashed with comments such as 'they don't listen to me any more' or 'if you tell them off, they rebel'.

All the fathers were deeply committed to their children's education and interested to find out more about specific ways in which they could contribute. The process of research and discussion it generated had a clear impact on men attending the centre, who saw their role being taken seriously.

Access to further training

The centre offers a number of ways in which parents can access further training. There is a well resourced information technology suit, which offers a range of courses as well as individual access to computers. Courses on topics such as food hygiene, community translating, first aid and crèche working have also been offered in response to community needs and give parents the opportunity to develop and extend skills ready for employment. Ongoing support and encouragement from staff are also important as returning to study can be a daunting experience.

Parental involvement in the management of the centre

Parents are also involved in the management of the centre. There are five parents on the governing body; one of whom is the deputy chair, and parents are represented on each of the four subcommittees, with two of the committees being chaired by parents. The parents forum, which is organised and chaired by the parent governors, offers an opportunity for those parents who wish to get involved with management of the centre. In order to get the views of as wide a range of parents as possible, the parents forum and others organise surveys of parents' views on key issues.

EVALUATION

Evaluating the success, or otherwise, of partnership work with parents is a complex task as it enters into so many aspects of the work of an early years centre. Numbers of parents who are involved at all different levels of activities are significant, but so too is the quality and nature of their involvement (see Wigfall and Moss 2001). We look at attendance figures for parents groups but we also ask questions about how much they have gained from that attendance. We make sure parents have a place on the governing body, but must also know that when they are there, they feel confident and able to contribute, and that their contributions are listened to and acted upon. We need to make certain not only that written information about the centre is available to parents, but that that information is in a language everybody can understand and which feels relevant to their concerns. It has been important to take into account the very wide range of parents – mothers and fathers, working and non-working parents, of different ages and ethnic backgrounds – and to consider whether the kinds of involvement we offer are appropriate to all their different needs.

As a well-known early years centre, we have been the subject of more evaluation projects than has always been easy to find the time for (see Draper, 2001), but the best and most useful of these have been those which have asked questions of the parents themselves. On the whole, so far, parents have responded positively, recognising this is a centre that takes them and their children very seriously.

CONCLUSION

At Thomas Coram we see one of our professional tasks as being to use our knowledge about what parents want and need – both individually and more generally – to work together with early years practitioners in the best interests of all. Parents' involvement with the centre will vary over time and from family to family, as will the nature of that involvement. We would argue that the opportunity to be involved, especially in their own child's learning and the management and development of the centre, must be open to all parents.

Points for discussion

(1) Are parents involved in all aspects of your setting?

(2) Are different kinds of parents equally involved, though not necessarily in the same ways?

(3) Does your setting have a policy on working with parents? Who has been involved in devising and developing it?

PART 3
RESEARCH

11

WHAT WORKS FOR FAMILIES OF CHILDREN WITH BEHAVIOUR PROBLEMS? EVIDENCE FROM RESEARCH

James Walker-Hall and Kathy Sylva

This chapter will describe programmes for parents that aim to help them improve their parenting skills. It is orientated towards families of 'hard-to-manage' children, specifically those who are exhibiting serious problems before the age of 6 years. The chapter begins with a description of behaviour problems and outlines the family and child factors that are associated with the development of the disorder. The evolution of programmes over the past 20 years is then discussed. Particular attention is given to the work of Carolyn Webster-Stratton, as her methods are the most commonly used, as well as the most supported empirically. Limitations of current programmes are addressed, as are recent developments that seek to improve the effectiveness and scope of parent training.

DEFINING PROBLEM BEHAVIOUR

The American Psychiatric Association, in *DSM-IV* (1994), identifies two different forms of child behaviour problems: oppositional defiant disorder, which is considered the slightly milder form; and conduct disorder, for more severe cases (generally, conduct disorder occurs more frequently in adolescents than younger children). DSM-IV has eight criteria for the oppositional category, of which four must be met throughout a six-month period. These include: frequent instances of anger, ill-temper and touchiness; spiteful, vindictive behaviour; and conflict with adults and other children. The conduct disorder category has 15 criteria, of which three must be met throughout a 12-month period. Reflecting the more extreme nature of the condition, they include bullying, fighting, cruelty to animals, criminal activity (e.g. theft, arson, physical/sexual violence), truancy and running away. Conduct disorder symptoms are more akin to adult anti-social personality disorder than those of oppositional defiant disorder, and its presence in the early years indicates a more pronounced risk for developing the adulthood manifestation.

These criteria seem largely to describe the characteristics of children who are referred for treatment for behaviour problems. For example, in a study of US preschoolers referred for treatment, 75% fulfilled the DSM-IV criteria for oppositional defiant disorder and 50% the criteria for conduct disorder (Keenan and Wakschlag, 2000).

RISK FACTORS AND CAUSES

Although studies of adult disruptive behaviours (e.g. anti-social personality) have revealed genetic influence, studies of children and infants with problematic behaviour suggest the causes are mainly environmental (Rutter *et al.*, 1990), of perhaps which parents are the most prominent source. Aggressive fathers (DeKlyen *et al.*, 1998), exposure to violence, high rates of maternal punishment (Eiden, 1999), mothers with psychiatric conditions (Harjan, 1993) and general marital discord/stressful home environment (Campbell *et al.*, 1996) have been associated with conduct problems appearing early in a child's life.

However, child behaviour problems are not limited to families with such extreme psychological profiles. Low-quality parenting has repeatedly been associated with behaviour problems (e.g. Stormshak *et al.*, 2000) and, while this may be more likely to occur in adverse familial contexts, it is to be found across the population. Low-quality parenting is characterised as being inconsistent, authoritarian, lacking in warmth, uninvolved, physically punitive, and by not providing adequate care.

Of course, hostile, poor-quality parenting may be in part a reaction to the child's conduct problems. However, studies of parental characteristics while the child is still in infancy (before any psychopathology develops) suggest that parenting style has a causal contribution. For example, Shaw *et al.* (1996) assessed mothers of children aged 1 and 2 years with a personality assessment known to measure characteristics linked to negative parenting style. At the age 5 years, the children of mothers who scored highly on the measure were more likely to have conduct problems. Further, Denham *et al.* (2000) found that, although problems tended to be fairly stable over time, the cases that worsened tended to be children of hostile parents, while those children who improved were more likely to be the recipients of supportive, structured and affectionate parenting.

Disorganised attachment is also commonly associated with conduct problems (Shaw and Vondra, 1995; Speltz *et al.*, 1999), and further illustrates the complex entanglement of negative child-parent interaction with cause and maintenance of early behaviour problems. Other child factors likely to play a more direct causal role are deficits in social information processing and problems in regulating emotion. For example, Webster-Stratton and Lindsey (1999) found that children (aged 4–7 years) with conduct problems tend to overestimate their own social competence, as well as mistakenly attribute hostility to others. It has also been shown that children with behaviour problems tend to have low frustration tolerance, poor impulse control and above-average activity levels (Zahn-Waxler *et al.*, 1996).

In his influential book entitled *Coercive Family Processes*, Gerald Patterson (1982) presented a comprehensive analysis of the interactions within disruptive families. Putting problem families under the microscope proved to be very fruitful, giving many clues as to how parent and child risk factors interact to cause and maintain a disruptive environment. Patterson concluded that parents of problem children ineffectively used punishment; he observed it was inconsistent, or too frequent, and often in extreme form following persistent nagging. Equally, parental positive reinforcers were used ineffectively: of touches, hugs, approval, attention, playing and talking – even the latter three tend to be sparse in disruptive families. By inadvertently responding in ways that reward disruptive behaviour, and by failing to encourage socially acceptable behaviour, parents can 'train' their children to behave anti-socially. As an example, consider a child who is persistently ignored but his or her continued whining eventually elicits a smack from the parent. This causes the child to whine more or tantrum, which finally results in the parent giving attention and talking to the child. In this instance the child's whining may be the only reliable method the child has of attaining some positive attention, even though it is mediated by an instance of physical punishment.

More recently, Gardner's (1994) observations of mother–child joint activity provided further insight into interactional patterns in families with disruptive children. She observed that mothers of problem children initiated less activity (see Figure 11.1) and made fewer attempts to keep it going once started. She also noted clear differences in the methods mothers use to control their children. As shown in Figure 11.2, mothers of disruptive children use more rigid instructions.

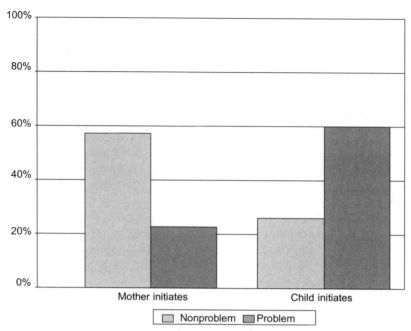

Figure. 11. 1   Initiation of joint activity.
Source: Gardner, 1994

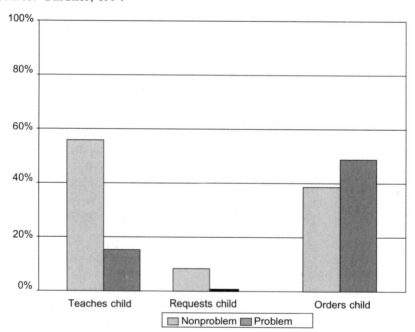

Figure 11.2   How mothers control children
Source: Gardner, 1994

WHAT HAPPENS TO THOSE WHO AREN'T TREATED?

The transition through preschool to the early school years is often cited as a particularly crucial time in the stabilisation of the disorder, and children who consistently exhibit problems throughout this time are at pronounced risk for continued problems in later childhood and adolescence (e.g. Richman *et al.*, 1982; Koot and Verhulst, 1992). Further, many studies have illustrated the potential severity of the consequences of prolonged conduct problems. Increased academic drop out (Kessler *et al.*, 1995), criminality (Rasmussen *et al.*, 1999), adult violence (Fulwiler and Ruthazer, 1999), substance abuse (Steele *et al.*, 1995; Bukstein, 2000) and suicidal tendencies (Hardan and Sahl, 1999) have all been linked with conduct problems in later childhood and adolescence.

Thus if problems are not tackled early, the child's developmental trajectory can veer off at an increasingly detrimental tangent. It is crucial, then, that early problems are addressed as soon as possible while they are still relatively malleable.

THE DEVELOPMENT OF
PARENT TRAINING PROGRAMMES

In the early 1980s, there were three distinct approaches to therapy, each stemming from a different scholarly tradition.

Behavioural approach

Behavioural training packages were developed by advocates of the behavioural modification tradition and used Skinnerian principles of reinforcement and punishment. Gerald Patterson pioneered this field, developing early programmes in the 1960s and 1970s (e.g. Patterson, 1974). Where successful these allowed parents, initially under the guidance of a therapist, to curb their own child's anti-social behaviour. Perhaps the most commonly used technique was the 'time-out' procedure (see below), which remains an important component of packages today.

The 'time-out procedure'

Time-out is essentially an extended form of ignoring, in which the child is removed from all sources of positive reinforcement for a preset period of time. It offers a non-violent method of stopping conflict and prevents further frustration from developing, allowing a cooling-off period for both the child and the parent. During time-out, the child is likely to reflect on his or her behaviour and consider other solutions.

As consistency in punishment is important, parents should predetermine which behaviours result in time-out. Initial candidates should be worst behaviours, and once these are reduced, time-out can then be used for less severe ones. The parent may decide that certain behaviours are allowed warnings first, while more severe ones result in immediate time-out.

The location of time-out should obviously be a safe place for the child to be alone, and as boring as possible. A general rule for time period is three minutes for 3-year-olds, four for 4-year-olds and five for 5-year-olds and over. No benefits are gained from increasing the time-out above five minutes.

Where time-out is challenged, the best response is to reiterate the request, adding an extra minute for refusals (up to eight minutes, after which other punishments such as loss of privileges should be issued).

Once the time-out period is finished, the parent should retry the original command that caused the conflict (e.g. 'OK, go and get dressed now'). This allows the child a second chance, having hopefully thought through what he or she did during the time-out.

(Adapted from Webster-Stratton, 1999.)

Consistent with the (then) culture of behavioural therapy, the leader of the behavioural programme was very much the expert and director, who 'taught' the more passive, 'novice' parent. The effectiveness of behavioural parent programmes is well documented and has been established for some time now. In 1972, for example, Berkowitz and Graziano reviewed 34 evaluation studies and concluded 'in light of the evidence, there is little doubt that behavioural techniques can be effectively applied to children's problem behaviours through the training of their parents...'

Community social work

In contrast to the behavioural approach, community social work programmes had developed a more collaborative process between parent and therapist, in which the leader was seen to work alongside the parents to identify and support their knowledge. The focus here was on developing the parent–child relationship in general, increasing communication and expression of positive emotion. Unlike behavioural parent training packages, which were initially designed solely to reduce child deviance, this approach sought to improve relationships in general; reductions in conduct problems *per se* were perhaps secondary to this. This may help to explain why this approach has been less successful than behavioural-based ones (Barlow, in press).

Cognitive-behavioural

The third approach stems from psychological and cognitive approaches to therapy and focuses on the child's social skills and cognition. There has been some evaluation of psychological, child-orientated therapy, but the results are far from convincing, as are the designs of the studies themselves. On the evidence available it would seem the benefits are limited to older children (for whom the programmes were initially designed), and those benefits are mainly in terms of social skills, which do not necessarily reduce actual conduct problems. Further, the benefits of improved social skills are mainly noticeable at school and do not transfer to the home situation so readily (Webster-Stratton and Hammond, 1997).

What works best?

Despite this, there would appear to be clear strengths in the social work and psychological approaches that the behavioural approach could benefit. First, they address other causes and risk factors behavioural parent training ignores. This offers potential improvements in the effectiveness of parent training which, at the same time, is likely to lead to the greater general well-being of the whole family. Second, the more involving, discursive nature of these approaches may be useful in increasing parents' understanding of the specific problem and perhaps the functioning of their family as a whole. While this may be considered desirable in its own right, it may also have implications for the breadth and longevity of improvements. Third, one might also speculate that what is arguably a more humanistic approach would be favoured by clients and lead to greater commitment, increased treatment adherence and satisfaction.

Not surprisingly, then, the trend in parent programmes for children's behaviour problems over the last 20 years can be essentially summarised as the mechanistic, behaviourist approaches evolving to embrace elements of the other 'softer' approaches. Building on Patterson's initial work, this gradual transition over the last 20 yeas is best exemplified by the pioneering work of Carolyn Webster-Stratton. Her work is among the best known and most effective parent training programmes available today.

THE WEBSTER-STRATTON APPROACH

By the early 1980s, the simplistic behaviour modification programmes had been transferred from their original therapist-to-parent form to the more cost-effective medium of videotape. While it had already been established that videotape was a preferred alternative to written and lectured packages, one of Carolyn Webster-Stratton's earliest contributions was to compare systematically the effectiveness of her own group videotape discussion therapy with traditional one-on-one therapy (Webster-Stratton, 1984) (see below).

The Webster-Stratton method

Group discussion videotape modelling (GDVM): developing parenting skills (from Webster-Stratton, 1994; Webster-Stratton and Hammond, 1997.)

The video series features 250 vignettes depicting various child–parent interactions. They address play skills, use of praise and rewards, limit setting and handling misbehaviour (e.g. time-out). After the presentation of each two-minute video vignette, the therapist leads a focused discussion and analysis, encouraging parents' reactions, ideas and questions. (See Webster-Stratton, 1981, for a more thorough description.)

Advancing GDVM: addressing parental and marital stress (from Webster-Stratton, 1994)

The basis of this additional component is 60 video vignettes, addressing five broad topics:

(1) Personal self-control (coping with anger, depression and stress).
(2) Communication skills (contrasting destructive with effective positive methods of communicating; skills to give and encourage support between partners).
(3) Positive problem-solving skills (skills to handle conflicts with spouse, employees, family and children effectively).
(4) How to teach children to solve problems pro-socially.
(5) Strengthening social support (general theme throughout sessions to encourage members to support one another).

'Dinosaur School': child-focused therapy (from Webster-Stratton and Hammond, 1997).

The first programme to use videotape modelling for children. It includes

---

more than 100 vignettes depicting children in a variety of situations (at home with parents, in classroom, in playground), which are discussed in groups with a teacher. As imaginary play is important to children, the videotapes also include films of life-size dinosaur puppets who present their 'ongoing interpersonal problems'.

The issues presented target problems with social skills, conflict resolution, loneliness, negative attributions, empathy, considering others and problems in the class. By use of modelling, they aim to teach the child a variety of techniques to control anger, solve problems positively, make friends and cope with teasing, etc.

The videotapes also include examples of children being sent to time-out, using self-talk to deal best with being there and receiving rewards for co-operating successfully.

Immediately after the course, mothers on both the individual treatment and group video-based courses had showed noticeable improvements in the quality of the interaction with their child, in addition to improved child compliance and reduced deviance, as independently observed by the researchers. An important part of the design of this study was the range of measures used (see below).

Evaluating treatment success

'...no single perspective really presents the whole picture...' (Patterson, 1994, p. 29)

Good evaluation relies on a range of sources. Generally the methods used fall into the following categories.

Parental knowledge of skills and techniques
Perhaps the weakest indicator of success – testing for knowledge of techniques is unlikely to be particularly informative about ability to use them in context.

Parental reports of child
Cheap and easy to administer and, due to the well designed structure, they provide a fairly good indicator of child behaviour. These questionnaires are likely to be prone to some material bias, expectations and 'social desirability' effects (i.e. telling the researchers what they think they 'want to hear').

Teacher reports of child
Teacher reports do not tend fully to correspond to mother reports or

observations in the home by researchers. Zahn-Waxler *et al.* (1996), for example, reported 20–30% agreement between teacher and maternal questionnaires.

This discrepancy may in part be due to teacher bias and expectations. However, problem behaviours are known to have a degree of specificity (i.e. children who are deviant at home may not be so bad at school, and vice versa; Farrington, 1994), and teachers are also likely to see different aspects of child behaviour, such as sociability and co-operation with peers. (Zahn-Waxler *et al.*, 1996). Thus, teacher reports provide a useful alternative perspective.

Independent home observation
Home observations are generally considered the 'best' all-round indicator. They are probably the most objective, as trained researchers tend to be less affected by bias, especially if they do not know which children received which treatment. They are also superior to observations in the clinic or lab, being in the more natural context. Still, they are not without limitations. One obvious influence is that some children may be more prone to 'playing up' to strangers in their home.

Long-term follow-up of families who had participated in the videotape discussion therapy revealed the strongest predictor of prolonged child deviance was marital distress and lack of a supportive partner. On the basis of this finding, the next major step for the Webster-Stratton programme was to add a component to address inter-familial 'communication, problem-solving and coping skills' (Webster-Stratton, 1994, p. 584). All families received the video-based group programme, and half received the new additional component on family communication and coping. Assessments were made in a comprehensive range of measurements both before and shortly after therapy.

Webster-Stratton found that both groups were equally successful in improving parental reports of child behaviour, and both groups showed comparable improvements in parental distress, quality of parental–child interaction and corresponding improvements in child deviance and non-compliance. However, the enhanced therapy was also associated with improvements in parental problem-solving, communication and collaborative skills. Likewise, only the enhanced programme was associated with improvements in the child's ability to suggest pro-social ways of solving problems.

An unfortunate limitation of the 1994 study was the lack of long-term follow-up. This raises questions as to whether short-term gains were retained and also does not permit examination of any potential delayed effects of the enhanced therapy to materialise. Indeed, Webster-Stratton speculated it may have taken time for the parents' new-gained problem-solving and communication skills to improve the behaviour of their child over what the standard therapy could achieve.

Such doubts were alleviated in the next study. Webster-Stratton and Hammond (1997) reported on an improved design (with follow-up at 1 year), and also added a separate child-focused component to the therapy. This was designed to address deficits in the child's cognitions; specifically, to improve 'social skills, conflict resolution skills, loneliness and negative attributions, inability to empathize or to understand another's perspective and problems at school' (*ibid.*, p. 96). Participating families either received the standard parent training, the child therapy component on its own, the full combined package or no therapy at all (but placed on a waiting list).

According to maternal and paternal report measures, behaviour had improved at post-test in all three conditions, the improvements most pronounced on the treatments involving parent training. In contrast, only the treatments including the child therapy component were associated with gains in child pro-social problem-solving ability. In home observations, both treatments involving parent training markedly improved mother and father parenting quality, while child therapy alone was associated with weak improvements on that aspect. Observations were also made in the child's home. In interactions with friends, all treated children exhibited improved positive conflict management skills, and this was more pronounced in the two treatments including child therapy. However, at immediate follow-up, observed child deviance had not been reduced by any of the conditions.

At one-year follow-up, all benefits found at post-test had been retained. Most importantly, however, it was also observed one year later that children in all three treatments had lower rates of observed deviance in the home – i.e. the therapy had a delayed effect. Further, the extent of these improvements is quite striking, especially for the combined therapy, in which 95% of children exhibited a 30% (or greater) reduction in observed deviance in the home (see Figure 11.3).

Clearly, then, there are advantages to adding a child-focused component to parent training. First, combining child therapy with parent training yields the best overall results in terms of reduction in actual deviance, and also the widest range of improvements across different measures. Second, as Webster-Stratton and Hammond point out, there are various reasons why some parents will never enter parent training programmes. These families could benefit the most from child therapy, which can be conducted at school and does not require parental participation, especially in view of the finding that at one-year follow-up, child therapy alone was superior to parent training alone in reducing observed child deviance (Figure 11.3).

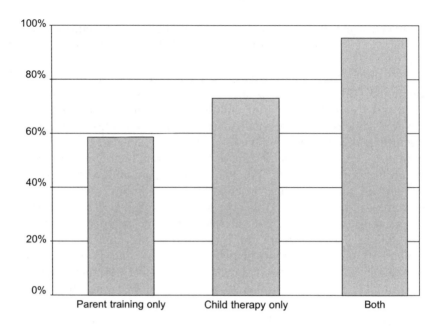

Figure 11.3. Percentage of clinically significant improvement at one-year follow-up

Source: Adapted from Webster-Stratton and Hammond, 1997

FACTORS RELATED TO THE
SUCCESS OF PARENT TRAINING

Furey and Basili (1988) revealed the potential role of biases in maternal perceptions on adherence to therapy. They employed a two-stage parent training package in which clinicians first worked one-on-one with mothers to improve parenting skills through instruction, modelling and role-playing to teach the use of positive social rewards, and 'time-out' disciplinary procedures. In the second stage, the mother was observed interacting with her child by the therapist behind a one-way mirror, who fed live feedback to her using a 'bug-in-the-ear device' to refine the techniques taught in the first stage.

Two months after therapy, mothers were categorised as either satisfied or dissatisfied based on their reports of the child's adjustment. Independent observations revealed, however, that the children of the satisfied and dissatisfied mothers had improved to equal levels, as had the quality of their parenting. The unnecessarily dissatisfied group was characterised by having children who were *initially* the most problematic at pre-treatment (although there were no differences post-treatment). They concluded that mothers of the most severe cases require follow-up therapy and support to ensure they continue using techniques, and, hopefully, will begin to realise the benefit of using them. If not, Furey and Basili (*ibid.*) speculated they would be likely to abandon them in time. Common sense suggests that dissatisfaction results in increased drop-out rates, as well as decreased compliance/persistence with techniques.

Carolyn Webster-Stratton acknowledges the role satisfaction may play in determining the programme's success. In 1989, she compared three versions of her treatment and found that parents preferred group discussion video therapy (GDVM) over both individually administered video therapy and group discussion therapy. Overall, parents were more satisfied with GDVM, found it easier to administer and believed it to be more useful, suggesting parents are happier with eclectic therapy and prefer to have a group leader. Webster-Stratton (1989) also demonstrated that parents found techniques designed to encourage desired behaviour (i.e. rewarding – e.g. positive emotional expression) easier to administer than those designed to decrease inappropriate behaviour (i.e. punishing – e.g. time-out, ignoring). This has been replicated elsewhere (e.g. Cross *et al.*, 1987), and the implications are clear in that parents should be given more support on the more difficult aspects to maximise the success of treatment.

Perhaps more worrying is the finding that the most vulnerable and needy families are the hardest to address. Several studies have found they are the least likely to enter therapy, the least likely to benefit from it and the most likely to drop out. For example, Kazdin (1990) found that those who failed to complete a programme were worse in terms of child symptoms, maternal stress and psychopathology, and the most disadvantaged socioeconomically. Furey and Basili (1988) also found that mothers who dropped out were more likely to be of lower socioeconomic class and had the worst parenting skills initially. Webster-Stratton and Hammond (1990), in a one-year follow-up study of the group-based videotape treatment, found that low socioeconomic status, single parenthood and negative life events were all predictors of treatment failure at one-year follow-up. Webster-Stratton and Hammond (*ibid.*) also found that parental perceptions of child behaviour were more closely linked to parental depression scores than their independent observations of deviance. This suggests depressed parents cannot accurately assess improvements in their child's behaviours and are therefore another group at increased risk of abandoning techniques.

FUTURE DIRECTIONS –
PROGRAMMES IN THE COMMUNITY

In an effort to address those most needy families who fail to respond to clinic-based programmes, the latest parent training schemes are being offered in community settings. In her paper entitled 'From parent training to community building', Webster-Stratton (1997) estimates that while the children of two thirds of treated families return to the normal range, a third of American families fail to respond. She mainly attributes this to factors associated with low socioeconomic status – such as poverty, lack of support, single parenthood and depression. Webster-Stratton (*ibid.*) strongly advocates community settings as the best way to address those disadvantaged families. She believes that through therapist support, group work and involvement with schools, much-needed social networks can be established that will have much wider-reaching implications for disadvantaged communities than just improved parenting skills.

Some empirical support already exists for the role community projects may have to play. In a Canadian study, Cunningham *et al.* (1995) invited families with conduct-disordered children to join one of two forms of therapy: either group-based therapy in a local community centre or clinic-based therapy at the university clinical psychology department. They found that families who chose the community-based therapy were more likely to have children with severe conduct problems and were more likely to be immigrants and have English as a second language. This study illustrates how community projects can successfully reach families that clinic-based programmes may miss.

The community setting also offers greater opportunity for prevention. Under the umbrella of a well developed mental health system, parenting groups in community settings could form a supportive network, allowing parents to discuss, support and develop skills that could prevent cases before they develop. Therapists and mental health professionals working in these settings could also screen and identify cases at particular risk for extra attention. Indeed this has long been a goal – in their early review back in 1972, Berkowitz and Graziano concluded (emphasis added): 'this new framework has important implications for future use in a systematic and *prevention-orientated* model.' Obviously, preventive programmes will always be preferable to treatment, not only in terms of time and financial resources but also by alleviating potential years of disruption and stress to families. Yet 30 years on, this vision is still to be realised, but as increasingly sophisticated community programmes are developed it edges ever closer.

All the studies discussed so far have been of North American origin.

Based in South London, the *Supporting Parents through Community Education* project (SPOKES) (Laurent, 2000) is one of the first to evaluate systematically the effectiveness of the Webster-Stratton approach in a UK community. Children in reception and Year 1 classes are screened through parent and teacher-completed questionnaires. The parents of children found to be 'at risk' of future behaviour problems are invited to take part in a parent training programme based on the Webster-Stratton videos and group discussion. Because the programme is based in local primary schools and aims at the 'whole child', parents are taught how to help their children's reading as well as a broad range of parenting skills related to children's behaviour. SPOKES is unusual in that it combines supporting parents in dealing with their children's behaviour, teaching parents specific skills to help their children read, and training parents how to problem-solve when difficulties arise in relationships with family members and teachers. This is a broad-brush programme that lasts almost a year and aims to take the Webster-Stratton programme into primary schools as a means of prevention. The children are not 'referred' and the schools offer it 'because so many children have difficulties making the adjustment to school'. The strong literacy element has been added to the 'standard' Webster-Stratton programme because children in inner-city schools often fall behind in reading – the key to progress in other subjects at school. Above all, the aim is to prevent and not to cure. Every effort is made to emphasise how 'normal' it is for young children and their parents to need extra help in the important transition to school – especially in inner-city ones.

CONCLUSIONS

There is good evidence that contemporary programmes can be very successful in tackling behaviour problems. This has been established by the effective treatment of real clinical cases, as evaluated by sound research designs, and further validated in real clinic settings. In a recent review, Serkeitch and Dumas (1996) discovered 26 evaluation studies (including four by Webster-Stratton and colleagues) that met rigid criteria for strong research design (e.g. use of control group) pooled the results statistically. They found that 77–80% of children who were treated were better off than those in control groups. They also found that 67% of parents finished treatment better adjusted than control parents.

While the initial focus of behavioural parent training packages was child deviance, contemporary programmes have been shown to benefit families across a whole spectrum of outcomes, including marital stress, inter-partner communication, problem-solving and family relationships; child conflict management and social skills; and increasing positive emotional expression between mother and child.

These findings are impressive, but it must be remembered they only include those who receive treatment in the first place. There is evidence that the most difficult cases are often missed by the traditional clinic-based system. At present, moving programmes into community settings offers the best hope of extending the benefits of parent training to families in deprived areas and those 'hard to reach'.

At the same time, looking beyond improving parenting skills, it is argued community-based schemes have the potential to help restore 'community' itself. This offers broad and extensive benefits to deprived communities at a psychological and, ultimately, sociological level. A bold aim, but none the less it is the target that leaders such as Carolyn Webster-Stratton have set for themselves. And given the steady progress of programmes over the last 20 years, who would bet against them?

PART 4
TRAINING

12

TRAINING TO WORK
IN THE EARLY YEARS:
DEVELOPING THE CLIMBING FRAME

Lesley Abbott and Denise Hevey

Practitioners in today's early childhood institutions are maybe facing some of the most demanding challenges in the history of their profession... Profound and interrelated change in our social, cultural, economic, political and technological environments, combined with a fundamental shift in the nature of work and employment patterns, are impacting on the lives of children and families (Oberhuemer and Colberg-Schrader, 1999).

Although written in the context of early education and care in Germany, the above statement has universal application. The challenges facing all those involved in the lives of young children and their families are immense.

A series of influential reports published in the last decade has highlighted the importance of high-quality training for those who work in the early years (DES, 1990; National Commission on Education, 1993; Audit Commission, 1996; DfEE, 1999b). Further, one of the most important conclusions reached by the RSA Early Learning Inquiry was that 'the calibre and training of the professionals who work with children are the key determinants of high quality provision' (Ball, 1994).

But what sort of training is appropriate to meet the challenges posed to and by families and children in the twenty-first century? Work with young children and their families has traditionally cut across bureaucratic demarcations between education, health and social services and has involved a wide range of different professionals from teachers and educational psychologists to health visitors and paediatricians and to social workers and community workers. Each of these different professional groups is rooted in a separate tradition with its own set of professional ethics and values, education and training requirements and career paths. These traditions permeate the language the different professionals use and the way in which they view and work with families and young children and the other client/user groups that are part of their wider professional roles.

However, the explicitly multidisciplinary nature of government initiatives in recent years and their focus on co-ordination and integration of early years services (such as the requirement for local Early Years Development and Childcare Partnerships and the Sure Start programme) require something more than benign co-operation across existing professions. These initiatives require a truly multidisciplinary response. Echoing the findings of the Rumbold Report (DES, 1990), successful work with young children and their families in the future requires support from highly trained professionals who possess a broad range of knowledge, a high level of skills and appropriate attitudes and values.

Some have argued that a multidisciplinary approach can be achieved through the provision of inter-professional training opportunities as part of continuing professional development programmes in order to overcome barriers to effective inter-professional collaboration. But this response can be criticised for not challenging the vested interests or viewpoints of existing professional groups or as 'tinkering at the edges' whilst accepting the status quo of agency-appropriate rather than age-appropriate services.

Moss and Penn (1996) provide us with an alternative vision of a new qualification of 'early childhood teacher' trained to work across the new services as they envisage them and only with children from 0 to 6 years of age. But this approach has been criticised for endangering the unique status of early childhood teachers in the UK who are technically qualified to work across, and hence influence, the wider primary phase of education. Others have argued for a radical solution in terms of the creation of a new multidisciplinary profession of 'educarer' incorporating the skills and knowledge of a variety of existing professional approaches within an exclusive focus on the early years (Calder, 1999). Use of accreditation of prior experience and learning, recognition of the need to bring together those working in different sectors and the determination of a committed group of early years trainers (Pugh, 1996) led to the development of the first 'multi-professional' early childhood studies degree programmes. By autumn 1997 there were 15 (Fawcett and Calder, 1998) and by 2000 the number had doubled.

As early as 1996 the Labour Party recognised the need to raise standards of education and training across the board and to promote a multidisciplinary approach at higher levels in order to provide appropriately trained staff to support their planned early years initiatives. As part of the strategy they explicitly supported the development of early childhood studies degrees: 'we will encourage the emergence of new courses which offer integrated training, like those at Manchester Metropolitan University and Suffolk College' (Labour Party, 1996, p. 14).

But the higher education approach to training for 'educarers' has met with criticisms from employers for not providing sufficient practical experience and for not being linked to nationally agreed vocational outcomes. There were also initial problems (since resolved) over recognition of an early childhood studies degree for progression to a postgraduate certificate in education because of the absence of substantive study of an academic subject (like maths, English or history) that is part of the National Curriculum.

Reflecting on the contribution of early childhood studies degrees in Britain, Calder (1999, p. 59) suggests that: 'although degree level training cannot ensure better pay, it is a way of recognising the skills involved and this makes more obvious the question as to why people in early childhood education and care are paid so little.'

The issue of pay and conditions is one reason why early years services have not been professionalised to any great extent to date. Despite high costs to individual families, Britain gets its childcare on the cheap. The vast majority of people who work with young children and their families in the UK are not trained to degree or professional levels. Nursery nurses, classroom assistants, playgroup leaders, crèche workers, out-of-school club workers, childminders and others who form the substantial cadre of para-professionals some 370,000 strong provide the lion's share of hands-on care and education for young children. It is, therefore, their 'calibre and training' that is likely to have the biggest impact on the quality of provision for young children in the immediate future. Hence it is their training (or lack of it) with which the next section of this chapter is concerned. Later in the chapter we examine teacher training in more detail to illustrate the difficulties in developing a multidisciplinary ethos for higher-level training within the constraints of existing professions and alternative routes to achieving Qualified Teacher Status. Finally, we consider the most recent developments in the 'climbing frame' of qualifications and the potential opening up of progression routes from para-professional to professional roles.

THE TRAINING OF CHILDCARE WORKERS

Over the past three years a series of six major national workforce surveys has been carried out under the auspices of the relevant national training organisations (see Table 12.1). These provide by far the most comprehensive picture ever collected of the characteristics, training and qualifications of the para-professionals who work in childcare and education and of their future training needs.

Table 12.1   Training of early years workers

Category of staff (volunteers/student placements in brackets)	No. in workforce	Turnover/ recruitment rates	% hold voc. qual.	% study voc. qual.	% interest in voc. quals.	% recent training	Source plus comments
Education support staff	121,500	9.7/22.6	63.4	10.7	32.6	86.0	*Survey of Education Support Staff and Volunteers in Nursery and Primary Schools,* Autumn 1999. *Comment:* paid staff include 34% with NNEB/CACHE or BTEC/National Diploma, 3% NVQ3 and 4% qualified teachers
(ES volunteers)	(178,800)	–	(19.4)	(8.2)	(20.5)	(37.1)	
Preschool/playgroup paid workers	80,440	20.3/22.5	74.1	15.9	11.1	56.9	*Registered Pre-School/Playgroup Survey,* 1998. *Comment:* paid staff include 11% with NNEB/CACHE or BTEC/National Diploma, 4% NVQ3, 18% Dip. in Playgroup Practice and 6% qualified teachers
(PPG volunteers)	(24,530)	–	(18.9)	(17.3)	(7.9)	(5.5)	
Independent day nursery staff	51,200	16.2/23.6	79.6	15.7	–	85	*Independent Day Nursery Workforce Survey,* 1998. *Comment:* paid staff include 45% with NNEB/CACHE or BETC/Edexcel National Diploma, 6% NVQ3 and 5% qualified teachers
(IDN placement students)	(7,770)	–	(0.0)	(100)	–	–	
Local authority day nursery staff (no info. on volunteers)	3,701	–	83.5	3.7	–	–	*Social Services Workforce Analysis,* 1997. *Comment:* includes 78% staff with NNEB/CACHE or BTEC/National Diploma, 1% NVQ3 and 0.4% qualified teachers and 2% qualified social workers
Local authority family centre staff (no info. on volunteers)	3,270	11.2/–	65.4	6.9	–	–	*Social Services Workforce Analysis,* 1997. *Comment:* includes 40% staff with NNEB/CACHE or BTEC/National Diploma, 1% NVQ3, 1% teachers and 19 qualified social workers
Childminders (no info. on volunteers)	93,300	18.3/14.4	30.3	7.4	28.5	100	*Registered Childminders Workforce Survey,* 1998. *Comment:* includes 9% with NNEB/CACHE or BTEC/Edexcel national diploma, 2% NVQ3 and 2.7% qualified teachers. Turnover based on no. working less than one year plus estimated fall in employment
Out-of-school clubs	13,550	20.3/30.2	55.9	19.8	12.8	50.0	*Registered Out of School Clubs Workforce Survey.* 1998. *Comment:* includes 15% with NNEB/CACHE or BTEC/Edexcel national diploma, 5% NVQ3 and 7% qualified teachers
(OoSC volunteers)	(2,120)	–	(18.9)	(18.9)	(17.4)	(8.3)	

Table 12.1 provides a comparative summary of information about training and qualifications based on all six surveys.[1] From this we can see that the total paid workforce in 1998/99 was 366,961 and growing and that this was supplemented by the participation of nearly 200,000 regular volunteers and students on placement. Turnover was running at up to one fifth in all types of setting apart from schools where it was considerably lower. Recruitment was buoyant in all areas apart from childminding and especially amongst infant/junior schools and out-of-school clubs – the latter experiencing rapid expansion.

Column three gives an indication of the percentage in each occupational category who had received training leading to some sort of qualification. With the exception of childminders and to a lesser extent out-of-school club workers, the figures give the impression that the workforce is already well qualified with roughly two thirds or more holding a relevant vocational qualification. However, these figures might be considered misleading since many of the qualifications reported in the survey required only a brief period of training and were below 'A' level or NVQ Level 3 in demand.

There is also considerable variation in the type and level of qualifications held by workers in different settings when judged by the relative percentage of workers holding the NNEB/CACHE or BTEC Diploma in Nursery Nursing (Level 3 qualifications) and higher-level professional qualifications such as teaching and social work. The variation partly reflects differential recruitment policies but it also reflects different career patterns and opportunities for training. For example, nursery nursing diplomas are predominantly studied full-time in colleges by 16–19-year-olds who have made an early career choice to work with young children. Those who complete such programmes tend to be recruited direct as qualified staff by day nurseries and others. On the other hand, playgroup leaders, childminders, staff in out-of-school clubs and, to some extent, education support staff, tend to be recruited from a different population of women who opt to take up work with young children once they have children of their own. The traditional nursery nursing diplomas may be less relevant to them and are frequently inaccessible through reasons of cost, college attendance requirements or time commitment.

The importance of alternative, part-time, setting-specific training is clear in this sector, particularly for older entrants. This sort of training includes the Introduction, Foundation and Diploma in Playgroup Practice or the new Certificate in Childminding Practice and National Vocational Qualifications (NVQs) in Early Years Care and Education and in Play Work:

---

[1] The surveys, though broadly comparable, did not cover exactly the same questions in all cases. For a detailed analysis of any one occupational group, reference should be made to the original.

NVQs...are suitable for those that can provide evidence of competence in the workplace. The level 2 qualifications are designed for those working under supervision, whereas the level 3 NVQs cover the competence required of those working without supervision, for example as playgroup or pre-school leaders (QCA, 1999b, p. 6).

NVQs are now the most common qualification aim amongst those currently studying/working towards a qualification while in work (column 4), and are increasingly widely accepted as qualifications for work in the early years[2] or in playwork.

Pent-up demand for training leading to qualifications is running at between 11 and 32% of early years workers (column 5) and is particularly strong amongst education support staff and childminders. Given the recent introduction of compulsory literacy and numeracy hours in primary schools, it is not surprising the main qualification of interest to the former in 1999 was the Certificate in Literacy and Numeracy Support (CLANSA).

The percentage of staff who have experienced recent non-qualification training,[3] according to the surveys, appears misleadingly high, ranging from 50% in out-of-school clubs to 100% amongst childminders. In reality 'recent training' usually boils down to the odd inservice training day or evening on a specific topic. For example, education support staff received on average 15.6 hours of training but the median figure (i.e. that achieved by 50% of the population) was only six hours. Further, since over 50% of childminders had been in the job for five years or less and the definition of recent in this survey was 'within the last three years', their basic induction course of 6–12 hours would have been counted as experience of 'recent non-qualification training' for many.

The combined evidence of those holding some sort of vocational qualification (30–83% depending on setting), those currently working towards qualifications (only 3% in best qualified settings – up to 20% in others) and the pent-up interest and demand for qualifications (11–32% of staff) demonstrates quite clearly that early years workers are committed to personal and professional development. So why is it the early years as a sector is widely perceived as under-trained and under-valued?

First, as has been pointed out, most of this training is short term, setting specific and at less than NVQ Level 3 or 'A' level equivalent. The percentage of staff with professional level qualifications is small and the low basic level of education and training creates problems for progression to higher-level, high-status qualifications.

---

[2] According to the ESS Survey (2000), 63% of schools now accept NVQ3 as a suitable qualification for education support staff; 12.5% do not and, 9 years since its introduction, 24.5% still don't know about it.

[3] This figure is based on last 6, 12 or 36 months depending on the survey.

Second, almost all the settings surveyed reported that lack of resources significantly restricted the availability of training opportunities. Whereas education and training for 16–19-year-olds is free, training for adult workers is largely assumed by the state to be the responsibility of employers. Early years settings that are small scale and often run on a not-for-profit basis or by community groups are also the ones that recruit predominantly from the unqualified adult population. The entire training budget of the majority of settings surveyed was less than £500 per year. In addition, childminders are technically self-employed and many earn below the threshold for income tax payment after allowable expenses. Yet, according to the relevant survey, more than half of those who had accessed qualification-related training in the last three years had had to pay for it entirely themselves.

A third factor might be described as barriers to access. Lack of time on top of the basic working week was a significant problem for childminders, playgroup workers and out-of-school club workers; whereas lack of information, availability and flexibility of courses and lack of incentives for better training were the main barriers for education support staff.

Many of the qualifications referred to earlier are relatively new but we can envisage the routes that might be opened up, for example, for a typical childminder – let's call her Jo:

Jo doesn't have good memories of school and left with qualifications which don't reflect her real ability. She married young and had two children by the time she was 20. She found she really enjoyed being with small children and didn't want to go back to work but, like most young families, money was short. Childminding was something she thought would fit in with her own family commitments. At first she didn't realise how much was involved. Whilst she was being registered, she took an induction course 'Introducing Childminding Practice', which formed the first unit from the NCMA/CACHE Certificate in Childminding Practice. She found this really helpful because it gave her an insight into how looking after other people's children was different from caring for your own and that being a professional involved being business-like as well as caring.

Once Jo was registered she started looking after a little boy, which was a change from her two girls. She was keen to learn more and progressed to unit 2 (Developing Childminding Practice), which covered the knowledge and skills needed by all registered child-minders. This gave her a real boost in confidence about her work as a childminder that helped her to have a more relaxed and equal relationship with parents. She realised she already had a lot of knowledge and skills which she was also able to build on with new information and ideas.

When one of her own children started school, Jo took on a second minded child. He seemed very anxious and insecure at first and his behaviour was quite challenging at times. The final unit on 'Extending Childminding Practice' helped Jo understand why he was being difficult and gave her some practical advice on how to manage his behaviour. She gained more in-depth knowledge of children's development that gave her confidence in communicating with other professionals. She also learnt more about the more specialised roles of a community childminder (caring for disabled children and children in need), or of an accredited childminder (providing early years education and promoting the early learning goals).

Completing all three units of the Certificate in Childminding Practice provided Jo with the underpinning knowledge for an NVQ Level 3 in Early Years Care and Education, which she was able to complete through compiling a portfolio of evidence based on the day-to-day work she was already doing with children.

Achieving an NVQ gives Jo a nationally recognised award based on her knowledge and experience of working with young children which is valid for work in any early years setting. It should also, as we shall see in the final section of this chapter, open up access to higher-level education and training opportunities should she choose to develop her career in early years services.

TRAINING FOR TEACHERS OF YOUNG CHILDREN

Achieving Qualified Teacher Status provides entry to a generic profession and, in theory, entitles the holder to teach across any age-range though, in practice, it is unlikely for primary-trained teachers to teach older children. This is something that distinguishes early years teachers in the UK from their counterparts in other countries who are restricted to teaching the youngest children. The upside of this is that early years teachers have equal status to other teachers and are open to take on positions of responsibility and to influence practice in the wider primary age-range. The downside is the assumption that those trained as educators of older children are equally well prepared to educate and support the development of our youngest children. In addition, until recently the requirement for a subject specialism imposed on all entrants to teacher training did not meet the wider needs of those wishing to train for work primarily in the early years.

After much lobbying, in June 1998 the Teacher Training Agency in England decided early years trainees could undertake an 'advanced study of early years' as an alternative to a National Curriculum subject. This opened the door to new specialist early years teacher training courses that also meet all the requirements for Qualified Teacher Status. This change was accompanied by the allocation to certain institutions of additional early years student numbers so that the new courses could contribute to fulfilling the UK government requirement for specialist early years teachers to be involved in all early years settings in future.

Specialist early years courses are now offered at undergraduate (Bachelor of Education or BEd) and postgraduate levels (the Post-Graduate Certificate in Education or PGCE) by an increasing number of colleges and universities. And, consistent with developing a multidisciplinary approach, students on such courses now experience work placements in a range of early years settings other than schools.

Practitioners themselves believe a specialist early years training leads to more appropriate curriculum planning (Blenkin *et al.*, 1996), and recent research findings highlight the significance of appropriately trained staff in the provision of quality experiences for young children (Abbott and Rodger, 1994; Pascal *et al.*, 1994; Sylva *et al.*, 1999). The introduction of a Foundation stage and early learning goals from September 2000 placed additional requirements on the training of early years teachers. There are concerns that the demands of the literacy and numeracy hour, the need for knowledge of National Curriculum up to Key Stage 2 and the requirement for some experience of working with children in the older primary age-range all eat into the time available in an already full PGCE curriculum to develop multidisciplinary approaches to work in the early years.

Recognition of early years as a specialist subject on a par with National Curriculum areas has also opened up access to postgraduate teacher training for graduates of early childhood studies degrees. This is particularly encouraging because it ensures those who go on to become early years teachers start from a sound grounding in all the disciplines relevant to work in the early years. However, whilst many early childhood studies degrees are offered on a part-time basis, at the time of writing there is an acute shortage of part-time PGCE courses. This has created a major barrier to access to the many early years practitioners with family commitments who are unable to travel long distances or attend full time or who simply '. . . could not afford to take time out to do traditional forms of teacher training' (DfEE, 2000c, p. 6.) And lack of funding, particularly to support low-paid staff on part-time courses, discourages many potential students from even beginning the education and training process that could lead eventually to Qualified Teacher Status. This is particularly regrettable in the light of recommendations by the Early Childhood Education Forum (1995) and the Pre-School Playgroup Review (DfEE, 1999b) that 'all managers of centres should be graduates'.

In order to improve access and encourage trainees from shortage subjects, the government is currently consulting on ways of enhancing employment-based routes into teaching (DfEE, 2000c). The existing Graduate and Registered Teacher Routes, which have only been successful on a relatively small scale to date, provide opportunities for funded school-based training for individuals who are already working in a school. The Registered Teacher Programme is designed for non-graduates with a minimum of two years' full-time equivalent experience of higher education, while the Graduate Teacher Programme offers an alternative, employment-based route to Qualified Teacher Status for graduates. This latter should be suitable for early childhood studies graduates lucky enough to be appointed as an untrained teacher to the staff of a state school. However, many schools are reluctant to take the risk of appointing someone who is untrained to their salaried staff. In addition the scheme does not meet the needs of those who work in independent nursery and infant schools that are not eligible for funding, and graduates from this background often find it difficult to gain access to schools willing to support them in the maintained sector. So, whilst considerable progress has been made in making teacher training more relevant to the needs of the early years sector and in opening up access to training, there are still issues to be considered.

WHY A CLIMBING FRAME?

Educationalists often use the analogy of a ladder of qualifications to represent systematic progression from basic to higher levels – academic progression from GCSEs to 'A' levels and on to degrees being the most obvious example. In terms of training to work in the early years we would argue that a 'climbing frame' is a much more useful analogy than a ladder (Abbot and Pugh, 1998). The survey results show that the majority of early years workers do not start on the bottom rung of a ladder at 16 years of age and work their way straight to the top. Many have worked initially in unrelated fields and gained experience as parents before entering the sector. Climbing frames in contrast to ladders are enabling rather than rigid and prescriptive and fit much better with the notion of life-long learning. Climbing frames have rungs of different size, shape and height and encourage horizontal as well as vertical progression. They are multi-dimensional and their variety and flexibility allow individuals to create their own routes and to exit at the level of their choice or to branch out in a different direction by, for example, extending their range of competence to include working with children with special needs, numeracy and literacy support, working with parents and so on. Where these sorts of opportunity have been provided there is convincing evidence that not only is individual confidence and self-esteem increased, but also that individuals have succeeded in achieving qualifications at the highest level (Graham, 1997; Powell, 1998; Abbott and Moylett, 1999).

One student who successfully accessed the 'climbing frame' via an innovative course developed in partnership between a local authority, a university and the Council for Awards in Childcare and Education (CACHE) was Sadja. As a language-support assistant in a local school she applied for an EU-funded course under the New Opportunities for Women (NOW) programme. She successfully completed the two-year part-time course and gained NVQ3, the Advanced Diploma in Childcare and Education (ADCE) and achieved credit at higher education level equivalent to the first year of the BA early childhood studies degree. At the end of the course her manager wrote of her:

> She is well aware of the way in which the course has changed her thinking. She has intelligence, sensitivity and experience which will enable her to become an enormous asset to any service operating in the area of support for children and families. She has the knowledge and commitment, but the existence of the right kind of opportunities has been an essential factor in allowing her to bring out these skills and develop them. First there was the 'doorstep' opportunity, the short basic course, friendly and informal with crèche on hand. Then there was the recognition and encouragement of her skills in helping others through interpreting, followed up by the possibility of much more in-depth study, but still in an environment which was supportive and enabled her to maintain full commitment to her family responsibilities.
>
> The availability of these opportunities has ensured that her unique combination of skills and experience will be used to give her increased personal fulfilment, her children a more knowledgeable and confident parent, while at the same time putting an enormous contribution back into society (Graham, 1997).

Sadja went on to join Level 2 of the honours degree programme in early childhood and has recently graduated. She was fortunate to work in an authority where access, funding and support for training were available.

Sadly this is not the case for many other students who, for a variety of reasons, are denied this opportunity. For them opportunities are needed for distance learning, access to supportive networks and links with centres, such as the recently established early excellence centres, as focal points for training and good practice.

In September 1999 the Qualifications and Curriculum Authority launched the first interlocking pieces of a climbing frame of nationally accredited qualifications for early years education, childcare and playwork

(QCA, 1999b) covering both vocationally related (i.e. preparation for work or extending knowledge) and occupational qualifications (i.e. NVQs) up to Level 3. This anticipated further developments at higher levels: 'When the new level 4 NVQs are available, these will provide a route for those working at senior management level or as specialist advanced practitioners in early years and playwork settings' (QCA, 1999b, p. 6).

In spring 2000 the new NVQs in Early Years Care and Education at Level 4 were indeed accredited. These are academically as well as practically demanding qualifications and are likely to be recognised as equivalent to a minimum of one-year full-time in higher education (120 CATs points)[4] with an exit level in terms of academic demand equivalent to the second year of a degree programme.

The new NVQ 4 has been designed around a common core for early years workers that includes the ability to operate as a reflective practitioner at a senior level, to make use of current and emerging theory and research evidence and to take responsibility for one's own continuing professional development. There are three professional pathways to suit different senior roles in the early years sector. These cover 'Management', 'Advanced or Specialist Practice' and 'Quality Enhancement' – the latter being suitable for those engaged in inspection, training and support of early years settings. Together they form the basis for a new multidisciplinary profession that is separate from, but complimentary to, the existing professions of teaching, social work and health visiting.

It has yet to be worked out how existing professional qualifications can be meshed together with higher-level NVQs to complete the climbing frame but the first moves are being made in relation to teaching. At the time of writing, discussions are in hand with the Department for Education and Employment and the Teacher Training Agency which hinge on the potential for integration of the NVQ 4 in Early Years Care and Education with a higher education qualification in a way that would result in eligibility for fast-track, employment-based routes to Qualified Teacher Status. This would put one key professional progression route in place within the climbing frame.

Figure 12.1 attempts to portray the developing climbing frame for the early years sector as of September 2000. Within a simplified, two-dimensional diagram it is not possible to represent all possible routes or the full variety of related vocational qualifications that could potentially be included within the nationally accredited 'Framework for Early Years, Child Care and Play Work'. However, the importance of the QCA framework embedded in the climbing frame lies in accreditation criteria

---

[4] Credit Accumulation and Transfer points form the common currency of higher education. One point is allocated for every 10 hours of notional study time at a designated HE level.

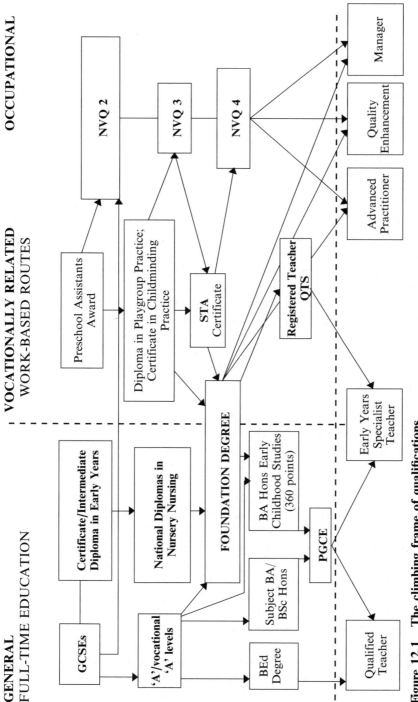

Figure 12.1 The climbing frame of qualifications

that should ensure relevance to national occupational and/or professional standards, location in terms of level and transparency in relation to progression routes.

As the climbing frame develops it will be important to clarify the relationship of the new higher-level NVQs to the early childhood studies (ECS) degrees which have done so much to promote multidisciplinary approaches to higher-level education and training in this sector. Early childhood studies graduates are now finding their way into employment in a range of areas, particularly the new roles created by the Early Years Development and Childcare Partnerships, but the 'currency' of the courses is still insufficiently established. Meanwhile entirely new forms of work-related higher education qualifications are to be launched from Autumn 2001 in England. These Foundation Degrees are being designed with the involvement of employers to provide a mix of work related specialist skills, academic learning and Key Skills such as team working and communication. They can be studied full time over two years or part time over an extended period and students will be able to 'top up' to a full honours degree with around 15 months additional study. In Early Years there are already moves afoot by the new DFES to kitemark those Foundation Degrees that meet national criteria as Senior Practitioner awards and there is the promise of bursaries to help low paid workers access them. The development of Foundation degrees will also meet the need for more flexible routes into teaching in order to increase the number of specialist early years teachers. Students who successfully complete a Foundation degree have a number of choices. They can either access the final year of a 3yr BA(Hons) Early Childhood Studies degree followed by a part-time or full-time PGCE course or the final year or years of a BEd(Hons) degree leading to qualified teacher status (QTS). A third option is to follow the school-based Registered Teacher Programme.

The completion of a climbing frame of qualifications for the early years sector will be a significant achievement that has the potential to raise the standard of education and training and to open up progression routes that have previously been blocked for the majority of early years workers. However, this is only a first step. Unlocking this potential for the benefit of a workforce who have been under-trained and under-valued for years requires a good deal more. The workforce surveys show that the vast majority of early years settings are small, many are community based or not-for-profit and their training budgets are tiny. There simply aren't lots of large employers to pick up the bill. This issue is finally beginning to be recognised and a national childcare training strategy is starting to emerge, backed by significant government funding and tailored to local needs through the Early Years Development and Child Care Partnerships. The next few years could turn out to see radical changes in the nature and availability of Early Years training and the professionalisation of the roles of early years workers. And, with the transfer of responsibility for regulation and inspection of all Early Years Services to OFSTED from September 2001, for the first time there should be a mechanism for evaluating the scale and quality of provision nationally. In the future the availability of OFSTED reports on an annual basis should enable us to judge to what extent investment in training for early years workers is really affecting the quality of care and education for our youngest children.

Points for discussion

(1) How far does the present range of training opportunities meet the needs of those wishing to pursue a career in early years care and education?

(2) There are those who claim we need a new type of early years worker. What kinds of knowledge and skill are needed to work with young children?

(3) Once trained, a teacher in the UK can teach any age-group – why should we think that teaching in the early years requires specialist skill and knowledge?

Further reading

Abbott, L. and Pugh, G. (1998) *Training to Work in the Early Years: Developing the Climbing Frame*. Buckingham: Open University Press.
QCA (1999) *Early Years Education, Childcare and Playwork: A Framework of Nationally Accredited Qualifications*. London: QCA.

REFERENCES

Abbott, L. (1998) *Pathways to Professionalism – Report of the European-Funded New Opportunities for Women Project*. Kirklees Early Years Service/Manchester Metropolitan University.

Abbott, L. and Alderson, P. (eds.) (1999) *Learning Inclusion: The Cleves School Experience*. London: David Fulton.

Abbott, L. and Moylett, H. (1997) *Working with the Under Threes: Responding to Children's Needs*. Buckingham: Open University Press.

Abbott, L. and Moylett, H. (1999) *New Millennium Series – Early Education Transformed*. London: Falmer Press.

Abbott, L. and Nutbrown, C. (2001) *Experiencing Reggio Emilia: Implicatons for Pre-school Provision*. Buckingham: Open University Press.

Abbott, L. and Pugh, G. (1998) *Training to Work in the Early Years: Developing the Climbing Frame*. Buckingham: Open University Press.

Abbott, L. and Rodger, R. (1994a) *Quality Education in the Early Years*. Buckingham: Open University Press.

Abbott, L. and Rodger, R. (1994b) *The Identification of Quality Factors in the Care and Education of Children under Five*. Manchester: Salford LEA/Manchester Metropolitan University.

Alderson, P. (1993) *Children's Consent to Surgery*. Buckingham: Open University Press.

Alderson, P. (1995) *Children, Ethics and Social Research*. Barnardo's.

Alderson, P. (2000) *Young Children's Rights: Exploring Beliefs, Principles and Practice*. London: Jessica Kingsley.

Alexander, R. (1988) Garden or jungle? Teacher development and informal primary education. In A. Blyth (ed.) *Informal Primary Education*

Today. Lewes: Falmer Press.

American Psychiatric Association (1994) *Diagnostic and Statistical Manual of Mental Disorders: DSM-IV*. Washington, DC: American Psychiatric Association.

Anning, A. (1998) Appropriateness or effectiveness in the early childhood curriculum in the UK: some research evidence. *International Journal of Early Years Education*, Vol. 6, pp. 299–314.

Archer C., and Lucas, R. (1994) *Women Managing Pack I, Pack 2*. Framework Press, Educational Publishing Limited, Lancaster.

Armstrong, D. (1995) *Power and Partnership in Education*. London: Routledge.

Arnold, C. (1996) Unpublished MA thesis, Leicester University.

Athey, C. (1990) *Extending Thought in Young Children: A Parent–Teacher Partnership*. London: Paul Chapman Publishing.

Audit Commission (1996) *Counting to Five*. London: Audit Commission.

Audit Commission (1999) *Children in Mind*. London: Audit Commission.

Balbernie, R. (2000) Violent behaviour: tracing its roots. *Young Minds Newsletter,* no. 46.

Ball, C. (1994) *Start Right: The Importance of Early learning*. London: RSA.

Ball, M. (1997) *Consulting with Parents: Guidance for Good Practices*. London: National Early Years Network.

Barlow, J. (1997) Systematic review of the effectiveness of parent-training programmes in improving behaviour problems in children aged 3–10 years. *Journal of Developmental and Behaviour Paediatrics*. Health Services Research Unit, Oxford University.

Barnardo's (1998a) *Attitudes Towards Parenting*. National Opinion Polls.

Barnardo's (1998b) *Children are Unbeatable*. Barnardo's.

Benn, M. (1998) *Madonna and Child. Towards a New Politics of Motherhood*. London: Jonathan Cape.

Bennett, J. (2001) 'Goals and Curricula in Early Childhood', in S. Kamerman (ed.) *Early Childhood Education and Care: International Perspectives*. New York: Institute for Child and Family Welfare at Columbia University.

Bennett, N., Wood, L. and Rogers, S. (1997) *Teaching Through Play*. Buckingham: Open University Press.

Berk, L. and Winser, A. (1995) *Scaffolding Children's Learning: Vygotsky and Early Childhood Education*. Washington, DC: NAEYC.

Berkowitz, B. and Graziano, A. (1972) Training parents as behaviour therapists: a review. *Behaviour Research and Therapy,* Vol. 10, pp. 297–317.

Bernstein, B. (1992*)* *The Structuring of Pedagogic Discourse. Volume IV. Class, Codes and Control*. London: Routledge.

Blenkin, G. and Kelly, A. V. (eds.) (1994) *Early Childhood Education: A Developmental Curriculum*. London: Paul Chapman Publishing.

Blenkin, G., Rose, J. and Yue, N. (1996) Government policies and early education: perspectives from practitioners. *European Early Childhood Education Research Journal*, Vol. 4, pp. 5–21.

Blyth, E. (1990) Assisted reproduction: what's in it for children? *Children and Society*, Vol. 4, pp. 167–82.

Brannen, J. and Moss, P. (1998) 'The polarisation and intensification of parental employment in Britain: consequences for children, families and the community', *Community Work and Family*, (1(3), pp. 229–247.

Brannen, J., Moss, P., Owen, C. and Wale, C. (1997) *Mothers, Fathers and Employment: Parents and the Labour Market in Britain 1984–1994* (DfEE Research Report No. 10). London: Department for Education and Employment.

Bruce, T. (1987) *Early Childhood Education*. Sevenoaks: Hodder & Stoughton.

Bruer, J. T. (1999) *The Myth of the First Three Years*. New York: Free Press.

Bruer, J. T. (2000) Education and the brain: a bridge too far. *Educational Researcher*, Vol. 26, pp. 4–16.

Bruner, J. (2000) Tot thought. *New York Review*, 9 March.

Bruner, J. and Haste, H. (eds.) (1987) *Making Sense*. London: Methuen.

Bukstein, O. (2000) Disruptive behaviour disorder and substance use disorders in adolescents. *Journal of Psychoactive Drugs*, Vol. 32, pp. 67–79.

Burgess-Macey, C. (1994) *Assessing Young Children's Learning*. In P. Keel (ed.) *Assessment in the Multi-Ethnic Primary Classroom*. Stoke-on-Trent: Trentham Books.

Butt, J. and Box, L. (1998) *Family Centred – a Study of the Use of Family Centres by Black Families*. London: Race Equality Unit.

Calder, P. (1999) The development of early childhood studies degrees in Britain: future prospects. *European Early Childhood Education Research Journal*, Vol. 7, pp. 45–67.

Calvert, S. and McMahon, R. (1987) The treatment acceptability of behavioural parent training programme and its components. *Behaviour Therapy*, Vol. 2, pp. 165–79.

Cameron, C., Owen, C., and Moss, P. (2001) *Entry, Retention and Loss: a Study of Childcare Students and Workers (DfES Research Report Series*, London: Department for Education and Skills.

Cameron, J. and Sturge-Moore, L. (1990) *Ordinary Everyday Families: Under Fives Project*. MENCAP London Division, 115 Golden Lane, London EC1Y 0TJ.

Campbell, S., Pierce, E., Moore, G. and Marakovitz, S. (1996) Boys' externalising problems at elementary school age: pathways from early behaviour problems, maternal control, and family stress. *Development and Psychopathology*, Vol. 8, pp. 701–19.

Carr, M. (1995) Dispositions as an outcome for early childhood curriculum. Paper presented at the 5th European conference on the Quality of Early Childhood Education, Paris. Available from Margaret Carr at the University of Waikato, New Zealand.

Carr, M. and May, H. (2000) Te Whariki: curriculum voices. In H. Penn (ed.) *Early Childhood Services: Theory, Policy and Practice*. Buckingham: Open University Press.

Ceppi, G. and Zini, M. (eds.) (1999) *Children Spaces and Relations: Metaproject for an Environment for Young Children*. Reggio Emilia: Reggio Children Domus Academy Research Centre.

Charles, E. (1994) *New Futures, at Whose Cost* in Boot et al op cit.

Committee on Right of the Child (CRC) (1995) CRC/C/Add. 34. February.

Committee on Child Health Services (1976) *Fit for the Future: The Report of the Committee on Child Health Services*. The Court Report London: HMSO.

Cousins, J. (1999) *Listening to Four-Year-Olds*. London: National Early Years Network.

Cowley, E. and Rouse Selleck, D. (1996) *Managing to Change. Module 4 – Playing and Learning*. London: National Children's Bureau.

CSIE (2000) *Index for Inclusion*. Centre for Studies on Inclusive Education, 1 Redland Close, Elm Lane, Redland, Bristol BS6 6UE.

Cullen, J. (1996) The challenge of Te Whariki for future development in early childhood education. *Delta,* Vol. 48, pp. 113–25.

Cunningham, C., Bremner, R. and Boyle, M. (1995) Large group community-based parenting programmes for families of preschoolers at risk for disruptive behaviour disorders: utilisation, cost effectiveness, and outcome. *Journal of Child Psychology and Psychiatry*, Vol. 36, pp. 1141–59.

Curriculum and Assessment Authority for Wales (1996) *Desirable Outcomes for Children's Learning before Compulsory School Age: A Consultation Document*. Cardiff: ASESU Cymru.

Dahlberg, G. and Asen, G. (1994) Evaluation and regulation: a question of empowerment. In P. Moss and H. Pence (eds.) *Valuing Quality in Early Childhood Services. New Approaches to Defining Quality*. London: Paul Chapman Publishing.

Dahlberg, G. (1997) 'Barnet och pedagogen som medkonstruktorer av kultur och kunskap' ('The child and the pedagogue as co-constructors of culture and knowledge'), in *Roster om den svenska barnomsorgen. SoS Rapport 1997:23 (Voices about Swedish child care, SoS-report*

1997: 23), Socialstryrelsen (National Board of Health and Social Welfare), Stockholm.

Dahlberg, G., Moss, P. and Pence, A. (1999) *Beyond Quality in Early Childhood Education and Care: Postmodern Perspectives.* London: Falmer Press.

David, T. (ed.) (1993) *Educating our Youngest Children: European Perspectives.* London: Paul Chapman Publishing.

David, T. (1996) Their right to play. In C. Nutbrown (ed.) *Children's Rights and Early Education.* London: Paul Chapman Publishing.

David, T. (1998) Learning properly? Young children and desirable outcomes. *Early Years,* Vol. 18, pp. 61–5.

David, T. (ed.) (1999) *Teaching Young Children.* London: Paul Chapman Publishing.

David, T., Raban, B., Ure, C., Goouch, K., Jago, M., Barrière, I. and Lambirth, A. (2000) *Making Sense of Early Literacy: A Practitioner's Perspective.* Stoke-on-Trent: Trentham Books.

Day Care Trust (2000) *Securing the Future 4. Making Childcare Sustainable in Disadvantaged Rural and Urban Areas.* London: Day Care Trust.

Day Care Trust (1999) *Listening to Children.* 4 Wild Court, London EC2B 4AU.

DeKlyen, M., Biernbaum, M., Speltz, M. and Greenberg, M. (1998) Fathers and preschool behaviour problems. *Developmental Psychology,* Vol. 34, pp. 264–75.

Denham, S., Workman, E., Cole, P., Weissbrod, C., Kendziora, K. and Zahn-Waxler, C. (2000) Prediction of externalising behaviour problems from early to middle childhood: the role of parental socialisation and emotion expression. *Development and Psychopathology,* Vol. 12, pp. 23–45.

Department of Health (2000a) *Protecting Children: Supporting Parents.* London: Department of Health.

Department of Health (2000b) *Tracking Progress in Children's Services.* London: Health Publications.

Department of Social Security (1993) *Households below Average Income 1979–1990/1.* London: HMSO.

DES (1989) *Circular 22/89. Assessment and Statements of Special Educational Needs. Procedures within the Education, Health and Social Services.* London: DES.

DES (1990) *Starting with Quality. Report of the Committee of Inquiry into the Quality of the Educational Experience Offered to Three and Four Year Olds, Chaired by Angela Rumbold, CBE, MP.* London: HMSO.

Desforges, M. and Lindsay, G. (1997) *Baseline Assessment: Problems and Possibilities.* Sevenoaks: Hodder & Stoughton.

de Zulueta, F. (1993) *From Pain to Violence: The Traumatic Roots of*

Destructiveness. London: Whurr Publishers.

DfEE (1988) *The Education Reform Act*. London: HMSO.

DfEE (1994) *The Code of Practice on the Identification and Assessment of Children with Special Educational Needs*. London: HMSO.

DfEE (1997) *Excellence for all Children: Meeting SEN*. London: HMSO.

DfEE (1998) *Meeting SEN: A Programme of Action*. London: HMSO.

DfEE (1999a) *Early Excellence Centres: First Findings*. London: HMSO.

DfEE (1999b) *Tomorrow's Children – Review of Pre-schools and Playgroups*. London: HMSO.

DfEE (2000a) *Making a Difference for Children and Families. Sure Start*. Nottingham: DfEE Publications.

DfEE (2000b) *A Guide for Third-Wave Programmes. Sure Start*. Nottingham: DfEE Publications.

DfEE (2000c) *Expanding Employment-Based Routes into Teaching: A Consultation Document*. Nottingham: DfEE Publications.

DfEE (2000d) *SEN Code of Practice on the Identification and Assessment of Pupils with SEN and SEN Thresholds: Good Practice Guidance on Identification and Provision for Pupils with SEN, for Consultation*. London: HMSO.

DfEE (2000e) *A training support framework for the Foundation Stage. Ensuring sound foundations: from principles to practice*. Training pack. Nottingham: DfEE publications.

DfEE (2001) *National Standards for Under Eights. Day Care and Childminding*. DfEE 0488/2001.

DfEE, EYNTO, IDeA, KCN and SPRITO (1999) *Registered Out of School Clubs Workforce Survey 1998, England*. London: Employers Surveys and Research Unit, Employers Organisation and Improvement and Development Agency.

DHSS (1989) *The Children Act*. London: HMSO.

Diamond, M. and Hopson, J. (1998) *Magic Trees of the Mind*. New York: Dutton.

Dickens, M. and Denziloe, J. (1998) *All Together – How to Create Inclusive Services for Disabled Children and their Families: A Practical Hand-book for Early Years Workers*. London: National Early Years Network.

Dobson, A., Jeavons, M., Lewis, K., Morahan, M. and Sadler, S. (1999) *Characteristics of Preschool Environments*. London: Institute of Education.

Dominelli, L. (1990) *Women and Community Action*. Birmingham: Venture Press.

Donaldson, M. (1983) *Children's Minds*. Glasgow: Fontana/Collins.

Dowling, M. (1995) *Starting School at Four: A Joint Endeavour*. London: Paul Chapman Publishing.

Draper, L. (2001) Being evaluated. *Children and Society,* Vol. 16, p. 1.

Dunn, J. (1987) Understanding feelings: the early stages. In J. Bruner and H. Haste (eds.) *Making Sense: The Child's Construction of the World.* London: Routledge.

Durrant, J. (1999) *The Status of Swedish Children and Youth since the Passage of the 1979 Corporal Punishment Ban.* London: Save the Children.

Dweck, C. S. and Leggett, E. (1988) A social-cognitive approach to motivation and personality. *Psychological Review,* Vol. 95, pp. 256–73.

Early Childhood Education Forum (1995) Draft discussion document. London: Early Childhood Forum (October).

Early Childhood Education Forum (1998) *Quality in Diversity.* London: National Children's Bureau.

Early Childhood Matters No. 95 (2000) *Parents and ECD Programmes.* The Hague: Bernard van Leer Foundation.

Early Education (2000) *Living, Loving and Learning. An Exhibition of Children's Learning from Birth to Three.* Early Education.

EC Childcare Network (1995) *A Review of Services for Young Children in the European Union, 1990–1995.* Brussels: European Commission Equal Opportunities Unit.

Eden, C. (1994) New futures: at whose cost? The nature and process of adult development. In J. Boot, J. Lawrence, and J. Morris (eds.) *Managing the Unknown by Creating New Futures.* London: McGraw-Hill.

Edgington, M. (1991) *The Nursery Teacher in Action,* (2nd edn). London: Paul Chapman Publishing.

Edwards, C., Ganderi, L. and Forman, G. (eds.) (1998) *The Hundred Languages of Children: The Reggio Emilia Approach to Early Childhood Education.* Norwood, NJ: Ablex.

Eiden, R. (1999) Exposure to violence and behaviour problems during early childhood. *Journal of Interpersonal Violence,* Vol. 14, pp. 1299–313.

Elfer, P. (1996) Building intimacy in relationships with young children in nurseries. *Early Years,* Vol. 16.

Elfer, P. (1997) *Attachment Theory and Day Care for Young Children. Highlight* 155. London: National Children's Bureau.

Elfer, P., Goldschmied, E. and Selleck, D. (2001) *Working with Children under Three: The Key Person Relationship.* Available from Peter Elfer at the University of Surrey.

Elfer, P. and Selleck, D. (1999) Children under three in nurseries: uncertainty as a creative factor in child observations. *European Early Childhood Education Research Journal,* Vol. 7.

EYNTO, DfEE, IDeA and PLA (1999) *Registered Pre-School/Playgroup Workforce Survey 1998, England.* London: Employers Surveys and

Research Unit, Employers Organisation and Improvement and Development Agency.

EYNTO, DfEE, NCMA and IDeA (1999) *Registered Childminders Workforce Survey 1998, England.* London: Employers Surveys and Research Unit, Employers Organisation and Improvement and Development Agency.

EYNTO, LGNTO and DfEE (2000) *Survey of Education Support Staff and Volunteers in Nursery and Primary Schools.* London: Employers Surveys and Research Unit, Employers Organisation and Improvement and Development Agency.

EYNTO, NDNA, DfEE and IDeA (1999) *Independent Day Nursery Workforce Survey 1998, England.* London: Employers Surveys and Research Unit, Employers Organisation and Improvement and Development Agency.

Farrington D. (1994) The Twelfth Jack Tizard Memorial Lecture. The development of offending and antisocial behaviour from childhood: key findings from the Cambridge Study in Delinquent Development. *Journal of child psychology, psychiatry and allied disciplines*, Vol. 36, pp. 929–64.

Fawcett, M. and Calder, P. (1998) Early childhood studies degrees. In L. Abbott and G. Pugh (eds.) *Training to Work in the Early Years: Developing the Climbing Frame.* Buckingham: Open University Press.

Filippini, T. and Vecchi, V. (eds.) (1996) *The Hundred Languages of Children: Exhibition Catalogue.* Reggio Emilia: Reggio Children.

Flekkoy, M. G. and Kaufman, N. H. (1997) *The Participation Rights of the Child: Rights and Responsibilities in the Family.* London: Jessica Kingsley.

Freeman, M. (1997) The new birth right: identity and the child of the reproduction revolution. *International Journal of Children's Rights,* Vol. 4, pp. 273–97.

Freeman, C. Henderson, P. and Kettle J. (1999) *Planning with Children for Better Communities.* Cambridge: Polity Press.

Fulwiler, C. and Ruthazer, R. (1999) Premorbid risk factors for violence in adult mental illness. *Comprehensive Psychiatry,* Vol. 40, pp. 96–100.

Furey, W. and Basili, L. (1988) Predicting consumer satisfaction in parent training for noncompliant children. *Behaviour Therapy,* Vol. 19, pp. 555–64.

Gardner, F. (1994) The quality of joint activity between mothers and their children with behaviour problems. *Journal of Child Psychology and Psychiatry*, Vol. 35, pp. 935-48.

Gardner, H. (1983) *Frames of Mind: The Theory of Multiple Intelligences.* New York: Basic Books.

Garner, P. and Sandow, S. (eds.) (1995) *Advocacy, Self-Advocacy and Special Needs.* London: David Fulton.

Gascoigne, E. (1995) *Working with Parents as Partners in SEN*. London: David Fulton.

Ghate, D. *et al.* (2000) *Fathers and Family Centres: Engaging Fathers in Preventive Services*. York: York Publishing Services.

Giddens, A. (1998) *The Third Way*. Cambridge: Polity Press.

Gillborn, D. (1990) *Race, Ethnicity and Education*. London: Unwin Hyman.

Gillborn, D. and Gipps, C. (1997) *Recent Research on the Achievements of Minority Ethnic Pupils*. London: HMSO.

Goldschmied, E. (1987) *Infants at Work* (training video). Available from the Early Childhood Unit, National Children's Bureau.

Goldschmied, E. and Jackson, S. (1994) *People Under Three. Young Children in Day Care*. London: Routledge.

Goldschmied, E. and Selleck, D. (1996) *Communication between Babies in their First Year*. London: National Children's Bureau.

Gopnik, A., Meltzoff, A. and Kuhl, P. (1999) *How Babies Think*. London: Weidenfield & Nicolson.

Graham, A.-M. (1997) Have experience: want to learn – creating a new pathway to professionalism with a little European money and a lot of hard work from our friends. In L. Abbott and H. Moylett (eds.) *Working with the Under-3s: Training and Professional Development*. Buckingham: Open University Press.

Grainger, T. and Goouch, K. (1999) Young children and playful language. In T. David (ed) *Teaching Young Children*, pp 19–29.

Grosberg. L. (1994) Introduction: bringing it all back home – pedagogy and cultural studies in H. Giroux and P. McLaren (eds) *Between Borders: Pedagogy and the Politics of Cultural Studies*, pp. 1–28. London: Routledge.

Grugeon, E. and Woods, P. (1990) *Educating All: Multicultural Perspectives in the Primary School*. London: Routledge.

Gunnarsson, L., Korpi, B. M. and Nordenstam, U. (1999) *Early Childhood Education and Care Policy in Sweden: Background Report Prepared for the OECD Thematic Review*. Stockholm: Swedish Ministry of Education and Science.

Hall, S. (1992) Race, culture and communications: looking backward and forward in cultural studies. *Rethinking Marxism,* Vol. 5, pp. 10–18.

Handy, C. (1994) *The Empty Raincoat*. London: Hutchinson.

Hardan, A. and Sahl, R. (1999) Suicidal behaviour in children and adolescents with developmental disorders. *Research in Developmental Disabilities*, Vol. 20, pp. 287–96.

Harjan, A. (1992) Children of parents with affective disorders: the role of an ill mother or an ill father. *European Journal of Psychiatry*, Vol. 6, pp. 74-87.

Hartley, D. (1993) *Understanding the Nursery School*. London: Cassell.

Henderson, P. *et al.* (1999) *Planning with Children for Better Communities.* Cambridge: Polity Press.

Henry, M. (1996) *Young Children, Parents and Professionals.* London: Routledge.

HERA 2 (1999) *Final Report: Childcare Training in the UK.* Ipswich Suffolk County Council.

Hodgkin, R. and Newell, P. (1998) *Implementation Handbook on the Convention on the Rights of the Child.* New York: UNICEF.

Hornby, G. (1995) *Working with Parents of Children with Special Needs.* London: Cassell.

Howells, J. (1974) *Remember Maria.* London: Butterworths.

Hyder, T. *et al.* (1997) *On Equal Terms: Ways to Involve Parents in Early Years Settings.* London: NEYN/Save the Children.

Hylton, C. (1997) *Family Survival Strategies.* Moyenda, Black Families Talking. Available from Coram Family.

James, A. (1998) From the child's point of view: issues in the social construction of childhood. In Panter-Brick, C. (ed.) *Biosocial Perspectives on Children.* Cambridge: Cambridge University Press.

Jamieson, A. and Owen, S. (2000) *Ambition for Change: Partnerships, Children and Work.* London: National Children's Bureau.

John, M. (ed.) (1996) *Children in Charge: The Child's Right to a Fair Hearing.* London: Jessica Kingsley.

Jordan, B. (1987) *Creative Social Work with Families.* Birmingham: BASW Publications.

Karlsson, M. (1995) *Family Day Care in Europe.* Brussels: European Commission Equal Opportunities Unit.

Katz, L. (1980) Mothers and teachers: some significant distinctions. In L. Katz (ed.) *Current Topics in Early Childhood Education. Vol. 3.* Norwood, NJ: Ablex.

Kazdin, E. (1990) Premature termination from treatment among children referred for antisocial behaviour. *Journal of Child Psychology and Psychiatry,* Vol. 31, pp. 415–25.

Keenan, K. and Wakschlag, L. (2000) More than the terrible twos: the nature and severity of behaviour problems in clinic-referred preschool children. *Journal of Abnormal Psychology,* Vol. 28, pp. 33–46.

Kessler, R., Foster, C., Saunders, W. and Stang, P. (1995) Kessler social consequences of psychiatric disorders. I. Educational attainment. *American Journal of Psychiatry,* Vol. 152, pp. 1026–32.

Khan, J. and Russell, P. (1999) *Quality Protects: 1st Analysis Management Action Plans.* London: Department of Health.

Kirkwood, A. (1993) *The Leicestershire Inquiry 1992.* Leicestershire County Council.

Koot, H. and Verhulst, F. (1992) Prediction of children's referral to mental health and special education services from earlier adjustment. *Journal of Child Psychology and Psychiatry,* Vol. 33, pp. 717–29.

Labour Party (1996) *Early Excellence – A Head Start for Every Child.* London: Labour Party.

Lambert, J. F. (1996) Des règles et du jeu. Paper presented at the European Seminar of OMEP, UNESCO, Paris, 24–27 October.

Lane, J. (1999) *Action for Racial Equality in the Early Years.* London: National Early Years Network.

Lang, P. (1995) The Place of PSE in the primary school. In I. Siraj-Blatchford and J. Siraj-Blatchford (eds.) *Educating the Whole Child: Cross-curricular Skills, Themes and Dimensions in Primary Schools.* Buckingham: Open University Press.

Lansdown, G. (1996) *Taking Part.* London: Institute for Public Policy Research.

Laurent, C. (2000) The real life class. *Guardian,* 11 April.

La Valle, I., Finch, S., Nove, A. and Lewin, C. (2000) *Parents' Demand for Childcare.* London: DfEE research report RR176.

Leach, P. (1999) *The Physical Punishment of Children.* London: NSPCC.

Levy, A. and Kahan, B. (1991) *The Pindown Experience and the Protection of Children: The Report of the Staffordshire Child Care Enquiry.* Stafford: Staffordshire County Council.

Lewis, A. and Lindsay, G. (eds.) (2000) *Researching Children's Perspectives.* Buckingham: Open University Press.

LGMB/ADSS (1998) *Social Services Workforce Analysis 1998.* Extracts reproduced in EYNTO, NDNA, DfEE and IDeA (1999) *Independent Day Nursery Workforce Survey 1998, England.* London: Employers Surveys and Research Unit, Employers Organisation and Improvement and Development Agency.

Lloyd, B. (1987) Social representations of gender. In J. Bruner and H. Haste (eds.) *Making Sense: The Child's Construction of the World.* London: Routledge.

Lloyd, B. and Duveen, G. (1992) *Gender Identities and Education.* London: Harvester Wheatsheaf.

Lloyd, E. (ed.) (1999) *Parenting Matters: What Works in Parenting Education?* Essex: Barnardo's.

Lloyd, T. (1999a) *Reading for the Future.* London: Save the Children.

Lloyd, T. (1999b) *Working with Fathers: A Strategy for Discussion.* Coram Family (unpublished).

London Borough of Hammersmith and Fulham/Early Years Development and Childcare Partnership (2000a) *London Borough of Hammersmith and Fulham (LBH&F) Early Years Development and Childcare Partnership Plan 2000–2001.* London: Hammerprint.

London Borough of Hammersmith and Fulham (LBH&F) Early Years Development and Childcare Partnership (2000b) *A Response to the DfEE Consultation on the Draft National Standards for the Regulation of Day Care.* Available from LBH&F/EYDCP Resource Centre at Randolph Beresford EYC, Australia Road, London W12 7PH.

Lubeck, S. (1986) *Sandbox Society.* Hove: Falmer Press.

Lutz, W. (1999) Will Europe be short of children? *Family Observer,* Vol. 1, pp. 8–17.

Macdonald, G. and Roberts, H. (1995) *What Works in the Early Years? Effective Interventions for Children and their Families in Health, Social Welfare, Education and Child Protection.* Essex: Barnardo's.

MacNaughton, G., Rolfe, S., Siraj-Blatchford, I. (2001) *Doing Early Childhood Research: International Perspectives on Theory and Practice.* Sydney: Allen & Unwin. Buckingham and Philadelphia: Open University Press.

Macpherson, W. (1999) *Report of the Stephen Lawrence Enquiry.* London: HMSO.

Mahony, P. (1985) *Schools for the Boys.* London: Hutchinson.

Marshall, J. (1994) *Re-visioning Organisatons by Developing Female Values* in J. Boot, J. Lawrence and J. Morris (eds.) (1994) *Managing the Unknown by Creating New Futures,* London: McGraw-Hill.

Marshall, K. (1997) *Children's Rights in the Balance: The Participation–Protection Divide.* London: HMSO.

Miller, J. (1996) *Never Too Young: How Children can take Responsibility and Make Decisions: A Handbook for Early Years Workers.* London: Early Years Network/Save the Children.

Miller, J. (2000) *All Right at Home?* London: Children's Rights Alliance for England/SCF/Children's Society/Barnardo's/NSPCC/NCH.

Miller, L. (2000) Play as a foundation for learning. In R. Drury, L. Miller and R. Campbell (eds.) *Looking at Early Years Education and Care.* London: David Fulton.

Moriarty, V. and Siraj-Blatchford, I. (1998) *An Introduction to Curriculum for 3 to 5 year-olds.* Nottingham: Education Now Books.

Morrow, V. and Richards, M. (1996) The ethics of social research with children: an overview. *Children and Society,* Vol. 10, no. 2, pp. 90–105.

Mortimer, H. (2000) *Developing Individual Behaviour Plans in the Early Years.* Tamworth: NASEN.

Moss, P. (1999) Renewed hopes and lost opportunities: early childhood in the early years of the Labour government. *Cambridge Journal of Education,* Vol. 29, pp. 229–38.

Moss, P. (2000a) Training of early childhood education and care staff. *International Journal of Education Research,* Vol. 33, pp. 31–5.

Moss, P. (2000b) 'From Children's Services to Children's Spaces', in K. White (ed.) *The Changing Face of Child Care, NCVCCO Annual Review Journal, No. 2,* pp. 19–35.

Moss, P. and Deven, F. (eds.) (2000) *Parental Leave in Europe: Progress or Pitfall? Research and Policy Issues in Europe.* The Hague and Brussels:

NIDI/CBGS.

Moss, P. and Pence, A. (eds.) (1994) *Valuing Quality in Early Childhood Services*. London: Paul Chapman Publishing.

Moss, P. and Penn, H. (1996) *Transforming Nursery Education*. London: Paul Chapman Publishing.

Moyles, J. and Suschitzky, W. (1998) Painting the cabbages red! In L. Abbott and G. Pugh (eds.) *Training to Work in the Early Years: Developing the Climbing Frame*. Buckingham: Open University Press.

NASEN (1999) *A policy on Partnership with Parents* from the National Association for Special Educational Needs, NASEN House, 4/5 Amber Business Village, Amber Close, Amington, Tamworth B77 4RP.

National Children's Bureau *Highlight* 170 (1999) *Evidence-Based Child Care Practice*. London: National Children's Bureau.

National Commission on Education (1993) *Learning to Succeed*. London: Heinemann.

National Family and Parenting Institute, Unit 431, Highgate Studios, 53–79 Highgate Road, London NW5 1TL.

National Institute of Child Health and Human Development Early Years Care Research Network (1999) Child care and mother child interaction in the first three years of life. *Developmental Psychology,* Vol. 35, pp. 1399–413.

National Playing Fields Association (1993) Statement at Launch event.

Newell, P. (1991) *The UN Convention and Children's Rights in the UK*. London: National Children's Bureau.

Norwich, B. (1990) *Reappraising Special Needs Education*. London: Cassell.

Nunes, T. (1994) The relationship between childhood and society. *Van Leer Foundation Newsletter,* Spring, pp. 16–17.

Nutbrown, C. (ed.) (1996) *Respectful Educators – Capable Learners: Children's Rights in Early Education*. London: Paul Chapman Publishing.

Nutbrown, C. (1997) *Recognising Early Literacy Development – Assessing Children's Achievements*. London: Paul Chapman Publishing.

Nutbrown, C. (1998) *The Lore and Language of Early Education*. Sheffield: University of Sheffield Division of Education Publications.

Nutbrown, C. (1999) *Threads of Thinking: Young Children Learning and the Role of Early Education*. London: Paul Chapman Publishing (2nd edn).

Nutbrown, C. (2000) Alex's story: literacy and literacy teaching in the earliest years. In E. Millard (ed.) *Enquiring into Literacy: Papers from the Literacy Research Centre Sheffield. Sheffield Papers in Education*. Sheffield: University of Sheffield, School of Education.

Oberhuemer, P. and Colberg-Schrader, H. (1999) The changing practitioner role in early childhood centres: multiple shifts and contradictory forces. *International Journal of Early Years Education*, Vol. 7.

Oberhuemer, P. and Ulich, M. (1997) *Working with Young Children in Europe*. London: Paul Chapman Publishing.

OECD (1999) *OECD Country Note: Early Childhood Education and Care Policy in Sweden*. Paris: OECD.

OECD (2001b) *Early Childhood Education and Care Policy in the United Kingdom*. Paris: OECD.

OFSTED (1998) *Guidance on the Inspection of Nursery Education Provision in the Private, Voluntary and Independent Sectors*. London: HMSO.

Organisation for Economic Cooperation and Development (OECD) (2001b) *Starting Strong: Early Childhood Education and Care*. Paris: OECD.

Owen, S. and McQuail, S. (1997) *Learning from Vouchers: An Evaluation of Phase One of the Voucher Scheme for Four Year Olds, 1996/7*. London: National Children's Bureau.

Pascal, C. *et al.* (1999) *Research to Inform the Evaluation of the Early Excellence Centres Pilot Programme*. Worcester: Centre for Research in Early Childhood, University College Worcester.

Pascal, C., Bertram, A., Mould, C., Ramsden, F. and Saunders, M. (1997) *The Effective Early Learning Project: A Professional Development Programme*. Worcester: Amber Publications.

Pascal, C., Bertram, A. and Ramsden, F. (1994) *Effective Early Learning: The Quality Evaluation and Development Process*. London: Amber.

Patterson, G. (1974) Interventions for boys with and without conduct problems: multiple setting, treatments and criteria. *Journal of Consulting and Clinical Psychology*, Vol. 42, pp. 472–81.

Patterson, G. (1980) *Coercive Family Processes*. Eugene, OR: Castalia.

Patterson, G. (1994) Some alternatives to seven myths about treating families of antisocial children. In *Crime and the Family Conference Report*, pp. 26–49.

Peers Early Education Project (1999) *Annual report*. Oxford: The Peep Centre.

Penn, H. (2000) *How Should we Care for Babies and Toddlers? An Analysis of Practice in an Out-of-Home Care for Children under Three*. Toronto: Center for Urban and Community Studies, University of Toronto.

Peters, D. and Kostelnik, M. (1981) Current research in day care personnel preparation. *Advance in Early Education and Day Care,* Vol. 2 pp. 29–66.

Phillips, A. (1998a) *The Beast in the Nursery*. London: Faber & Faber.

Phillips, A. (1998b) *Monogamy*. London: Faber & Faber.

Pollard, A. with Filer, A. (1996) *The Social World of Children's Learning:*

Case Studies of Pupils from Four to Seven. London: Cassell.

Powell, J. (1998) The Pathways to Professionalism Project – a case study: making an early childhood studies degree accessible. In L. Abbott and G. Pugh (eds.) *Training to Work in the Early Years – Developing the Climbing Frame.* Buckingham: Open University Press.

Preschool Learning Alliance (1999) *Inclusion in Preschool Settings.* Available from 69 Kings Cross Road, London WC1 X9L.

Pugh, G. (1988) *Services for Under Fives: Developing a Coordinated Approach.* London: National Children's Bureau.

Pugh, G. (ed.) (1992, 1996) *Contemporary Issues in the Early Years: Working Collaboratively for Children.* London: Paul Chapman Publishing.

Pugh, G. (1996) Four year olds in school: what is appropriate provision? In *Childfacts.* London: National Children's Bureau.

Pugh, G. (1999) Young children and their families: a community response. In L. Abbot and H. Moylette (eds.) *Early Education Transformed.* London: Falmer Press.

Pugh, G. and McQuail, S. (1995) *Effective Organisation of Early Childhood Services: Summary and Strategic Framework.* London: National Children's Bureau.

Purves, L. and Selleck, D. (1999) *Tuning into Children.* London: BBC Education Productions.

QCA (1997) *The National Framework for Baseline Assessment: Criteria and Procedures for the Accreditation of BA Schemes.* London: QCA.

QCA (1998) *Baseline Assessment: Baseline Assessment Schemes Accredited by QCA, Final List, April 1998.* Middlesex: QCA.

QCA (1999a) *The Early Learning Goals.* London: QCA/DfEE.

QCA (1999b) *Early Years Education, Childcare and Playwork. A Framework of Nationally Accredited Qualifications.* Ref QCA/99/435.

QCA (2000a) *Curriculum Guidance for the Foundation Stage.* London: QCA/DfEE.

QCA/DfEE (2000b) *A Training Support Framework for the Foundation Stage.* London: QCA.

Raikes, H. (1996) A secure base for babies: applying attachment concepts to the infant care setting. *Young Children,* Vol. 51, pp. 59–67.

Rasmussen, K., Storsaeter, O. and Levander, S. (1999) Personality disorders, psychopathy, and crime in a Norwegian prison population. *International Journal of Law and Psychiatry,* Vol. 22, pp. 91–7.

Report of Inquiry (1988) *Report of the Inquiry into Child Abuse in Cleveland, 1987.* London: HMSO.

Richman, N., Stevenson, J. and Graham, P. (1982) *Pre-School to School: A Behavioural Study.* London: Academic Press.

Roaf, C. and Bines, H. (eds.) (1989) *Needs, Rights and Opportunities.*

Lewes: Falmer Press.

Roberts, R. (1998) Thinking about me and them: personal and social development. In I. Siraj-Blatchford (ed.) *A Curriculum Development Handbook for Early Childhood Educators*. Stoke-on-Trent: Trentham Books.

Robertson, J. and Robertson, J. (1989) *Separation in the very young*. Free Association Books.

Robinson, A. (2000) *Working Parents' Cuttings, 2000* (a synopsis of contemporary issues and parents' perspectives taken from press cuttings). Available from the National Children's Bureau.

Rodd, G. (1994) *Leadership in Early Childhood*. Buckingham: Open University Press (2nd edn 1998).

Roffey, S. (1999) *Special Needs in the Early Years*. London: David Fulton.

Rose, N. (1990) *Governing the Soul: the Shaping of the Private Self*. London: Routledge.

Rouse, D. (ed.) (1991) *Babies and Toddlers: Carers and Educators – Quality for the Under Threes*. London: National Children's Bureau.

Russell, P. (2000) Developing a comprehensive and integrated approach to early years services for children with SEN: opportunities and challenges in current government initiatives. In B. Norwich (ed.) *Early Years Development and SEN. Policy Paper* 3. Tamworth: NASEN.

Rustin, M. (1997) in Miller, L., Rustin, M. and Shuttleworth, J. (eds.) *Closely Observed Infants*. London: Duckworth.

Rutter, M. (1995) Clinical implications of attachment concepts, retrospect and prospect. *Journal of Child Psychology and Psychiatry,* Vol. 36, pp. 549–71.

Rutter, M., Macdonald, H., le Couteur, A. and Harrington, R. (1990) Genetic factors in child psychiatric disorders. II. Empirical findings. *Journal of Child Psychology and Psychiatry and Allied Disciplines*, Vol. 31, pp. 39–83.

Sammons, P., Sylva, K., Melhuist, E., Siraj-Blachford, I., Taggart, B. (1999) *Characteristics of the EPPE project sample at entry to the study* Technical Paper 2. London: DfEE and Institute of Education.

Sayeed, Z. and Guerin, E. (2000) *Early Years Play: A Happy Medium for Assessment and Intervention*. London: David Fulton.

SCAA (1996a) *Desirable Outcomes for Children's Learning on Entering Compulsory Education*. London: SCAA.

SCAA (1996b) *Baseline Assessment – Draft Proposals*. Middlesex: SCAA.

SCAA (1997a) *The National Framework for Baseline Assessment*. Middlesex: SCAA.

SCAA (1997b) *Baseline Assessment Scales*. Middlesex: SCAA.

Schools Council (1981) *The Practical Curriculum*. London: Schools Council.

Schweinhart, L. *et al.* (1993) *Significant Benefits.* Ypsilanti, MI: High/ Scope Press.

Scott, W. (1996) Choices in learning. In C. Nutbrown (ed.) *Respectful Educators – Capable Learners.* London: Paul Chapman Publishing.

Sebba, J. and Sachdev, D. (1997) *What Works in Inclusive Education.* Essex: Barnardo's.

Serketich, W. and Dumas, J. (1996) The effectiveness of behavioural parent training to modify antisocial behaviour in children: a meta-analysis. *Behaviour Therapy,* Vol. 27, pp. 171–86.

Sharpe, K., Broadfooot, P., Osborn, M., Planel, C. and Ward, B. (1999) Young citizens: young children's development of national identity. In David, T. (ed.) *Young Children Learning.* London: Paul Chapman Publishing.

Shaw, D., Owen, E., Vondra, J., Keenan, K. and Winslow, E. (1996) Early risk factors and pathways in the development of early disruptive behaviour problems. *Development and Psychopathology,* Vol. 8, pp. 679–99.

Shaw, D. and Vondra, J. (1995) Infant attachment security and maternal predictors of early behaviour problems: a longitudinal study of low-income families. *Journal of Abnormal Child Psychology*, Vol. 23, pp. 335–57.

Shropshire and Telford & Wreakin EYDCP joint training initiative (2000) *Staff Development for Baby and Toddler: Observations in Group Care.*

Siraj-Blatchford, I. (1994) *The Early Years: Laying the Foundations for Racial Equality.* Stoke-on-Trent: Trentham Books.

Siraj-Blatchford, I. (1996) Language, culture and difference. In C. Nutbrown (ed.) *Children's Rights and Early Education.* London: Paul Chapman Publishing.

Siraj-Blatchford, I. (ed.) (1998) *A Curriculum Development Handbook for Early Childhood Educators.* Stoke-on-Trent: Trentham Books.

Siraj-Blatchford, I. and Clarke, P. (2000) *Supporting Identity, Diversity and Language in the Early Years.* Buckingham: Open University Press.

Siraj-Blatchford, I. and Siraj-Blatchford, J. (eds.) (1995) *Educating the Whole Child: Cross-curricular Skills, Themes and Dimensions in the Primary Schools.* Buckingham: Open University Press.

Siraj-Blatchford, I. and Siraj-Blatchford, J. (1999) Race, research and reform: the impact of the three Rs on anti-racist pre-school and primary education in the UK. *Race, Ethnicity and Education,* Vol. 2, pp. 127–48.

Smith, A. (1999) Quality childcare and joint attention. *International Journal of Early Years Education*, Vol. 7.

Smith, F. and Barker, J. (2000) *Child-centred After-School and Holiday Childcare.* Children 5-16 research programme. Edinburgh: ESRC.

Solity, J. (1995) Psychology, teachers, and early years. *International Journal of Early Years Education,* Vol. 3.

Special Educational Needs Tribunal annual reports, available from DfEE Publications, PO Box 5050, Sudbury, Suffolk, CO10 6ZQ.

Speltz, M., DeKlyen, M. and Greenberg, M. (1999) Attachment in boys with early onset conduct problems. *Development and Psychopathology,* Vol. 11, pp. 269–85.

Stacey, M. (1991) *Parents and Teachers Together.* Buckingham: Open University Press.

Steele, M. *et al.* (2000) *Strengthening Families, Strengthening Communities: An Inclusive Parent Programme.* London: Racial Equality Unit.

Steele, R., Forehand, R., Armistead, L. and Brody, G. (1995) Predicting alcohol and drug use in early adulthood: the role of internalising and externalising behaviour problems in early adolescence. *American Journal of Orthopsychiatry,* Vol. 65, pp. 380–8.

Stepney and Wapping Community Child Health Project, Stepney Community Nursing Development Unit, research and development programme, 1993–95.

Stormshak, E., Bierman, K., McMahon, R. and Lengua, L. (2000) Parenting practices and child disruptive behaviour problems in early elementary school. *Journal of Clinical Child Psychology,* Vol. 29, pp. 17–29.

Strand, S. (1996) Value added analysis of the 1995 Key Stage 1 results: an LEA case study. Paper presented to the British Educational Research Association Conference, September, Lancaster University.

Strandell, H. (2000) What is the use of children's play: preparation or social participation? In H. Penn (ed.) *Early Childhood Services: Theory, Policy and Practice.* Buckingham: Open University Press.

Sure Start (1999a) *A Guide for Trailblazers.* London: DfEE.

Sure Start (1999b) *A Guide to Evidence Based Practice.* London: DfEE (2nd edn).

Sure Start (2000) *Providing Good Quality Childcare and Early Learning Experiences through Sure Start.* London: DfEE.

Swann, M. (1985) 'The Swann Report': *Education for all: report of the chairman of the Committee of Inquiry into the Education of Children from Ethnic Minority Groups* Department of Education and Science (DES). London: HMSO.

Swedish Ministry of Education (2000a) *Maximum Fees and Universal Pre-school: Fact Sheet (May 2000).* Stockholm: Ministry of Education.

Swedish Ministry of Education (2000b) *A New System of Teacher Education: Fact Sheet (August 2000).* Stockholm: Ministry of Education.

Sylva, K., and Siraj-Blatchford, I. (1996) *Bridging the Gap between Home and School: Improving achievement in primary schools.* Paris: UN-

ESCO.

Sylva, K., Siraj-Blatchford, I., Melhuish, E., Sammons, P. and Taggart, B. (1999) *Effective Provision for Pre-school Education Project. Technical Paper* 6. London: DfEE and Institute of Education, University of London.

Sylva, K. (2000) What Works Best for Parents and Children? Evidence from Research, Keynote Lecture at 'Parent Child 2000', London.

Taggart, B., Sylva, K., Siraj-Blatchford, I., Melhuish, E. and Sammons, P. (2000) *Technical Paper* 5. London: DfEE and Institute of Education, University of London.

Thomas, N. and O'Kane, C. (1998) The ethics of participatory research with children. *Children and Society*, Vol. 12, pp. 336–48.

Tobin, J. J., Wu, D. Y. H. and Davidson, D. H. (1989) *Preschool in Three Cultures: Japan, China and the United States*. London: Yale University Press.

Tomlinson, J. (1986) The co-ordinator of services for under fives. *TACTYC*, Vol. 7, no. 1, autumn.

Trevarthen, C. (1992) An infant's motives for speaking and thinking in the culture. In Wold, A. H. (ed) *The Dialogical Alternative*, pp. 99–137. Oxford: Oxford University Press.

Trevarthen, C. (1999) An interview recorded and scribed for BBC Radio 4 by Angie Mason in the BBC Radio series *Tuning into Children*. Extracts in Purves and Selleck (1999).

Troyna, B. and Hatcher, R. (1991) *Racism in Children's Lives: A Study of Mainly White Primary Schools*. London: National Children's Bureau and Routledge.

UNICEF (2000) *A League Table of Child Poverty in Rich Countries: Innocenti Report Card, Issue No. 1*. Florence: Innocenti Research Centre.

Utting, D. (ed.) (1999) *A Guide to Promising Approaches*. London: Communities that Care.

Utting, W. (1997) *People Like Us*. London DH/Welsh Office.

Vernon, J. (1999) *Parent Partnership and SEN: Perspectives on Developing Good Practice. Research Report* 162. Sudbury: DfEE Publications.

Vygotsky, L. (1978) *Mind in Society: The Development of Higher Level Psychological Processes*. Cambridge, MA: Harvard University Press.

Wade, B. and Moore, M. (2000) Starting early with books. In S. Wolfendale and J. Bastiani (eds.) *The Contribution of Parents to School Effectiveness*. London: David Fulton.

Wardle, F. (1999) *Tomorrow's Children: Meeting the Needs of Multiracial and Multiethnic Children at Home, in Early Childhood Programs and at School*. Colorado: Center for the Study of Biracial Children.

Warnock, M. (Chair) (1978) *Special Educational Needs*. London: HMSO.

Waterhouse, R. (2000) *Lost In Care* (the tribunal of inquiry into abuse of children in care in Clywd and Gwynedd). London DH/Welsh Office.

Webster-Stratton, C. (1981) Videotape modelling: a method of parent education. *Journal of Clinical Child Psychology,* Vol. 10, pp. 93–7.

Webster-Stratton, C. (1984) Randomised trial of two parent training programmes for families with conduct disordered children. *Journal of Consulting and Clinical Psychology,* Vol. 52, pp. 666–78.

Webster-Stratton, C. (1989) Systematic comparison of consumer satisfaction of three cost-effective parent training programmes for conduct problem children. *Behaviour Therapy,* Vol. 20, pp. 103–15.

Webster-Stratton, C. (1994) Advancing videotape parent training: a comparison study. *Journal of Consulting and Clinical Psychology,* Vol. 62, pp. 583–93.

Webster-Stratton, C. (1997) From parent training to community building. *Families in Society: The Journal of Contemporary Human Services,* pp. 156–71.

Webster-Stratton, C. (1999) *How to Promote Children's Social and Emotional Competence.* London: Paul Chapman Publishing.

Webster-Stratton, C. and Hammond, M. (1990) Predictors of treatment outcome in parent training for families with conduct problem children. *Behaviour Therapy,* Vol. 21, pp. 319–37.

Webster-Stratton, C. and Hammond, M. (1997) Treating children with early-onset conduct problems: a comparison of child and parent training interventions. *Journal of Consulting and Clinical Psychology,* Vol. 65, pp. 93–109.

Webster-Stratton, C. and Lindsey, D. (1999) Social competence and conduct problems in young children: issues in assessment. *Journal of Clinical Child Psychology,* Vol. 28, pp. 25–43.

Weinberger, J. (1996) *Literacy Goes to School.* London: Paul Chapman Publishing.

West, M. (2000) A case study of the key person approach. Available from Dorothy Selleck.

Whalley, M (1999) Women Leaders in Early Childhood Settings. PhD Thesis, University of Wolverhampton.

Whaley, K. L. and Rubenstein, T. S. (1994) How toddlers do friendship. *Journal of Social and Personal Relationships* 11.3 pp. 383–400.

Whalley, M. and the Pen Green Centre team (2000) *Involving Parents in their Children's Learning.* London: Paul Chapman Publishing.

Whalley, M. and the Pen Green Centre team (1997) *Working with Parents.* Sevenoaks: Hodder & Stoughton (2nd edn 2000).

Whitaker, P. (1997) *Primary Schools and the Future.* Buckingham: Open University Press.

Widdows, J. (1997) *A Special Need for Inclusion.* London: Children's

Society.

Wigfall, V. and Moss, P. (2001) *More Than the Sum of Its Parts? – A Multi-agency Childcare Network*. Joseph Rowntree Foundation/National Children's Bureau.

Williams, P. (1994) *Making Sense of Quality: A Review of Approaches to Quality in Early Childhood Services*. London: National Children's Bureau.

Willis, P. (1977) *Learning to Labour*. London: Saxon House.

Willow, C. (1997) *Hear! Hear!*. London: Local Government Information Unit.

Willow, C. and Hyder, T. (1998) *It Hurts You Inside*. London: National Children's Bureau/Save the Children.

Wilson, B. (1998) *SEN in the Early Years*. London: Routledge.

Winnicott, D. W. (1965) *The Maturational Processes and the Facilitative Environment*. New York: International Universities Press.

Wolfendale, S. (1993) Involving parents in assessment. In S. Wolfendale (ed.) *Assessing Special Educational Needs*. London: Cassell.

Wolfendale, S. (ed.) (1997a) *Working with Parents of SEN Children after the Code of Practice*. London: David Fulton.

Wolfendale, S. (ed.) (1997b) *Meeting Special Needs in the Early Years: Directions in Policy and Practice*. London: David Fulton (reissued 2000).

Wolfendale, S. (ed.) (2000a) *Special Needs in the Early Years: Snapshots of Practice*. London: Routledge.

Wolfendale, S. (ed.) (2000b) Special needs in the early years: policy options and practice prospects. In B. Norwich (ed.) *Early Years Development and SEN. Policy Paper* 3. Tamworth: NASEN.

Wolfendale, S. and Cook, G. (1997) *Evaluation of SEN Parent Partnership Schemes. Research Report* 34. Sudbury: DfEE Publications.

Wolfendale, S. and Einzig, H. (eds.) (1999) *Parenting Education and Support: New Opportunities*. London: David Fulton.

Woodhead, M. (1991) Psychology and the cultural construction of 'children's needs'. In M. Woodhead, A. Light, and R. Carr (eds.) *Growing up in a Changing Society*. London: Routledge and The Open University.

Woodhead, M. (1996) *In Search of the Rainbow: Pathways to Quality in Large Scale Programmes for Young Disadvantaged Children*. The Hague: Bernard van Leer Foundation.

Zahn-Waxler, C., Schmitz, S., Fulker, D., Robinson, J. and Emde, R. (1996) Behaviour problems in 5-year-old monozygotic and dyzygotic twins: genetic and environmental influences, patterns of regulations and internalisation of control. *Development and Psychopathology*, Vol. 8, pp. 103–22.

Index